GW01605892

MRS. MARY REIBEY

From the original miniature in the possession of the
Mitchell Library, Sydney

MARY REIBEY — MOLLY INCOGNITA

A Biography of Mary Reibey 1777 to 1855, and her World

by Nancy Irvine

LIBRARY OF AUSTRALIAN HISTORY
NORTH SYDNEY
1987

LIBRARY OF AUSTRALIAN HISTORY – Publishers
17 Mitchell Street, NORTH SYDNEY, NSW. 2060

First Published 1982
Reprinted with Expanded Preface 1987
ISBN 0 908120 46 X

"To green the memory"

Lovingly dedicated to my daughters Elizabeth Richards and Christine Lawrie

Printed in Australia by The Book Printer, Lane Cove, NSW. 2066

CONTENTS

ILLUSTRATIONS

FOREWORD

Mary Reibey – Molly Incognita was originally published five years ago and has established itself as a valuable biography of one of the most interesting female convicts to be transported to New South Wales. The broad features of Mary's life had long been known, but Nancy Irvine's meticulous research into a wide range of primary sources, located here and overseas, enabled her to correct earlier misconceptions and present a fuller, more detailed picture of her subject. She shares with her readers the excitement associated with the search for fresh material and provides guidance of value to those interested in following genealogical trails of their own. She presents her findings in a narrative that is at once lively, vivid and colourful. Her illustrations are well chosen and contemporary material is reproduced to give further backing to her conclusions.

The decision to re-issue the book needs no justification. In order to appreciate the richness and complexities of life in New South Wales it is important that biographical studies should continue to be made and that they should remain available. The present study makes a contribution to family history and to the expanding field of women's history. It illuminates the growth of commercial activity and highlights the opportunities that were available to the enterprising emancipist. In its republished form it contains a new preface incorporating recently discovered letters that provide additional information about Mary and her husband. Such material enhances the importance of a book which has already heightened our understanding of a number of features of economic and social conditions in early New South Wales.

The University of Sydney — Brian H. Fletcher

ACKNOWLEDGEMENTS

This biography of Mary Reibey was made possible by the continuous encouragement and unstinted assistance given to me by so many people. Amongst them are: Dr. Ron Traill and Laurel Heath, who never lost faith in the historical value of the story; the good natured highly skilled Mrs. Gay Hayden, who cheerfully typed and retyped the changing format; Messrs Keith Johnson and Malcom Sainty of the Library of Australian History, Publishers, who patiently shepherded this brash author through the publishing maze; my family, who for three long years have endured the endless repetition of doubts and fears; the academic friends who have provided valued professional criticism; helpful archivists and librarians of the Hobart and Launceston Libraries, of the Mitchell Library, of the State Library of New South Wales, of the Archives Office of N.S.W., Sydney, of the National Library of Australia in Canberra, of the Library of the Canberra College of Advanced Education, of the Lancashire Archives Office in Preston, Lancashire, and of the British Museum Library (where a kindly attendant directed me to 'turn right at Magna Carta, Ma'am' to reach the room holding some of our early records!) Finally, I must thank the Mitchell Library for permission to use the charming miniatures as cover illustrations; The National Library for permission to copy the valuable early prints which illustrate the text; the Public Record Office, London, for permission to include copies of the original parchment records of the trial at the Summer Assizes in August, 1791 and David Hardy for his helpful proof-reading.

PREFACE

I 'turned right at Magna Carta' in the British Museum, and the gestation of the story was assured! For, sensing that the fascinating history of Mary Reibey had some tantalizing gaps which needed to be filled, a routine search was made in many Public Offices of Archives, in order to make a faithful biography of Mary Reibey 1777-1855. In 1978 I found, whilst searching through the *original* government records in Chancery Lane, London, what appeared to be a discrepancy with current 'received' accounts. This discovery triggered off a paper chase and led me to my affair with the locale of the young lady; to my affair with the people and customs of the late 18th century, which was when Molly Haydock ran away into such incredible trouble in 1791; finally to my affair with life in the early days of New South Wales. As a result this account of the life of Mary Reibey (a woman important in Sydney's early history) falls naturally into two parts.

Part I, set vividly against the Hogarthian background of the era, relates the piquant adventure story of the runaway girl who succeeded in hiding her identity and maintaining her disguise, as a boy, for more than four long months. And that difficult feat was carried out in an 18th century prison. The young girl deluded captors, court officials, judge, jury, and gaolers for long after the trial and commutation, until at last she was forced to make an appeal when officials finally rumbled her charade. Transported to New South Wales, arriving in October 1792, she survived as a housekeeper, until her marriage with Tom Rabey in September 1794.

Part II tells of the continued, discreet and plucky management of her life, from the firm change of her baptismal name of Molly Heydock to Mary Reibey (so spelt in later years). Mrs. Thomas Reibey, widowed later and left to handle a growing business and a young family of seven, battled with the emancipist image and succeeded as a respected and wary proprietor, equal to any of the shrewd businessmen of the young Colony.

Mrs. Reibey died in 1855, misleading family and future historians with her own conservative and romanticised version of the whole epic saga of 1791-1794.

This is an historical project, bestrewn with many minute details about people and their habits, using available resources. Many of these clues were provided by her own cooperative descendants, who adopted me into the Reibey Clan, whether I was meeting them in Devon (U.K.), Queensland, Victoria, Tasmania, or New South Wales — a charming family trait.

The surname was pronounced Rabey, as in 'may be'. Tasmanian and Devon descendants politely insist that all their own immediate grandparents pronounced their parents' name in this way. The last person with this surname, a descendant of Thomas Reibey I, was Emily Charlotte Reibey of Devon who became Charlotte William-Powlett of Cadhay, Ottery St. Mary. She was Mary Reibey's great-great-granddaughter, dying in 1954, 100 years later than her famous ancestor. She is affectionately remembered as 'Sugar-Plum' by her grandson Oliver William-Powlett, present owner of Cadhay; he remembers well how Charlotte Reibey pronounced her maiden name. The wedding certificate of Thomas and Mary Reibey was signed by Thomas himself as 'Thomas Rabey', in September 1794.

Nancy Irvine,
Canberra

December 1981.

PREFACE TO SECOND EDITION

Since publication of my biography in 1982 newly discovered letters and newspaper accounts of Mary Reibey have given some further details about the merchant lady. I refer to the recent sale by auction in London of some more of Mary Reibey's letters. There is her exciting letter as a young lass, Molly Haydock, on the second day of arrival on the waters of Port Jackson. There is the 1986 publication of her 1818 letter when widowed Mary Reibey, business woman of Sydney Town. In addition during the last two years I have unearthed further facts concerning her husband, Thomas Reibey and his (Tom's) boyhood in Entally, near Calcutta, India.

Descendants of Mary and Thomas, many of whom I have met and quite a few of whom have become friends, have delighted in the story of Australia's first mercantile lady – convict Molly Haydock, who became Matriarch of Sydney Town.

The earlier legends surrounding Mary were dealt with in the first edition of my biography, to which Sothebys, London, have referred in their July catalogue. The newly discovered facts as we now understand them, add a lot to our picture of this remarkable woman. I quote her view of Sydney Cove from the deck of the *Royal Admiral.* The ship had arrived at the heads of Sydney Harbour at midday on the 7th October, 1792. It is written to her Aunt Hope, presumably wife of Adam Hope who had headed the list of Blackburn persons applying, unsuccessfully, for Mary's pardon before leaving England. (see p.20) This and subsequent letters are reproduced in near original form with minimal interpretation of spelling and punctuation, allowing for irregularities in handwriting. Explanatory notes follow each letter.

October 8th 1792 bottany bay.[1]

'My Dear Aunt[2]

We arrived on the 7th and I hope that it will answer better than we expected for I write this on board of ship but it looks a pleasant place Enough we shall have a pair of drawer to make a week[3] *(see p.37)* and we shall have twenty pounds [about 8 kilograms] of rice a week and 2½ pound of pork[4] besides Greens and other Vegetables the[y] tell me I am fore life wich the Governor told me I was for 7 years. wich Grieves me very much to think of it but I will watch every oppertunity to Get away in too or 3 years But I will make myself as happy as I Can In my Present and unhappy situation I will Give you Further satisfaction when I Get some and is setty [settled?] I am well and hearty as every I was in my Life[5] I desire you will answer me by some ship that is Coming and lett me know how the Children[6] is and all inquiring friends so I must Conclude because we are in a hurry to go to shore remember My Love to my sister[7] and Aunt Wamsley[8] and My Cousens so no more at present from your Dutiful neice Mary Haydock Mr Scott[9] Took 2 Guineas of me and said he would get me My Libberty [Parting?] ... with my sister has been very ...[cruel?]... To Me & I must never see you again...'

Notes:

1. Location was actually Port Jackson. Interesting to note that the Convicts had been sentenced to 7 years beyond the Seas to Botany Bay in 1791 – that of course was what was then generally accepted as the name of the Colony.
2. Prior to this letter becoming public (June 1987), there was no evidence to show that Mary Reibey corresponded with her Lancashire family during the voyage. Here however, is the missing evidence that Molly Haydock was corresponding with her Aunt Hope at least from her first day in New South Wales. And yet, that Aunt had not volunteered to undertake responsibility for the girl for four years in 1791 and thus save Mary from transportation for seven years. The 1818 letter (acquired by the State Library of New South Wales in 1986) is further evidence of the correspondence and there are the revelations in Mary Reibey's little daily book of remarks made in 1820 when she finally visited England.
3. The convict women made clothes from Osnaburg and other types of cloth, for the residents of the Colony. Hence they, as on page 37, were supplied with thread etc. for sewing garments. Apparently the convict women have been briefed before landing. Their quota was to be the making of one pair of draw(?) (trousers?) remembering the long shirts over bunched trousers that were worn in the late 18th century.
4. The rations appear to be fairly liberal considering that the Colony was still struggling to be self supporting. Pork meant salt pork in strips, mostly months old.
5. This is a particularly interesting report upon her health. Governor Phillip (page 44) commented that too many people had been crowded into the small *Royal Admiral* including 289 male convicts and 47 female convicts. On arrival the sick were taken to hospital, the healthy to the settlement at Rose Hill (Parramatta). It also shows that Mary at least and no doubt many other women, other than the pregnant and sick, were relatively well treated on the voyage. We know they were allowed most of the time, on the deck with the free women travelling on board. (see p.42)
6. Also Notes 7,8. These reveal that Mary felt very keenly about her immediate family even though she had run away from her 'situation' in Blackburn, Lancashire. In fact,

this letter changes the original perception of her as a girl who did not want her family as such. It was they who dared not keep her. See Chapter 4.

9. Mr Scott's identity remains a mystery. However, it was probably the last time Mary Haydock was conned by anyone. No wonder she managed her monetary affairs so well in later life!

★ ★ ★

The second letter, bought in December 1985 by the State Library of NSW, also requires footnotes to illustrate the contemporary scene, as it affected the Reibey family and discusses esoteric family details. This is quoted in full under the editorial conditions as previously mentioned.

Sydney NSW August 12, 1818

'Dear Cousin Alice[1]

by a Gentleman Who Expects to come to Liverpool and which I believe is a resident their I avail myself of the opportunity of letting you know that with myself my Family are all well and that of Announcing the safe arrival of my dear sister[2] and Family all well except herself which suffered severly during a paſsage of Five Months and 2 days[3] but now thank God she is perfectly Recovered and which added more to her disappointment was when she arrivd I was Absent at Vandiemans Land[4] wither I had gone to settle my affairs previous to my Coming home [England] as I had Let my shop and Whare houses as also my Farms but her arrival will detain me sometime longer as I do not wish to leave her and Mr Foster Expects to get his Land[5] and Indulgences and proceed with the cultivation of it so that he can either let or sell it I intend bringing my Eldest Daughter Celia[6] and youngest son George and I believe my three little ones...that I am preſsent Deveided about my Son George I was thinking of placing with Mr ... of Manchester Should we agree & should it Lye in your way to mention it to him I Whould thank you to send his Terms so that I may hasten his Comeing home [England] as he is getting so big I had him at a Latin School till within this 9 months ever since he [Thomas 2?] came from England my eldest[7] Son [Thomas Reibey 2] is Married and become the father of a fine Daughter my other Son James which I let your ever to be Revered Mother know of his Marriage is now on a visit to us and on Busineſs but George is now at Vandiemans Land as I left him to Collect the Remainder of my Debt and Rents when I heard my sister had arrived I was very Impatient to see her so that she has not yet seen him I went down their in a brig of my own[8] Commanded by my Son Thomas and brought her up Loaded [probably later] with which she is now gone after a cargo of Cedar Wood[9] for Building Mr Foster is gone in her I expect him in the Course of six or Eight weeks I have also got a Small

Schooner but Trade and Commerce is getting so bad that I Cannot sell anything or I Should have been Home [England] long before now   I have enclosed you a Couple of our Sydney Gazettes where you will see an advertizement of mine but their is no person here able to purchase them so I must give over the Idea of selling[10] and live on my income   but I had forgot 2 Farms one of 100 & one of 40 acres at Hawkesbury and the Estate that I have lately purchased at Vandiemans Land of 2000 acres[11]   as an entail on my Children forever and one Agoining [adjoining?] I Purchased when I was down their of 40 acres   so that my yearly income is one Thousand pounds [in 1818!] and should I Come to England Immediately I could have – Remitted home seven hundreds pounds per Annum after leaving a little for my sons and paying agency – therefore I think it will be as well to leave them [the farms?] as to Sell to make a Sacrifice   my sister [Elizabeth Foster] begs of me to mention a Book Entitled the History of N.S.Wales [?] that she left with a man in Byron's [shop?] next door to the first House as you turn the Corner   that is all the description she can give   she wishes you to get it for her if you Can   she Whould do very well here Could she have her own way at her Busineſs and Mr Foster too but noone will do well that is not thrifty Correct and Sober *(see p.84)*   this place is not like England you are under the Eye of every one and your Character Scrutinized by both Rich and poor[12]   altho you may have a different Oppinion of it through the different Characters that Comes here   but they are Kept in Regular order by our Good Governor Laclan Macqurie[13] he has been here these eight years altho it is the orders from home that no Govt should be kept here more than five years but through his good Conduct is Solicited from England to Stay longer   the young man that I wrote my sister sometime ago by the Name of James Foster Which She tells me she understood to be the same person which Mrs Hilton Interceded for is doing very well and a very Respectable young man he is   before my sister Came he told me he knew your Brother John very well   those Houses[14] in Salford which did belong to me & my sister and which she has made over her Interest in to your Mother I should wish if agreeable to Repurchase on my arrival in England   the Bill is against me I have Recd by the hands of my sister which shall be attended too   I can aſsure you my poor sister never mentions your Mother[15] but with Tears and the Deepest Sorrow for her loſs and altho I had not seen her for 27 years[16] it had a great effect on me for almost the first interchange of words with my sister was to know if my aunt Hope was alive   I do aſsure you the meeting of her was one of the happiest moments of my life and still more so knowing it was in my power to aſsist her as I Consider her so deserving the protection of me and every one who knows her *(see p.84, James' later letter)* She did not meet as good Treatment as might be expected on her paſsage Considering what she paid but had I been at home [Sydney] while the Capt of the ship was here I Whould have actioned him but he sailed the day after I came home little Eliza and James [Foster] go to the same school as my 3 children[18] who are Boarders they are fine company for each other and are very fond of each other little Eliza [Foster] is ... notice by everyone she is such an agreeable little thing my youngest little girl [Elizabeth] and her are very much alike and is remarked almost by everyone my sister wished me particularly to mention to you how my Husband came here he was 2d officer and ... of the *Brittania* Whaler ship which was laying in the Harbour when I came here and he prevailed on the Captain to let him stay here [who was Guardian to him][19] I hope dear Cousin altho unknown to you but for the sake of your dear Mother you will write by every opportunity and by sending your letters to Mrs Smith in London Where my sister stayd She will be remitted I have nothing more at present to say except my sons and all my children desires their love to you and all your brothers [David and John Hope] my sister desires her Respectful Compliments to Miſs Ward, Mrs Wood, Mrs Aspinall, Mrs Parkinson, and my Aunts Hind [Hindle] *(see p.88)* and Ramsbottom and to all Inquiring Friends and pray Remember me to them likewise and my sincere love to yourself and brothers Jane and Eliza[20] send their love to you I am Dear Cousin yours Affectionately M.Reibey My sister thinks it whould be the best way to pay the postage to the Lands end of England and they are sure to come safe'

The important news in this letter confirms assumptions made from Mary Reibey's advertisements in the *Sydney Gazette* that she meant to go to England. Home as she calls it. It confirms that Tom 2, her eldest son, had visited England.

The letter gives a very conservative valuation of her property and cash flow of £1000 per Annum income, very considerable in 1818. It shows how much education Mary had absorbed when compared to her letter as a fifteen year old convict girl. It shows her goodwill towards her sister and husband though this attitude did change later.

It indicates how carefully she was obliterating her early sentence of deportation back in 1792 by sending her three young children to a Boarding school, and her son to a Latin school. It gives her version of meeting Tom Reibey, though we know that he went with the *Brittania* to Cape Town in 1792, that he and Mary did not marry till September 1794, when he was granted his first land at the Hawkesbury settlement.

Notes:

1. Cousin Alice, daughter of Adam Hope. Two years later, in 1820 when Mary finally reached England, Alice Hope became a close friend.

2. Mary's sister – Elizabeth Foster formerly Elizabeth Haydock, five years senior to Mary and apparently reared by her aunt, Mrs Hope while Mary was cared for by her Grandmother Law in Bury. Married to Charles Foster, Elizabeth with her husband and her three children arrived in the Colony in February 1818. They settled in Van Diemen's Land near Launceston.
3. Mary's 1792 journey had taken just under six months; not much improvement despite the 25 years that had elapsed.
4. By 1818, as well as those interests in NSW, Mary Reibey had consolidated land grants, mortgage settlements and built quite a business in Van Diemen's Land on the banks of the Tamar and the Esk, where Entally House was to be built. The brothers, Thomas 2 and James, had staithes or wharves on the river banks and the Reibey schooners berthed there with their cargo.
5. Her two daughters, Celia and Eliza, accompanied Mary to London in 1820.
6. The *Sydney Gazette* advertises several schools at this time for the 'colonial gentry.'
7. Thomas Reibey 2, apparently returning from England, married one of the most eligible young ladies in the Colony, Richarda Allen. They settled at Hadspen on the River Esk south of Launceston and began building Entally House, now famous as a designated State historical property.
8. This says it all – Mary Reibey travelled to Tasmania in her own brig commanded by her eldest son.
9. The small schooner had been built at the Wills-Reibey shipyard before Tom 1 died in 1811.
10. These advertisements are well documented.
11. The 2000 acres was purchased near to grants to her sons and which became Entally.
12. Governor Macquarie favoured the Emancipists. However it appears that Mary Reibey did not tell of her emancipist status.
13. Legend talks of her popularity with Macquarie, no evidence so far uncovered.

14,15,16. Mary talks of the 26 years since she was transported in this private letter. She is preparing the way for her trip to 'Home'.

17. Her protection for her sister.
18. The careful schooling.
19. Records show that Tom Reibey 'jumped' ship with his commander's permission but this was in 1793. He was allowed a small grant of land.
20. Eliza and Jane Penelope Reibey. Eliza travelled to England with her mother.

★ ★ ★

There are three later letters recently auctioned by Sothebys, London, 1987. From these extracts which follow are some known facts which can be added to the letters already given in the first edition.

Letter A, dated 5 August 1825.

> 'theire is great alterations here now with the Clergy. Mr McAuthur *(sic)* Certainly is a very Clever man [1] and I think a very good one... he is rather too violent in the Pulpit I am afraid it will Engure his lungs. we are now dayly expecting our new Governor... I suppose their will be great alterations in our Government but all the same to me I never meddle in politics'[2]

Notes:

1. Rev. Archibald Macarthur first Presbyterian minister in Australia was appointed to Hobart in December 1822.
2. This was not true as Mary Reibey was very supportive of Wentworth.

As shown on page 103, Mary was complaining of being short of cash to pay her accounts according to her letter discovered in 1981 in Devon.

Letter B, dated October 1829 (Read James' letter dated 1829 p.84 together with these extracts)

> 'I have had the first legal Advice in the Colony and they say they are of opinion that I can refuse to receive them after such a length of time... I realy do not know what to do with them their is no money in the Colony noone will buy under 12 or 18 months credit here even my poor Eliza has now got 5 children... he[1] is very kind and affectionate to her but that is not all... she is quite a slave to them... had she a Husband equal to herself they might have been amongst the first people in the Colony but he is fit for nothing...'

Notes:

1. Formerly Lieutenant Thomson who had squired Mary and the girls in London and assisted them all the way home to New South Wales, shared a big wedding to Eliza in Launceston but, who had then embezzelled from the Government some £3000, which Mary Reibey made good.

Mary died in 1855. She had been troubled by the Cobbold tarradiddle about Margaret Catchpole... (see p.109)

Letter C, dated 21 June 1845

> 'I am Obliged to exercise the greatest prudence and econimy still in my old age and so many years of perseverance and industry it is hard to be deprived of the many Comforts I have been accustomed too but that I do not think so much of as the unprincipled feeling towards me in the matter... I open my mind to you more than to anyone else since the Melancholy death of all my sons' [Thomas died in 1842 and James in 1844].

It is hard to reconcile these thoughts of penury with her very substantial estate, with the then magnificence of Entally, Tasmania and her holdings in Sydney and on the South Coast of New South Wales.

* * *

Finally I come to the interesting tale of Thomas Reibey 1, the first mate on the East India Company licensed whaler *Britannia*, captained by the part owner and friend of Tom, Captain Raven.

By chance Mary and Tom's grandson, Thomas Reibey III, Premier of Tasmania, was interviewed in 1876 at Entally House, Hadspen Tasmania, by a reporter from the Hobart newspaper, *The Mercury*. The newspaper account reveals how Premier Reibey explained that this Entally, as was the house in Macquarie Place, Sydney also known as Entally, were both named after the district of Entally near Calcutta in Bengal. His grandfather, the Premier said, had been wrecked as a boy Marine off the Bengal coast, rescued and cared for by Bengal people at Entally. He, Thomas I, had believed that his father was drowned.

With this slim clue, I searched in the India Office Library in Blackfriars Road, London for evidence of wrecks off Bengal between the relevant years 1748 to 1800. Likewise I looked in the Press Lists of Calcutta from 1748 to 1800 and found the letters of Tom's father addressed to the East India Company after his spell as a prisoner of the French. He was Edward Raby (for one spelling of Reibey) younger son of a Cobham, Kent family, second officer of the East India Company schooner *Tannah.* This English vessel of the hated East India Company was caught by the French and burned to the water line on 24th January 1781. The boy, Thomas, who was twelve years and a midshipman on his father's boat escaped when wrecked. He was fortunately rescued by the Bengal family or people from Entally.

Thomas I, when Mary's spouse, remained a frequent visitor to Entally in Bengal, eventually there contracting an illness which killed him in 1811 after his last visit in 1810. Edward Raby, Tom's father had been taken prisoner by the French, being released after the treaty of Versailles of 1783. Edward Raby made his way to Fort William, the Calcutta Base of the East India Company only to find that all his friends were either dead or returned to Europe. I quote the two letters as discovered in the India Office Library in London.

Fort William 23rd February 1784

> 'Hon'ble Sir & Sirs,
>
> I beg leave to lay before your Hon'ble Board that I was made prisoner by the French on 24th of January, 1781 being at that time 2nd officer on board the *Tannah* schooner, belonging to the Hon'ble Company's Bengal Marines and that after a severe imprisonment I am at length arrived at this place distitute of every neceſsary where to add to mortification those Friends I left here in whose power it was to assist me are either dead or gone to Europe. I therefore Hon'ble Sir & Sirs look up to you for assistance hoping you will enable me by an order from your Hon'ble Board to receive my pay as second officer of the above mentioned Vessel during the time of my imprisonment to furnish myself with such neceſsarys as I am immediately in want of trusting in the Generosity of the Hon'ble Board.
>
> I remain &ca Edward Raby'

The order of the 'Hon'ble Board' reads;

February 1784

> 'Agreed that mr Raby be put on the same footing with others in a similar Situation and Ordered that notice thereof be sent to the Marine Paymaster.'

Edward made his way home to England where he made his will naming his brother Alexander Raby, Gentleman of Cobham, Kent as his executor. He returned to India on the *Deptford* 16 August 1786 bound for Diamond Head, port for Calcutta as a saloon passenger; he having first been to see the top management of the Company's affairs in London to secure his promotion. Cudbert Thornhill, Supervisor of the Bengal Marines wrote "that on enquiry it appears that Mr Raby deserves to be reinstated with his rank as Officer commanding".

A search of contemporary sources reveals no record of his death, certainly not on board the *Deptford*, nor any record of his marriage. But there can be little doubt that he was Tom's father after such evidence of that of Tom having been wrecked at that time as a Marine seaman. Interestingly Mary never sought out any Reibey connections when visiting England, yet pursued every Haydock relative in 1820. Even more interesting that Thomas Reibey I had such a strong affection for Entally, Calcutta. I tend to think his mother was a high caste Indian lady as was the case with so many officers in the East India Company. He was always a brave sailor, suffering pirates, native uprisings on the Pacific Islands as well as his experience as a boy midshipman. Mary may never have known of Edward Raby, only of the Entally connection.

These newly-found letters of the Reibeys and the Hopes, coupled with records of the East India Company and the reminiscences of the great Thomas Reibey III, Premier of Tasmania in 1876, do much to add in a valuable way to the data gathered for my biography of Mary Reibey...Molly Incognita.

Nance Irvine
Elizabeth Bay, NSW. 1987

PART I
MOLLY HAYDOCK — GIRL AS BOY

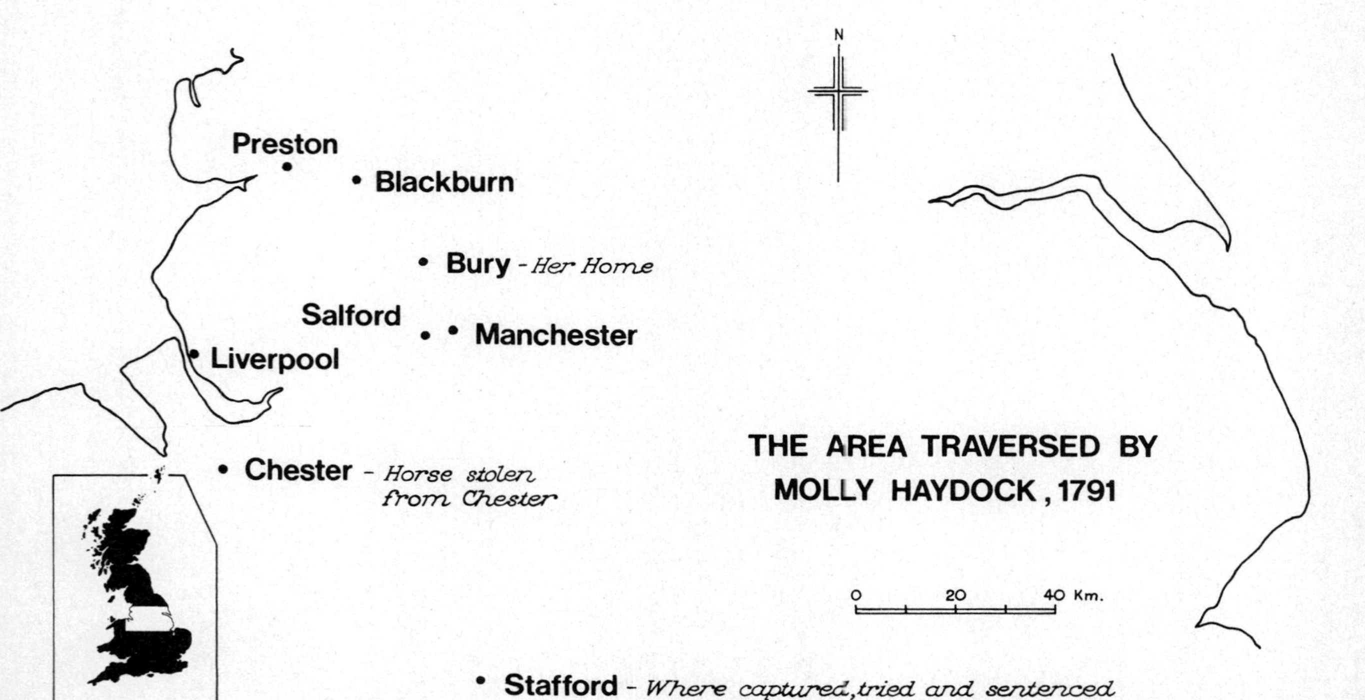
N
Preston
Blackburn
Bury - Her Home
Salford
Manchester
Liverpool
Chester - Horse stolen
from Chester
THE AREA TRAVERSED BY
MOLLY HAYDOCK, 1791
0
20
40 Km.
Stafford - Where captured, tried and sentenced

Chapter 1

PRELUDE . . . TO 1791

The Missing Detail — the discrepancy.

For Sydney people the well known name, Mary Reibey, probably conjures up visions of the historic Rocks area to be found near the present Harbour Bridge. Some may visualize hazy pictures of 18th century Colonists, a motley group sharing a precarious existence, all tenaciously establishing the infant nation. Reibey Place near Pitt and George Streets, at Circular Quay, close by the site of Governor Phillip's first brave flag-flying, may recall the Reibey family store. There have been many cogent reasons for the varying accounts of this splendid lady's history: accounts, however, which were often based upon incorrect romantic reports; reports handed down through the years, perhaps indeed from Mary herself.

It would be folly to talk of the daring deeds and disastrous experiences of the teenaged Molly Haydock without first looking at her old world of Lancashire, Bury-Blackburn in the 18th century, her family, and her early environment. Accordingly, for the purpose of this biography, a search was commenced in 1978 in relevant archives. In the Public Record Office, Chancery Lane, London, an interesting discrepancy was discovered: a discrepancy from the 'received' accounts and records of the childish escapade which culminated in transportation in 1792. The Muster of the Colonial Secretary (Reel 2427, Archives Office of N.S.W.) of the convict personnel of the transports, for the voyage of the *Royal Admiral* in 1792, records:

> '119, Mary Haddock, [sic] al James Burroughs, County Stafford Assizes, on 10/3/1790 for seven years.'

The Muster is incorrect in two details; the trial took place at the Stafford Summer Assizes on 24 August 1791; the surname should read Haydock, (Molly), as on her birth certificate.

A routine search of the original government records of that trial failed to reveal the name Molly Haydock (or Haddock), though the names of several girls were listed amongst the thirty-six people accused. Peripheral searches which followed were fruitless. However, repeated checking threw up the name James Borrow; but there was *no* indication that this was an alias. (Note — the same court records do indicate another prisoner's alias *and* his correct name.) Indeed, if the search in the Mitchell Library of the Colonial Secretary's Muster had not recorded the 'Burroughs' alias, this interesting story would never have been detected.

For, most oddly, the original pathetic conviction, and the evidence, the application for commutation from the death sentence to 'transportation beyond the seas' are *all* concerned with a young boy named James Borrow, labourer of St. Mary's Parish, Stafford, 1791 — so where was the recorded evidence of the 'girl', Molly Haddock? Why hadn't the blunt and factual Court proceedings of the Summer Assizes of Stafford, England, of 1791, recorded the trial of a girl from Bury, Lancashire? She simply wasn't there, according to all the evidence; or was she?

Mary Reibey was born in Bury, England and christened Molly Haydock, 1777. The background to her childhood and her adventure becomes extremely important when putting into perspective the traits of that indomitable personality whose subsequent colourful maturity makes such a success story in the early commercial history of Sydney and, indeed, of New South Wales, and also of Tasmania (Van Diemen's Land). Her story clearly demanded objective research into the life of Molly Haydock who became Mary Reibey.

Family History.

Her tough little ghost persistently followed me through Great Britain to her childhood locale: Preston, Blackburn, Bury, Darwen. Paradoxically, in the Lancashire Archives Office, Preston, though it was an unbelievably cold September day, I was warmed by those relevant records; records redolent with Lancashire names from centuries back. Those families (as shown later) that were connected with Molly Haydock's genealogy were incredibly dynastic. These names — Haydock, Hindle, Hope, Hargreaves and Law — popped up periodically from the thin pale parchment rolls — rolls yards long,[1] on to which the good Bishop, 'Gerald Clayton, Wigan, of the Parish of Walter le Dal', had transcribed Blackburn District records of all Christening, Marriage and Burial services dating from 1609 to 1812. Reverently handling these rolls, I wondered whether my Lord Bishop had used a quill when executing that impeccable spidery copperplate script. Confronted by such a mammoth search the brain stuttered, but that girlish ghost, by now a 'familiar', pressed alongside demanding a true and fair report of her 18th century Bury-Blackburn background. A fascinating picture comes alive as one reads reports of this busy, populous 18th century Lancashire area.

Historian Will Abram[2] has traced some of these families back to the 14th century. Nowadays the local Blackburn telephone book is a Who's Who of Haydock (Heydock)[3], Law, Hindle, Hope and Hargreaves families — families important to this story since these names occur in the Travel Diary Notes[4] made by Mary Reibey some thirty years later during her return visit to England in 1820-21. The locality (near Liverpool, England) includes Darwen Street near Pleasington, and which was an 'appendage' of Bury; Mellor and all places 'continguous' to Blackburn. Shaw[5] most interestingly identifies Darwen as Over Darwen, a Norman settlement of the 11th century and as being in 1702 the home of coal cutters, with a population of 600 souls. By Molly Haydock's time, the district sported two printing works, many shops, and a population of 3,587 — getting quite crowded. The yeoman family of Haydock, variously spelt as Heydock, is recorded sporadically, from Roger Haydock, 1342; John, who (predictably) was taxed in 1690; Lawrence the same in 1701; and John in 1729.[6] In 1740 Thomas Haydock by licence married Mary Bracewell of Goosnargh.[7] (What a lovely name! One may still visit Goosnargh, go into a spooky old monastery and shiver while looking at the priest hole and fear a visitation of the well known ghost of a long since perished, walled up priest.)

Mary and Thomas Haydock's children included William, born 1746(7), **and James** who became the father of Molly, our heroine. Historically there is no mystery about the Haydock ancestry; they were sound, uncomplicated Lancastrian yeomen, living in a village that reached back into the times of the roving Norman settlers. There is no evidence available that James Haydock was other than a yeoman of the district.

Molly's mother was Jane Law.[8] She had lived with her family about twenty yards past the Grey Mare Inn near Darwen Street, Bury.[9] The Law family have an equally long established residency in Bury — the name first figuring on a Blackburn church tombstone, to wit — 'Chris Law 1500'.[10] Aunt Hindle Brown, lovingly referred to in 1820 by Mary Reibey,[11] was descended from Hindle of Hind Fold, by way of Christopher Hindle of Bradley Hall and Higher Croft and eventually of a 'mansion' of Lower Darwen. Similarly the other named relatives can be traced.[12] One comes to wonder, rather cynically, as to the whereabouts of these people when Molly so desperately needed them in 1791.[13]

Such is the background to the family of this girl. Such is the stuff of history, the 'genes', dare one say, of some first comers to our nation. For Molly was to come to 'Botany Bay' as a convict in 1792, and to become the wife of the free man Thomas Raby (Reibey) in 1794.

Her Childhood, 1777-1791.

Born on 12 May 1777, christened Molly Haydock on 29 May, father James Haydock,[14] Molly is quite clearly identifiable as the daughter of James Haydock and Jane Law.[15] There was one little sibling who had survived the infant mortality lists of those records; this was Elizabeth, born 1771[16] and now five years old. There has to be some careful speculation or extrapolation about these childhood years, drawn from the meagre crumbs unwittingly dropped by Mary Reibey in her 1820 Travel Diary. (It is deemed an unwitting act, as the lady has so carefully omitted all mention of her early defection from the family circle.) That she was an orphan is apparent. James Haydock, yeoman of Bury, Pleasington[17] died in 1779. From the tantalizing official early records innocent of antecedent generations, save the name of the father, it is still possible to assume that there were two other little daughters born to the Haydock menage; one, Dolly, who died at birth on 6 January 1773, and a Mary, who died on 25 November 1774.[18] It appears that her mother also died during the children's infancy, since she, Molly, lived with her grandmother and had a nurse. (*Vide* the Diary[19]: she writes '. . . on entering my Grandmother's House where I had been brought up . . .'; she also speaks of meeting her old nurse.[20]) There is no mention of that other little sister, Elizabeth, being around in those days; indeed the Diary makes only two brief mentions of Mrs. Elizabeth Foster.[21] Possibly Molly was a frequent attendant at some church services. She was christened at Bury, her parents' marriage took place in St. John's and her later Travel Diary is full of Church references. Yet the minister, the Reverend Thomas Harkie, minister at Blackburn in 1791, when sending the Petition (Chapter 3) on its way, does add a rider '. . . not knowing the young girl personally I could not with propriety put my name to the petition.'[22] But the friends allege 'Her Grandmother had used every endeavour . . . to enjoin her [Molly] to the practice of every moral religious duty.'[23]

Most important to this research is the comment in the 1820 Diary:[24]

'. . . and [I] whent [sic] to see the first stone laid of the old church at Blackburn. It is somewhat singular that nearly thirty years ago before that Mr. David Hope and myself was at the September 2nd [1790] laying of the first stone in St. John's Church.'[25]

So Molly and David had stood together in 1790. How much for them to remember in 1820. Molly was a girl of eleven years in September 1788, when Governor Phillip had commenced that tremendous adventure in the South, in which, so shortly, she was to be involved.

It appears that relatives had secured a good education for the orphaned child. Children of yeoman stock were fortunate in the late 18th century, according to Trevelyan,[26] as they, as a class, had money to invest both in land and the new industrial scene and in the education and upgrading of their families. Mary Reibey's Travel Notes reveal a good hand, and an intelligent grasp of written expression which must have stemmed from an early family environment of literate people and from a thorough schooling. As a random example from her Diary, written when she was forty-three years of age, note her comments when visiting Glasgow in 1820:

'we availed ourselves of their kind invitation to dinner . . . after taking a glass of wine and a little Bride cake (they being lately married) the Gentlemen took us to see the different manufactorys and . . . the sounding Ile attached to the old Abbey . . . and returned and dined from a very sumptious dinner provided by our friendly host.'[27]

The same Diary shows a familiarity with Gibbons, Grecian History, Walter Scott, and British Essayists. Her schooling looks to have been with the local Grammar School, of which school the Headmaster, the Reverend Samuel Dean saw fit to add his name to the 'humble' petition of 5th November, 1791, petitioning for Molly Haydock's freedom.[28] It seems fair to deduce that she had been a pupil up to early 1791, and had been a respected school member. The Blackburn Grammar School had evolved from a school founded in 1514 according to *A Brief Sketch of Schools*[29] — and was a well established school. As a child it appears she had endeared herself to her nurse, as evident in two Diary entries. Mary visited the old lady in 1820 at her home in Openshaw-folie near Bury, and the nurse

'in her 81st year of her age (with her husband) was so gratifyed hardly knew how to contain themselves with joy . . .'[30]

And again, in the cold of New Year's Day, January 1821, these old people walked the nine miles from Bury to see her at Manchester, Salford. As Mary Reibey writes:

'A more venerable and better looking old man I never saw and a more healthy old woman at her age . . . indeed she looked likely to live twenty or thirty years more.'[31]

Certainly not the actions of a celebrity seeker, one would think, but rather those of a still loving nurse.

Agent-Provocateur or Simply Galvanized by Misery?

Apart from her schooling, her Grandmother's home, her church activities, an intelligent lass like Molly must have heard much talk of the district. The roads were still nightmare experiences for travellers; mud and highwaymen were the norm. Circulating libraries spread the Gothic horror stories, the adventure stories and the love stories of the late 18th century. The nearby shipping port of Liverpool, recorded a growing population of 78,000 in 1770, with Manchester-Salford, not far away, listing 140,000 people. From the Liverpool trading port 'slavers' were regularly sailing to North America and West Africa. One hundred and seven of these ships left Liverpool in 1777 on their round trip, selling finished cotton goods, buying and selling slaves and buying raw cotton for the mills.[32] Molly would have heard of the prison hulks, of the muddled laws of the times which demanded the death penalty for sheep and horse stealing, of sentences to transportation for petty thieving. She must have been aware of the public hangings.[33] There is little early evidence of family concern other than that outlined already, apart from the care given by her Grandmother, who as noted died before the 1791 affair.[34] Concerning her childhood memories, one sentence in the 1820 Diary suggests earlier family disunity. Mary Reibey is with her Hope cousin in Darwen Street on 6 August 1820. She writes:

> 'It is impossible to describe the sensations I felt when comeing [sic] to the top of Darwen Street . . . my native home . . . and amongst my relatives [that is 1820 relatives] and on entering my once Grandmother's House where I had been brought up, and to find it nearly the same as when I left nearly 29 years ago, and all the same furniture and most of them standing in the same place as when I left *but not one person I knew or knew me*.'[35] [Author's italics.]

In the Diary one playmate of the past is mentioned:

> '[There] was a Deaf and Dumb woman whom I had often played with when a girl, came to see me, she appeared to be overjoyed.'[36]

Yet, despite schooling, family, church, despite the risks both known and unknown, Molly Haydock ran away from Bury in June 1791. The petition of friends quotes Molly Haydock as having been 'prevailed on by another young girl [no name given] to leave her situation in June 1791.'[37] So the possibility exists that upon the demise of Grandma Law, the thirteen year old Molly had been placed in service, in a situation. Perhaps she fled in misery. Obviously she disliked her new situation, so possibly fired with adventurous dreams of the great Southern capital, London, and perhaps in fact influenced by an agent provocateur, Molly 'threw her cap over the windmill' and vanished. She was to disguise herself in boy's clothing and take the name of James Borrow. There had been a boy of this name born a month before her,[38] who, if records are correct, had died in 1789 — significantly two years prior to this adoption of a most convenient alias. She used his name for months. Despite all the well known dangers of the Highway, Molly Haydock, now known as James Borrow, ran away to encounter a heap of trouble. So much for the Bury-Blackburn childhood scene.

Staffordshire. The Jurors for our Lord the King upon their Oath present . . . Guilty; to be hanged no goods that James Burrow late of the parish of Saint Mary in the Borough of Stafford in the County of Stafford Laboror on the thirteenth Day of August in the thirty first Year of the Reign of our Sovereign Lord George the third King of Great Britain etc with force and arms at the Parish aforesaid in the County aforesaid one Bay Mare of the price of Ten pounds . . . of the Goods and Chattels of John Sorton then and there being found feloniously did steal take and lead away against the peace of our said Lord the King his Crown and Dignity.

W.J.

John Williamson Esq., Joseph Dickenson, Clerk — "two of his Majesty's Justices of the Peace for the s[d] county of Stafford" etc. on the Assizes record of 29 September 1791.

On the back, "A True Bill — John Sorton Hughes — Robert Silvester — Francis Emborton — William Moore — John Commander 5 sworn in Court" (Signed individually.)

P.R.O. London Assi 5/111 4181

Chapter 2
BAKER MAN — BEGGAR BOY — THIEF

The Restless Teenager — Reckless or Calculating?

Although this account is biographical, and provenance is documented, relying strictly on legitimate sources, let it not be deemed a mere tedious barebones picture — a skeleton without the flesh of personality. In another 'biographical' account of a man-woman charade, Virginia Woolf clearly states the dilemma, the limitations of the genre when she complains:

> 'our simple duty is to state the facts and so let the reader make of them what he may'[39]

but adds:

> '[the subject] from the rumours, legends, anecdotes of a floating and unauthenticated kind . . . will have the power to stir the fancy . . . to keep a memory green, [will have] a mysterious power we may call glamour.'[40]

For some living in this contrived, mechanical world of the late 20th century, the memory of Molly Haydock generates this power, this kind of glamour. Let us 'green the memory'! We need to discover that girl, just fourteen years of age, who abandoned her 'situation' in 1791.[41] Perhaps the Petition story[42] that another (significantly unnamed) lass went with her, persuading her to a male masquerade and to a journey south, has some grains of truth. But this I find is doubtful on the evidence of her later actions; actions sometimes unwise, which appear to be based on Miss Haydock's own initiative. Allegedly, the "girls'" partnership dissolved upon reaching Chester.[43] In appearance it is reasonable to assume Molly was flat chested, therefore boyish, small in stature: girls in the cold North, it is claimed by medical savants, are late in maturation, often in their sixteenth and seventeenth year of life. Further, the extant portrait of the subject when a middle-aged forty years, shows a small rounded face, implying a small short frame.[44] The question is, was this girl hot-headed, heedless, daring? Was she a fool-hardy romantic child easily influenced by another? Or was she a cool determined young girl who took this daring, calculated plunge into an unsheltered life on the roads? I opt for the last plucky hearted character! She has an attractive image which stubbornly persists throughout her story.

The social historians, writing of the late 18th century give a grim picture of the chaotic, unpoliced, crowded industrial and agricultural north.[45] Manchester and district was a mere nine miles away, with a reportedly recorded populace of 137,201,[46] being the second largest city (of Great (Britain), the first being the Queen City of London with its one million inhabitants (in 1790). Agreed then that Molly Haydock would have reached her early 'teens', accepting as normal the world 'outside'; an environment of seamen from the Liverpool 'slavers', the local and foreign traffic on the Canals, the easy acceptance of smuggling,[47] the 'recruiting' habits of the military press gangs. She would have known of transportation prior to the American Wars, the Independence Declaration almost coinciding with her birth; of the unreal 'capital' crimes and the consequent public hangings[48] or, very recently, the alternative transportation to Botany Bay. Blackburn-Bury was not a village hidden in the hills — it was on a travellers' trunk road, mud and dirt though it may be.[49] There were, note, some 4,000 talkative village and town souls to tell of highwaymen attacking coaches, of stolen horses — horses which were the country's most valuable asset before the days of steam and mechanised wheels. But still she went adventuring into this violent social maelstrom.

The Clever Alias — the Beggar Boy and the Old Mare.

Camouflaged as a boy, she most skilfully succeeded in adapting to the role, and as noted in Chapter 1, named the miscreant young fellow as James Borrow. A neat choice, possibly a childhood companion;[50] the carefully chosen pseudonym again shows a forward planning, rather than an impetuous flight. 'James Borrow' in this disguise, is described with certainty[51] as having the appearance of a possible horse thief — and as looking very much a boy, and 'tho' very young as to age, an old offender'.[52] It's a goodish step from Blackburn to Chester, around or across the Mersey. According to the Petition,[53] Molly, now 'James', 'left [Blackburn] her situation in the month of June (1791) . . . that they immediately came for Chester and the next day they parted . . .' (i.e. Molly parted from the unnamed girl companion). So 'James Borrow' was somewhere on the road from June to August, (his name variously spelt as Burrow) and admittedly had reached Chester and 'went' on 'his' way to Stafford — forty miles away. It so happened that a ten years old mare, spavined and all, belonging to a Chester glover, John Sorton,[54] 'was stolen out of a Field adjoining the City of Chester in the night of the eleventh of August [1791].' The Petition[55] asserts that Molly Haydock disguised as James Burrow was on 'his' way to Stafford and 'was accidentally overtaken by a man with 2 horses who desired 'him' [James] to ride one and he would please 'him' and that the man fearing a discovery left 'him' in Stafford with the horse.' So reads the Petition. From this point one must think only of a small ragged scrawny young fourteen year old boy to appreciate to the full the happenings from June 1791 to November 1791.

In actual fact, John Sorton's mare arrived in Stafford in the charge of the boy, James Borrow, towards evening on Friday 12th August 1791. If these sworn statements of John Sorton Hughes[56] and Robert Silvester[57] are correct, then that old mare logged a pretty good day's trot from Chester to Stafford. Did James in fact, in desperation, 'collect' the mare from Chester? Actually Mr. Justice Heath's report appears to give a more reasonable account:

> 'She [the mare] was stolen off a Common near Chester and was missed on the 12th August 1791'[58]

— 'missed', mark you, or so deposed the nephew of the glover. Stealing a horse was an act punishable by death: in the 18th century, the horse was everyone's joy and need. (Without good work horses, agricultural activities would revert to primitive practice: likewise the well bred blood thoroughbreds of the age were big business in George III's day. Trevelyan writes of the equine importance:

'from the race horse to the hardly less noble carthorse. The horse was essential to sport, travel and agriculture and to all these the English gentlemen of the age were devoted.'[59]

The bakers, the yeomen, the merchants, the exporters, the stage coachmen and the highwaymen all needed the transporting horse: and all enjoyed the sporting activities engendered by fine animals — as can be seen in Phillip's and Pollard's aquatint of May 1786[60] where a lively motley of all classes enjoy a race meeting. Trevelyan claims 'riding was the commonest act of the day' among the upper and middle classes.[61])

To return to the two days, 12 and 13 August 1791. Either James Borrow 'collected' the mare from the Chester Common, or, as claimed in the Petition, was left in Stafford with the stolen animal. However, the sequel shows no sign of James abandoning that animal, probably knowing it to be stolen, or of James running for cover. He shows a reckless disregard for foreseeable and, possibly, terrifying consequences.

According to the evidence,[62] on that high summer day, going about his duties was Robert Silvester, who kept the Swan Inn at Stafford. Towards evening on Friday 12 August he saw a young boy on horseback approaching his Inn, and the boy accosted him. The boy, afterwards identified as James Borrow, asked Silvester if he would buy the mare. For, claimed James, the horse belonged to 'his' Uncle Darbin who 'lived about five miles from Chester.' Silvester noted the animal 'was a Bay horse with a longish tail'. He told the boy to get along — to go about his business. But James was apparently desperate for a sale, and 'he' hung about the stables till very early next morning, 13 August, a Saturday morning at a bright summery 5 a.m. The fully detailed events[63] demand dramatizing to bring the reckless, determined courage of young James Borrow to the forefront of this account.

Francis Emborton, the hostler of the same Swan Inn, met James Borrow riding the mare at 5 a.m. James Borrow offered Francis the mare by sale — and no, '[I'd rather] stand the Horse Market with Her' replied Francis. James was tenacious in 'his' anxiety to sell, saying 'he' only asked Thirteen Pounds (a lot of money surely in 1791!) for the mare, 'she was aged about four past'. No, replied the hostler Francis, looking into the mare's mouth, adding 'he thought she was [as] old as he [Francis] was'. What's more, Francis began to suspect 'her to have been stolen, and that [James] tho' very young as to age was an old, old offender.' Francis, the hostler, examined the young salesman 'more strictly', enquiring as to the ownership of the animal. James answered that 'the mare was the Property of his Uncle who lived at Darbin'. Francis questioned 'How [does] it happen that one so young should be entrusted with selling a horse?' Loudly and roughly one can imagine him growling at the boy 'Huh, a young'un like ye wouldn't be trusted to take a horse for sale.' James courageously (and pertly) countered that he 'had sold a horse for [my] uncle for more money than [Uncle] could get for her' and for that reason he, James, was employed again, audaciously adding 'It's Four Pounds for the saddle and bridle.' How confident was that 'boy'! — standing 'his' ground and bargaining for Seventeen Pounds. The evidence states that the animal was a Blood Mare, hence very valuable, though 'she had a spavin on one leg and the remains of a spavin on the other hind leg'.[64]

Well, 'James' slipped away from that suspicious hostler and, undeterred, 'walked the mare into Stafford'. It is no surprise that Mary Reibey, twenty years later as a youngish widow, became a most successful dealer in money and property. This tenacity of purpose was evidently very strong when she was a youngster of fourteen years. Molly Haydock — note you — was so well disguised and so adapted to the role of the young boy, James Borrow, that she completely misled all the dealers 'he' approached. An amazing histrionic feat! The boy sought still another possible purchaser.

Baker Man.

This was to be the Baker Man, John Commander, of St. Mary's Parish, Stafford.[65] The Baker's handwritten evidence shows a literate man, well aware no doubt of his importance as a baker in the town. (Trevelyan tells of the high necessity of bread to 18th century England — 'many lived mainly on bread and cheese'[66] — and of the young German traveller, Moritz, who in 1792 wrote of 'the fine wheaten bread I find here [England] besides excellent butter and cheese which makes up for scanty dinners.'[67]) Straight from the Swan Inn débâcle went James at 5 a.m. leading the mare in the streets of Stafford, and, most unluckily, intercepted this Baker Man 'to offer a bay mare to sale'. John Commander, much sharper than the hostler of the Swan Inn, 'seized the boy with the mare' and called to Yeoman William Moore, who happened to pass by at the time when 'James Burrow offered to sell the . . . Mare.'[68]

Now really in trouble — the boy, on being quizzed, asserted to William Moore[69] that 'he' 'brought the Mare from [my] Uncle, a grocer at Darbin, one John Burrow'. William Moore sought out the Chester Carrier (also handy on that bright Saturday morning) for corroboration, but the Chester Carrier didn't know of any John Burrow, Grocer, of Darbin.

Further complicating the situation and literally, at this moment, condemning 'himself', James Borrow argued that 'Uncle kept the Black Crow and let[s] out a post chaise.'[70] No, said the Carrier, there was no such inn — and the three men, Baker, Yeoman and Carrier, still pressed the poor little Beggar Boy to tell from whence he got the mare. But James didn't give up. 'He' said 'he' 'bought the mare from Thos. Lyster who keeps the White Lyon at the Back of the Exchange in Chester'.[71]

The Vagabond Thief.

Well, that was enough obvious fabrication for the three law abiding citizens. Horse stealing was rife, evil, disturbing to society, and had to be stopped. Although the offender was young, and the penalty was Capital, the boy showed signs of becoming a dangerous vagrant, from his appearance,[72] and was tossed into the town prison. Next, the mare was taken to be identified. When his 'mare' was missed from the Chester Common, John Sorton Hughes had obviously made public his loss, even as far abroad as Stafford. Therefore, on the following Thursday, 18 August 1791, the mare having been identified by his nephew John Hughes[73] 'by her marks and particularly by the spavins', the three Informants, Baker, Yeoman, and Glover's nephew, went before the Mayor, John Wright

Esquire, taking an oath on their evidence. This evidence was sufficient to send James for trial for the crime of horse stealing. Clam-like, 'James' still concealed 'his' real identity — undetected action sufficient to raise a lot of questions about the late 18th century prisons and upholders of the law.

The full horror of the situation must, by now, have begun to loom pretty realistically in front of Molly. She appears to remain struck dumb, and in fact remains incognito till mid-November 1791. Her terror, her silence, her stubborn pluck, reaches out over the one hundred and ninety years, in an awesome wave.

Chapter 3

STAFFORD NIGHTMARE . . . 1791

The Gaols.

Whilst recording these Stafford experiences, that ambivalent duo Molly Haydock and James Borrow have become almost as identical twins, and just as 'troublesome'. So often the girl's thinking, which explains the boy's action, confuses the issue. Thinking of the youth of that child, yet a bare fourteen years, the stark dilemma of the boy 'James' arouses cathartic emotions. There 'he' is stun-shocked and despairing on that Saturday morning, 18 August 1791. Locked into the awful bedlam of the 18th century prison in St. Mary's Parish, Stafford, 'he' had to tumble to the terrifying truth that the so cleverly planned adventure somehow had come adrift — seriously adrift! A horse had been stolen and 'James' had been caught red-handed whilst offering that old blood mare for sale. Full well 'he' knew the severe English laws which made the perceived punishment fit the crime — moreover this particular crime was 'capital'.

Authentic sources record a pretty grim picture of the 18th century prisons in which no segregation by age or sex was practised (with the exception of the 'male only' hulks).[74] Conditions of overcrowding and filth, with attendant gaol distemper, of perversion and immorality, were the norm. Felons, so called, came mostly from the poor hungry ranks of petty thieves, prostitutes, and highwaymen. Those prisoners without private means to gain favours found their pastimes were confined to debauchery, perversion, and further exchanges of information on the survival art of robbery. Therefore the inmates often fulfilled their expected role of illiterate, belligerent, thieving unruly persons. Conditions of detention in holding gaols were of no matter to the 18th century general public. True, John Howard[75] and others were attempting to stir the nation's dormant sympathies, but actual reforms were not to come about till well into the 19th century.[76]

'James's' Prison Masquerade.

Young 'James' was tossed into one of these hellish halls of detention, places designed to protect the public from the evil of infecting and offending criminals. Fortunate indeed for Molly Haydock that she so convincingly impersonated a young lad; she appears to have come through this whole experience without physical harm, if the inferences of 'young', 'innocent' and 'simple' in the future Petition are properly interpreted. In the prisons, sanitation was minimal; 'easing chairs' or necessarys, as lavatories or water closets were so euphemistically known, were common areas for both sexes. An 18th century universal labouring smock overdress or tunic with peg top pantalettes would have made good cover for Molly's small, flat, immature young boy's figure. There could never have been any girlish curls or protruding breasts. Did she/he keep a hat crammed on his head for the four long months of disguised identity in that gaol? How did 'he' sleep? Was 'he' friendly with any special prisoner? Did anyone know 'his' secret?

Contracts for the care and victualling of prison inmates were let to private civilian gaolers by the Government — gaolers who were minimally supervised. Apart from London's Bow Street runners, no police force was around at that time. The military served as press gangs and supporters of the local Sheriff and County Magistrates. The prison overcrowding problem was due to two circumstances. One was the refusal by the newly independent American colonists to pay for and accept any more convicts as servants; the second circumstance was the tremendous increase in the proclaimed number of citable offences. Gaolers therefore, were faced with worsening situations in the Bridewells, Newgate and early Millbank and County holding prisons as the law breakers were caught in ever increasing numbers. Prisoners with private means could buy privileges for a 'consideration'; privileges such as extra comforts, better quarters; others languished in the overcrowded situations awaiting their trial, their punishments or transportation. Sometimes whole families were involved, the poor-work-house being the only other alternative for people without any breadwinner.

Society's Dilemma — What to Do?

There is really nothing specifically English or new in a society's traditional imposition of retribution upon breakers of that society's code of laws. It is endemic in man's long history, mythological and recorded. Offenders, unlucky enough to be caught, were always eliminated or ostracized, sometimes such people were stigmatized with a body brand.[77] One shudders to read of the earlier vengefully branded 'A' upon detected offending womenfolk by the more fantical sects, as, for example, by some of the Pilgrim Fathers. The 18th century approved of publicly administered corporal punishment, whether by stocks, pillory, whipping post, or the gallows.[78] The old motto — 'an eye for an eye, a tooth [or even two teeth] for a tooth' — lurked in their respected philosophies of law and order. As a handy expedient punishment, banishment had enjoyed a long run of popularity: the Greeks sent their controversial opponents to the galleys, a habit copied by the Romans. For the Elizabethan English and Scottish nobility, exile was an opportune punishment.

By the 18th century it had been convenient for the British Government and for the collective conscience to serve two purposes by banishing criminals by transportation to America; purpose one was to deter criminals (by example), and purpose two was to supply the colonists with labour.[79] Since Americans would no longer co-operate, Botany Bay, opportunely sighted by Captain Cook in 1770, became the venue for convict transportees — a new expatriation became a necessity. Moreover by the late 18th century, no less than 231 offences had been proclaimed as capital, and banishment beyond the seas was considered a merciful reprieve when the monarch commuted the attainted prisoner's grim sentence. Society deemed that all crime was deliberate misconduct, that the law as it stood was there to enforce the view that the community was stronger than the culprit — a possible vindication for the long list of offences.

To some 20th century eyes bizarre anomalies appear in the ranking of 18th century crimes. Until 1803 attempted murder was regarded as a mere misdemeanour; paradoxically 'felonies without benefit of clergy'[80] such as stealing property as gates, fruit, timber, coins, food, furniture, livestock, or clothing, were punishable by death. Such an overall picture of 18th century law and punishment may never have been really understood by Molly Haydock in her childhood days, but she must have overheard Grandma Law talking with her friends, mainly church-going old lady-gossips, discussing Blackburn criminals, their crimes and subsequent punishments. These wicked malefactors would have been the shop lifters, horse, sheep and cattle stealers, forgers and common thieves. One can guess that James Dean, the school master, would have added his quota to the 'moral instruction' mentioned in the Petition.[81] But in 1791 despite her own early training in rectitude, Mary as 'James' is now found 'holden at Stafford [Gaol] in and for the County of Stafford'.[82]

'James' on Trial — the Nightmare Increases in Horror.

The subsequent official Court proceedings drag out 'his' nightmare, for as we already know (Chapter 2) some six days after that disastrous early Saturday morning dénouement 'James' found 'himself' before the Mayor, John Wright, and the young prisoner is still assumed to be what 'he' claims — a vagrant labourer, James Borrow. Just how did Molly manage this? Did she huddle in a corner of the crowded gaol, day and night, insignificant looking, silent, quietly mulling over the likely outcome. One can imagine the situation: after reading the given evidence from those original precious parchment documents (see Appendix A), all so beautifully handwritten by the long-dead Clerk of the Court. (The Public Record Office, London, allow biographers to handle these old records; they gave me a fey feeling.) We, like James, are back with the past, with the noisy legal proceedings in Stafford; with the preliminaries and trials of the Summer Assizes; and we can watch 'James' who is standing very still, ill at ease and listening, silent.

A personal empathy is taking over from bare history, yet the truth is never thereby distorted, the picture becomes sharper. Here is a slip of a girl, who in her vastly improved understanding of life has decided that, as a boy, she possibly is relatively safe from sexual molestation by male prisoners. She has realized it is wiser to silently acquiesce to all the accusations being solemnly made by John Commander and Co., possibly then no interrogation will follow, for interrogation may lead to the discovery of 'James's' sex.

In Chapter 1, the character of a plucky sagacious girl with a certain amount of reticence was preferred to that of a romantic adventuress. This chosen prototype still holds good. It is the quintessence of many early enduring pioneers. A romantic, flighty, impulsive young adventuress never would have had the necessary iron nerve to stand quietly in that old court facing her accusers without argument. Were the appeal's plausible facts true (see Appendix A), an adventuring Molly Haydock would at this point have told all about the other 'evil intentioned' persons who had caused her so much trouble; she would have confessed her identity and appealed for aid from Blackburn.

Not so. It is obvious that she did stand quietly, dumbly, for she retained her assumed identity. Listen to John Commander and William Moore repeating on oath the story of their experiences to Mayor Wright. The baker has no doubts in his mind, concerning James' sex: his evidence reads:

> 'This informant saith that a young man who calls himself James Burrow [sic] did . . . offer a bay mare to sale to this informant . . . from the appearance of the said James Burrow suspecting that the said mare was stolen . . .'[83]

signed with a flourish in a very firm hand — John Commander.

Nor does the corroborating witness show any doubts. Yeoman William Moore 'who was passing in the street' testifies:

> 'Suspecting that the mare was stolen [he] immediately seized the said James Burrow with the mare in his possession.'[84]

Written on the outside of this original rolled parchment record is: 'Informations ag^{s} Jas Burrow for Horse stealing, 18th Augt 1791.' It is obvious that neither clerk nor witnesses, nor yet again the Sheriff Mayor, had looked very attentively at that vagrant little horse-thief, tattered and torn 'labourer', possessing 'no goods'.[85]

'James' was committed for trial at the Summer Assizes to be held on Wednesday 24 August 1791, so back 'he' went to that prison and still made no plea, no terrified confession, sent no SOS to whatever extended family there was in Blackburn. Molly Haydock, so far, has shown little trust and maintained little hope of help from her relatives, which rather explains her original flight from her situation in June 1791.[86]

Her Fellows in Crime.

Incredulity piles upon incredulity in this continuing Stafford prison saga. There were some thirty-six prisoners, men and women, summoned to appear at the Summer Assizes. Their accusers were also listed and summoned to appear and 'prosecute and give evidence . . . with Informations, Depositions and Confessions'.[87] Of these prisoners one, Thomas Watton, is shown with an alias of Guy, presumably known as Thomas Guy. There is no other name shown in that list with an alias alongside. Although there are six girls — females — amongst those thirty-six names, there is no Molly or Mary Haydock listed — only a young boy's name, 'James Burrow'. And this, of course, is the nub of the whole story. For those ten days she had hidden in that crowded prison, still successfully impersonating the dead boy, James Borrow.

There is simply no other satisfactory explanation for these authentic court lists of persons arraigned for the Summer Assizes. Molly kept her own counsel and had planned perhaps some future move. Obviously there had been no thorough medical check, as yet, of the inmates. It seems that her companions do not appear to have noted any odd characteristic of the small, quiet vagabond, 'James'. After all, inmates ate together whatever victuals came their way; presumably the situation would be discussed, cursed, debated, as the days went by. Still 'James' as a young boy would not be encouraged to 'put in his oar' nor join in the extravagant roistering and cursing of the older men. Speculation as to possible sentences to be handed down by the well known visiting Westminster J.P.'s — Sir James Eyre and Justice Heath for the County of Stafford, of the Oxford Circuit, would be prophesied by the sophisticated criminal cognoscenti. Hence in this gaol melée, more than at any other time, Molly needed her reserves of steely determination: she must not chatter, nor when questioned by her fellow inmates answer with any clear details concerning her crime or background. She must not show any of her Blackburn Grammar School education or middle class yeoman family training. She was among some pretty sharp customers, well tutored in the criminal lore of the crowded Staffordshire streets. 'James' needed to appear as one of the frightened, insignificant lesser rabble. 'He' needed constantly to anticipate awkward situations and thus not by any mistaken action to become conspicuous.

Marvellous to relate, Molly did just that; she weathered those closely confined days, continuing successfully in her male role, one she had sustained since leaving Blackburn-Bury in June 1791. Some of her fellow prisoners had been awaiting trial for nearly one year; as with James' crime, all offences had had to have been committed in the precincts of Stafford — to thus be eligible for trial at the Stafford Assizes.

'James', Labourer of St. Mary's Parish meets Judge and Jury.

Fortunately for her, when 'James Borrow's' name appeared upon a certain select list of ten prisoners to be tried by Justice Heath on the Wednesday, 'his' was the only name allegedly from the Parish of St. Mary's, Stafford. This meant there could be no neighbourly common discussion, about that locality, with any other likely St. Mary's lad. The list (see Appendix A) asks for a 'general delivery of the gaol' of these ten persons.[88] Justice Heath reporting later, wrote (see Appendix A):

> 'I report the case of a person (who answered to the name of James Borrow) who was tried before me at the last Stafford Assizes.'[89]

Of the ten prisoners, four were other girls. Amongst the ten names appears the bare charge:

> 'James Burrow for feloniously stealing — Bay Mare Val. Ten Pounds, property of John Sorton, parish of Saint Mary — 13th August, 31st yr. Geo 3rd [1791]'.

The four girls, or women (no ages shown) were arraigned for crimes typical of the era.[90] Sarah Bull was an expert pickpocket — she had 'privily' stolen from 'John Harris without his knowledge, one Silver Watch Val. 40 shillings.' Jane Watt had taken her chance and broken into Henry Clenyon's empty dwelling house. She had made a rich haul of velvet waist coats, linen shirts, silver sleeve buttons, silk handkerchief, cotton stockings, and two muslin aprons. Ann Thompson, another shop lifter, had carried away yards of cotton and nankeen. However, they all had been apprehended, it seems! Priscilla Cockin was a wild girl — not on one, but on two occasions she had set fire to haystacks — and once it had been on a cold icy January night. One wonders why. Was the 18th century Priscilla a political terrorist?

Amongst those four women, Molly Haydock would most certainly have been subjected to ridicule, abuse and spite. Better as 'James' the boy. Yet the other males, the five men, appear to be fairly rough types. Tom Jones was a highwayman who had put a traveller, William Millington 'in fear', taking from him and 'against his will one pistol mounted with silver'. Tom Jones must have been 'quicker on the draw'! Job Bratt was the petty thief of 24 iron locks. Thomas Baxter was an 18th century version of a 'mugger'. Strangely enough he was the only one of the ten to eventually win a 'Not Guilty' verdict. Thomas' indictment reads:

> 'for unlawfully assaulting Jos. Watson a . . . Keeper of Barton Ward in Reedward Forest and feloniously beating and wounding him.'[91]

John Brough foolishly had robbed

> 'the most noble Granville, Marquis of the County of Stafford' on the previous 24th October (1790), having stolen '60 lb. weight of lead, value Five Pounds.'[92]

Like Ann Thompson, Peter Burnside was a shop lifter — again the goods were of cotton and nankeen.

This tough school of 'professionals' in the art of robbery and assault must have been puzzled at the enormity of the theft — of a horse — carried out by the young weedy insignificant boy 'James'. Amongst those nine companions on the trial day, where could he have found a sympathetic mate? One thing, it seems, 'James' did realize; he had talked too much and too fancifully when pushing the sale of that old mare to the Saint Mary's men. One surmises that this is the reason why there is no defence recorded at the trial, which is almost a non-event in modern parlance. 'James Burrow's' crime was attested before Mr. Justice Heath. The authorities had rounded up all five witnesses, four of whom could swear to "James'" persistent efforts to sell the mare — bakerman, yeoman, innkeeper and hostler. The charge is written, in beautiful script, on a narrow parchment strip measuring about 12 inches wide by 3 inches long.[93] On the back is inscribed the names of the five witnesses, all signed in their own differing styles:

> 'A True Bill
> John Sorton Hughes,
> Robert Silvester,
> Francis Emborton,
> William Moore,
> John Commander.
> 5 sworn in Court.
> J.P.'

The charge in part reads:

> 'The Jurors for our Lord the King upon their oath present that JAMES BURROW, labourer of the Parish of Saint Mary . . . with force and arms . . . a Bay Mare of His price of Ten Pounds . . . did steal take and lead away against the peace of our said Lord the King . . .'

Note how 'James' has continued to let it be supposed he was a labourer of St. Mary's Parish. To this thin slip of parchment with the charge are added two sad little memos. In one handwriting is noted 'Guilty', in another 'To be hanged: No goods'. What, not even a scanty bag of personal goods? Poor James, poor Molly — a young boy to hang.

Commenting on the sentence Mr. Justice Heath, much later, in November 1791 when reporting to His Majesty per Lord Granville, wrote:

> 'The Jury found the prisoner guilty on this Evidence and I was [as the presiding Judge] perfectly satisfied with the Verdict.'[94]

It might now be expected, with that terrible spectre of imminent death by hanging confronting her, that Molly would succumb to panic, appeal to some gaol officer for help or perhaps even identify herself. But not she — as 'James' the labourer she toughed it out for another five weeks. One can only speculate as to the possible reactions of the other attainted prisoners. On enquiry as to her possible reactions, a modern redhead, some fourteen plus years (in 1978) argued that were she Molly she would have buried herself in her, by now, established prison corner to think out the problems, 'How did I get into this mess?' and more importantly, 'How do I get out of it?'[95] So also, possibly, would Molly; no tears but a relatively careful scrutiny of her present imminent peril. This grim tenacity still fits with the original analysis, our concept of the girl's character. Even now she still preferred not to seek help from Bury; she probably underestimated the Hope family. Molly however was aware that she had 'cut the painter', disappeared, and now she apparently feared the consequence of being found as a condemned prisoner. Illogical maybe. Throughout her life, on what evidence there is, the adult competent Mary Reibey was reticent, fearful of family censure, concealing whatever could be concealed: and she was so minded in 1791 in that prison.

There were, of course, some helpful interventions occurring at the same Court Assizes. For example, Jane North, murderess, attainted on the evidence of no less than six people, was unconditionally pardoned (by Mr. Justice Heath), upon the not unfamiliar opportune intervention of medical advice. Her reprieve reads in part:

> 'As to the prisoner Jane North [a pardon] without any condition whatever, it having appeared to me by the examination of the Surgeon, who could not attend at the trial to give his evidence, that the prisoner Jane North was insane at the time of committing the Act.'[96]

The Commutation of the death sentence for that vagabond boy.

The Unmasking.

Some six weeks later, Molly's charade still not rumbled, the Magistrate, on 29 September 1791, made the customary appeal for the condemned, asking for the commuting of certain capital sentences, declaring to the 'King's most excellent Majesty' that he:

> 'Humbly recommended them [certain attainted persons] . . . diverse favourable circumstances appearing, as fit subjects to receive your Majesty's pardon on the sev^{l} conditions following, if your Majesty shall so think fit.[97] (see Appendix A)

Wonderfully, but perhaps predictably, clemency is asked for 'James Burrow of stealing a mare . . . on condition as to being transported beyond the Seas for . . . the term of 7 years'. Later Judge Heath declared clemency was shown to James on account of his extreme youth.

So 'James' was bound for 'Botany Bay'.

During the next five weeks, at some time in October, the expected/or/unexpected suddenly happened, for the whole charade is unmasked and the boy 'James' is no more! One can only presume that the authorities began to sort out those sentenced to transportation and to apply the usual medical checks. (Manning Clark describes the joy of the Irish at Cork, when those awaiting transportation lived like fighting cocks, well fed, and what's more, bathed and clothed — they having endured poverty for so long before during their lives.[98]) This hygenic sluicing and preparation was due to Phillip. In 1787, whilst still loading at Portsmouth, when reporting to Secretary Nepean, he had complained:

> 'Unless orders are being given for their [the prisoners] being washed and cloathed [sic] on their leaving the prisons or the hulks . . . we may see the seamen belonging to the transports run from the ships to avoid fatal distemper.'[99]

Convicts were accordingly ordered to be cleansed, if not necessarily quite healthy, in body before being entrusted to 'merciful administration' on board for so long a voyage. The Stafford Nightmare must surely have reached its apex of horror for young James when lined up for his 'cleansing'. To the insignificant vagabond suddenly to have been so confronted, the imminent rumbling of his/her masquerade must have been a mind shattering blow, a complete collapse of all her dogged intention. The terror or her changed relations with both women, who would become (mostly) rather spiteful at such a long hoax, and with men who, unless the girl was very small and unbecoming, would offer her several sexual suggestions, must have acted as a goad. Indeed, it was a traumatic enough situation for Molly, now listed as Mary Haydock, to finally seek help from 'home'. At all events an appeal, dated Blackburn, 5 November 1791, was rapidly organised by certain residents, headed by one relative.[100]

The Petition.

The appeal is couched in plausible terms, which are calculated to make the situation appear as the unfortunate result of a simple accidental happening. The later highly embroidered stories of the young lady using the squire's horse in a mischievous half hour, resulting in the transportation of an innocent child, obviously are pure fiction. The Blackburn Petition alone puts paid to that fabrication. It is an honest attempt by friends to rescue the girl, stating she was:

> 'a poor helpless orphan prevailed upon by another young girl to leave her situation in the month of June last [1791] . . . to purchase boy's clothing and change name . . . Mary Haydock then assuming the name of James Burrow they [the girls] parted . . . 'the said Mary Haydock then Burrow in boy's clothing . . . was accidentally overtaken by a man with 2 horses who desired her to ride one . . . the man fearing discovery left her in Stafford with the horse and she showing inexperience in offering it for sale was apprehended upon suspicion of having stolen it and committed to the prison under the name of James Burrow.'[101]

Well, perhaps this is what could have happened, but as already shown, events in St. Mary's Parish on that August Friday evening and Saturday morning do not reveal that sort of girl. It must be stressed that, if so naive, she would not have held her impersonation for nearly five long months. Our Molly had courage and brains; had she been so simple and had she been so easily influenced, she must surely have 'cracked' long before the first trial. Note, in her efforts to sell the mare, how readily she concocted fabrications as fast as she was questioned — she never gave up her intention of selling that mare. Moreover, irrespective of any man 'saddling' her with it — she made no attempt earlier to abandon the animal and to run away from trouble. If there was indeed such a wicked man, was he somewhere waiting for his share? She doesn't say, and no such gentry was mentioned in Court. He never appeared.

The Petition further argues:

> 'It does not appear that she had any hand in the original Act of stealing the horse . . . she was drawn in by the wicked contrivance of some evil minded person(s) . . . it appears still more unlikely that she alone could have formed a scheme so daring as that of stealing a Horse . . .'

The Petition asserts that her 'lately deceased Grandmother . . . enjoin(ed) her to the practice of every moral religious duty' — the petitioners prayed that 'she may not be doomed to be a miserable exile . . . but be freed . . . and be restored to her relations and friends'.

Adam Hope, most interestingly, is the name at the top of the 'humble petition'. Not one of the relatives Haydock, Hargreaves, Hindle, Brown or Law appear on the list. Maybe it is not a mere coincidence that Mary Reibey explicitly records her admiration and affection for the cousins Hope, in her 1820 report of her warm welcome by these Hope relatives.

The Petition of 1791 is an impressive one, signed by a surgeon, several manufacturers, three drapers, a tea dealer, several merchants, attornies at law, the Reverend Samuel Dean who was Headmaster of the Free Grammar School (one has presumed this was her school), and most delightfully a Jane Austen character, Robert Smalley, Gentleman, and the Reverend Richard Smalley. Two ministers of religion had generously added their names to this petition, which was to be forwarded by the Minister at Blackburn, the Reverend Thomas Harkie, to the Right Hon. Henry Dundas (Secretary of State). But, Harkie — surely a narrow nasty sanctimonious Godfearing minister! — saw fit to add that unpleasant memo of his:

> 'Not knowing the young girl personally I could not with propriety put my name to the Petition.'

He does, however, add:

> 'Her relations in this town are very respectable people and I hope her extreme youth will entitle her to the Royal Mercy. Signed: Thos Harkie.'

Evidence shows that she was kept in the gaol, but there's no guessing as to what really happened to the girl Molly in the ensuing weeks. That she was now listed as a girl would have become common knowledge amongst her fellows. Were they friendly and admiring, or jealous and spiteful? How did the men behave?

Two weeks later, 18 November 1791, Mr. Justice Heath the Trial Judge reported on the case and the Petition of 5 November, through Lord Granville to His Majesty. (As an interesting side comment one might compare the same Mr. Justice Heath's recommendation written some three weeks earlier granting an absolute pardon to the murderess, Jane North. Still, after all, it was the 18th century and Molly had stolen a horse — now that surely was a real crime — that was abuse of property, not to be so lightly pardoned as was the murder of a child.)

On this petition from Blackburn, from Molly's friends, Justice Heath reports to His Majesty in a very restrained manner. He writes:

> '. . . I report the case of a Person who was tried before me at the Summer Assizes for stealing a Bay Mare . . . which person then answered by the name of James Burrow . . . but . . . is a Girl of the name of Mary Haydock![102]

The report then details the evidence of Robt. Silvester 'who keeps the Swan Inn at Stafford'; of Francis Emborton the hostler of the Inn who 'saw the Prisoner [James/ Molly] between the hours of 5 and 6 in the morning of the 18th inst. [August 1791]'; of William Moore, the Yeoman to whom James/Molly had spun the varied tales about his/her uncle John Burrow, uncle's Inn the Black Crow, and so on.

The evidence is fairly put and is accurate according to all the facts which this biography has previously detailed. However, Mr. Heath turned 'thumbs down' and ruled 'A Capital Respite not recommended for further extension of Mercy'; that is, she was to be transported, and it was to be the Colony's gain. Mr. Heath's argument (see Appendix A) is lucid and logical; he had already on account of 'the tender age of the prisoner' recommended earlier that the capital sentence 'be mitigated to Transportation'. Replying to the Petitioners' suggestion that Mary Haydock was a girl 'of perfect innocence', Heath finds their claim to be at variance with 'her artful manner' when endeavouring to sell the mare to those witnesses, Silvester, Emborton, Commander, and Moore. The Judge agrees with Francis Emborton that 'she is an old offender'. (I have to say James-Molly was too good an actress in that role — she enjoyed, apparently, her adventure! Who would have thought it of Mary Reibey, looking at her quiet guarded eyes in that lovely little miniature of 1820?)

The final paragraph of the report sadly puts the whole miserable experience into proper perspective. There was no one who really cared, and that may have been the original spur for the planned flight from her 'situation', her town, her family connections and from her friends.

Judge Heath concludes:

> 'If there were any respectable persons who would take charge of her and enter into the cognizance that she shall not commit any Felonies for 4 or 5 years to come . . . she might be justly entitled to the Royal Mercy. Otherwise I am humbly of the opinion . . . it is more advantageous for the prisoner herself and expedient for the PUBLIC EXAMPLE that she should be transported.'[103] (Author's capitals.)

The Judge was right — it would be and it was advantageous for the prisoner to go to a new place. The settlement in New South Wales was only four years old, but already, some food was growing at Rose Hill, there were some possible situations awaiting in the new Colony which might not be available in that old conservative town of Bury near Blackburn, especially if no family member would volunteer 'to take charge of her'. This refusal is not to be condemned — after all, Molloy, had shown strange, odd but tremendous spirit and with it, rebellion. She had run away, spent five months amongst the rather horrible unfortunates in the crowded gaol; who could guarantee she wouldn't commit another terrible felony, such as this present crime — the stealing of a horse for dishonest sale? What a responsibility — but what a weak-kneed lot were those chaps who signed the Petition for merciful release. Hadn't Adam Hope really thought out the possible final consequences? It's comforting for the reader to realize there was to be a bright future. Of course poor Molly didn't know what would happen after her Stafford nightmare, and there were six more months to spend in that wretched holding prison.

Chapter 4

THE THORNY PATH TO TRANSPORTATION

The Family Problem — What Should They Do?

Without resorting to the 'biographer's subjunctive' — maybe this, maybe that — one feels pretty positive that Molly Haydock must have been a thoroughly deflated, disillusioned young teenager during those long months after the unsuccessful appeal in November 1791.[104] She was now some fourteen and a half years of age. It indeed appears, to sympathetic 20th century readers, to be unforgivable to send such a young girl to such a dreadful fate. There she stands, unwanted, condemned to months in the Stafford holding prison, to still further months as a convict in a small uncomfortable transport, and finally to continue to languish till the expiration of her sentence in 1798, under terrible conditions in that far away New South Wales settlement 'beyond the seas' at the world's other end!

It might be wise, therefore, before outright condemnation, to take an objective glance at both family and judicial problems and their 18th century solutions to such a situation. We've noted that her horrifying future appears to have left unmoved any responsible relative who might have been expected to offer succour. In November 1791 there lived in Blackburn, amongst others, Uncle William Haydock and his son William; Aunt Hindle Brown; the cousins, Hope and Hargreaves; as well as Adam Hope. Aunt Hindle Brown and Uncle William Haydock, who were both then aged forty-nine years were evidently unable to help.[105] Had any one of them offered lawful sanctuary to Molly Haydock she would have been immediately pardoned and released into the sponsor's custody as explained by Justice Heath (Chapter 3).[106] But no one came forward to guarantee guardianship for that young girl to the criminal court authorities.

It's easy enough to follow the 'reasonable' arguments of that family group of Hopes, Hindles, Laws, Haydocks and Hargreaves, a reputable established clan whose history reached back a hundred years or more, steeped in traditional 18th century mores.[107] The family were mostly solid, middle class educated yeomanry. The young cousins Hope and Hargreaves were to become a lawyer and a surgeon;[108] Mr. William Hope himself became a pillar of the Bible Society.[109] Later, in 1820, Cousin John's wife, Aunt Hindle Brown, was a septuagenarian, a kindly helpful Quaker, and all these friendly kin are much in evidence in 1820 when Mary Reibey returned to her native Blackburn in Lancashire — as a wealthy Antipodean, a highly respectable widow. But in 1791 the mothers of Molly's young contemporary relatives might well have had doubts if asked to include the orphaned cousin within their family circle. Note that prior to her absconding, for reasons of their own which are not clear to us, no one had, most surprisingly, befriended this child upon the death of her Grandmother Law. She had run away from her situation, whatever that might have been, in June 1791.

Her contemporary (1791) young cousins Hope, Alice and brothers, were to become such very close, welcoming relations in 1820.[110] These appear to have been the children of the Adam Hope who so bravely headed the list of petitioners seeking the Royal Clemency.[111] Did Adam, however, consult his helpmeet and family on the possible conditions which obviously would become automatic with the granting of a pardon? Problems would have confronted Adam's wife, if asked to add Molly to the family table, alongside Alice and David and John. Indeed the parents might well cringe, fearing they would all attract the shame incurred by the disgraced rebel. As her relatives they would keep reminding themselves that all Molly's connections were church people. As noted previously their Christening, Marriage and Burial ceremonies appear in the Bishop's Transcripts.[112] The girl had been a pupil at the Free Grammar School, the family would argue, a member of St. John's Church of England, Blackburn, and had been well tutored by Grandma Law in the principles necessary for her survival as an 18th century young lady.[113] Yet, it would have appeared to the clan, such instruction had been all to no avail.

Female relatives would be more concerned, however, with the exploits of the young lady since quitting Blackburn in June 1791, than with generously assessing the unhappy causes of her flight. That, of course, was the critical point in the argument; the flight from Blackburn. Molly had 'flown the coop', decamped secretly, and what's more, shamefully disguised as a lad.

True, the boyish charade probably shielded her virtue, but . . . Then there was that wicked horse-thief, who was alleged to have met her on the Chester highway and was therefore, of course, responsible for all her peculiar crimes;[114] what other tricks might not he have taught her? Certainly, when attempting to sell the old thoroughbred mare to no less than five different men, she had shown great skill in fabrication. Had all that sharp practice been learned in Blackburn? And how had she dared to commit that ultimate crime, the stealing and selling of a horse? One tends, rather sadly, to conclude it was probably the women of the family who proscribed their young relative. They knew also of the girl's long sojourn amongst the degraded men and women in 'the filthy verminous gaol', which had probably alerted Molly to a very seamy side of life, possibly to have taught her undesirable habits.

The Public Attitudes of the Old World towards Prisons, Prisoners, and the Necessity for Such Punishments.

The British public, well informed by such 18th century journals as the *Edinburgh Magazine,* the *London Evening Post,* the *Dublin Chronicle,* and local tabloids, were well aware of the continuing overcrowding of the prisons and all the attendant abounding troublesome complications. Indeed the public community was afraid. Authoritative historian, Manning Clark, quotes:

> '. . . the several gaols and places for the confinement of felons were so crowded that the greater danger was to be apprehended not only from their [the felons'] escape, but from infectious distempers [spreading from the gaols]'[115]

Bridewell, once Cardinal Wolsey's palace, had its cells filled with prisoners, vagrants and prostitutes. Dundas sums up the generally held opinion that all criminals came from an impoverished class which had to be suppressed by severe punishment. He claimed that:

> 'Death, transportation and the Bridewell are the only varieties of punishment the manners of our country will admit of.'[116]

Speaking of the prisoners sentenced to transportation, Manning Clark writes that:

> 'All evidence emerging from the study of official and unofficial descriptions of convicts suggest the high proportion of men and women transported to New South Wales from England and Scotland from 1788 to 1823 belonged by taste and circumstance to the criminal class — people dependent upon crime.[117]

At that time, it has been estimated, some 115,000 persons depended for a living upon crime, according to Manning Clark. Collins points out that transportation came next to death as the most severe punishment and was intended 'to purge, to deter and to reform';[118] transportation it was believed would prevent the commission of murder and theft. The late 18th century social laws were largely protective for the society, and were never of the narrow hypocritical colour of the future 19th century: these unwritten laws were influenced by the conditions spawned by the Industrial Revolution. The perceived right of each individual to paid employment in urban areas, hence to food and shelter, was now simply not available, due to the improved standards of health, the rapidly increasing urban populace, and the introduction of cotton mills.

In the days of quid pro quo in the rural village complexes, security, though humble enough, had been a common right for most of the agricultural workers. But not in the late 18th century. Petty thieving, pilfering, brutality and murder had become the necessary norm for a great number of desperate people, as well as for those who preferred that way of life. The yeomen, the gentle folk, and the new industrial merchants, had become the targets for the depredations of these criminals who had been tutored in the seedbed ghettos of the large cities. Lancashire, the industrial centre, and London, provided the largest percentage of rogues to be transported. Property thefts and damage to property had become of greater concern to the law than acts of violence; thefts were accordingly punished with greater severity.

It was a hopeless predicament for lower class females who lacked employment in the new factories, or were not engaged in that old reliable alternative, service with the upper classes. Well, what could a girl do, not so employed, other than join the prostitutes' squad? There had to be a limit to the numbers of females who found refuge in religious establishments in the 1790s, and in any case 'Hie thee to a nunnery' was generally an historical order for the disgraced upper class lady; she, generally speaking, brought money with her.

The Lonely Prison Sojourn — Step 1 on the Long Weary Road to Botany Bay.

It was with some of these outcasts that Molly must surely now have been familiar. Since her petition had been dismissed she had nowhere to go and like the others was bound for 'Botany Bay'. In time the causes of such degradation and sorrow of so many of her fellow travellers must surely have become evident to her. Did she feel pity or was she afraid of them?

There is no written evidence available to show any concern for or contact with convicted persons, throughout Mary Reibey's history. Certainly her family were reared carefully as exclusives, and duly trod the socially mobile marriage ladder of the Colony, just as did some other free persons including Elizabeth Macarthur, also of British yeoman stock.

There were a small percentage of convicts, like Molly, who came from a gentler background than the majority of transported felons. However, this was no advantage in gaol, and the code of the 18th century prison life was harsh. As a reputed wily convicted young female thief she would endure a very hard time in the holding gaol of Stafford until sailing in April 1792. No personal reminiscence by word of mouth through descendants, no letter of hers, remains to tell of these five months. The inference of the romantic stories circulated in Australia for so many years has been to suggest an 'overnight' transfer from Blackburn, Bury to 'Botany Bay' — the girl carefully screened from her surroundings — which of course is not feasible; she was part of that transported gang.

Romantic novelists have not done justice to our pioneers when painting scanty, effete, and often false pictures of their early experiences. The true, painful story of transportation, of what really happened to people who were apprehended and convicted in the last years of the 18th century, reveals their native hardiness as well as their superficial weaknesses. Manning Clark succinctly sums up this paradox, writing:

> '. . . convicts often had the strength of their hands and the sharpness of their wits, which in their new environment would help them to create wealth, which would buy property, respectability, and to found families to find indeed a different lifestyle.'[118]

Writing realistically, tantalizing questions arise, which a biographer must ponder honestly on paper. In truth Mary Haydock's one desperate contact with her home town had resulted in that rejected petition to the Crown, and that is fact. It seems fair to assume possible future meetings with, and messages and helpful gifts from, her family. Prisoners were allowed visitors, even when awaiting departure on the actual transports;[119] under supervision prisoners could receive gifts. Perhaps, during those six months of waiting, the young girl made friends with others sentenced to be transported to New South Wales. Who were they? Did they become friends? On board the *Royal Admiral,* eventually, would be forty-six other females, apart from the travelling free settlers and troops, in addition to the male convicts. Reports, letters,[120] show generally that prisoners were not informed of their travel arrangements much before their actual removal to Portsmouth. In this case the order to board the *Royal Admiral* may have been equally precipitate for the convicts.

The Speculative Internees.

Since so many letters and articles were reported in the press in 1790-1791,[121] it seems fairly certain that discussion in the immediate gaol circle must have speculated on the conditions of the forthcoming journey. This sharp-witted group slept, ate, brawled, existed, in a tight gaol situation and questions and answers would fly around. Molly Haydock would therefore have to know that in New South Wales, males would outnumber females by six to one; that convict women could be and were sorted out by the military and civil gentlemen, mostly as concubines, rarely with View Matrimony if Suitable. Obviously with such a preponderance of males in the Colony, prostitution, though officially frowned upon and severely punished, was physically forced upon some of those women, especially if unable to liaise with a protector on shore. On board the transports, sailors often had access to the women, though male convicts were kept apart from the women's quarters. Watkin Tench comments:

> 'while they [the convicts] were on board ship, the two sexes were kept most rigorously apart: but, when landed, separation became impracticable . . . and wrong. . . . To palliate . . . evils, marriage was recommended.'[122]

Prior to the embarkation of the prisoners, often to occur weeks before actual date of sail, the Clerks of the prisons were responsible for those convicts due for transportation.

According to A. G. L. Shaw:

> Clerks of various courts sent lists of such persons to the Lord Lieutenant, who would then supervise their transport to a port town, their confinement there and contract for a ship for their transportation overseas, expenses being paid by the Treasury.[123]

In our particular area of enquiry as to what might have happened to Molly Haydock, there is the extant Staffordshire report dated 29th September 1791. Officer Price records:

> 'the gracious extension of His Majesty's royal mercy to them [several persons named including the boy James Burrow] for the term of seven years . . . on condition of the prisoners being severally transported to the eastern coast of New South Wales . . . It is therefore ordered that the said [prisoners] be transported [to New South Wales] accordingly as soon as conveniently may be . . . and that John Williamson Esq., and Joseph Dickenson, Clerk, [both J.P.'s of Stafford] . . . do contract with any person or persons for the performance of the said transportation and order such and sufficient security to be taken for the same [prisoners] & also cause the said persons . . . to be delivered over by the gaoler of the . . . County of Stafford in whose custody they [prisoners] now are . . . to the person Contracting for them and security so to be taken . . . at the next gaol delivery, to be holden for the said County of Stafford.'[124]

So Molly, recorded as James Burrow, officially for the last time was 'holden' in the Stafford gaol as shown in Chapter 3, while routine preparation and medical checks were to be undertaken preparatory to that embarkation in April of the following year, 1792.

The Government's Efforts.

In all sincerity a Committee of the House of Commons, when drawing up a plan for the penal settlement of a far distant land, endeavoured to organize what they believed to be a reasonable exile. They argued that

> 'The climate ought to be healthy: . . . their [the convicts'] Transportation shall not expose them to any imminent Danger of their Lives.'

and that they would be

> 'removed to a considerable Distance whence the Means of returning may be rendered difficult . . . a Coast situation is preferable to an Inland one . . .'[125]

This committee also recognised that there would be found 'both Husbandmen, and Artificers among them, as well as Men of Talents and Education.' Naively these men of Government believed

> 'that an Aversion to Labour and the Inequality of Fortunes, which stimulate Men at Home to the Commission of Crime . . . could have no operation [in a primitive distant penal settlement] . . . They would remain honest for Want of a Temptation to be otherwise . . . the most refractory [of the felons] might gradually be reformed.'

In fact, indeed, some were able to use their native good sense and strength of endurance; others remained what they were, products of criminal ghettos in the large British cities.

At first the government let out contracts to, often, unscrupulous ship owners and contractors. Those tough little sailing ships, as transports, sailed stuffed with convicts, crammed with provisions of salt beef, pork, biscuits, flour, peas and butter, plus necessary tools for construction and agriculture. Comparable in size with the 'Lady' ferries now on the Sydney Harbour[126] averaging about 400 tons, these small barques, with magnificent seamanship, were skilfully guided on their uncomfortable voyage, down to Rio, across to the Cape, across the stormy southern reaches of the Indian Ocean, around Van Dieman's Land, finally to make port at Sydney Cove, New South Wales. The voyage ranged in time from six to twelve months, depending on storms, upon the humanity of the Masters in allowing plenty of time for recuperation in the ports en route. But what a journey; what superb navigation, all without any communication lines unless, by chance, returning trade ships were met in the South American or South African ports. By comparison, the moon voyage, as a project monitored from take-off to return to earth, looks a much safer bet.

'Mary Haddock al. James Burrough' was rostered to make this long journey to New South Wales by the Government chartered British East Indiaman, the *Royal Admiral*; Captain Bond, Master. The ship eventually left Portsmouth in May 1792 and made landfall in Sydney on 7 October 1792.

Just five years earlier, Captain Arthur Phillip had led the First Fleet, that original brave Armada, to found a Colony in New South Wales. Indeed, incredibly he seeded a nation with the penal settlement at Sydney. Australia was the romantic result of these coldly brutal, awful sea journeys, made between 1787 and 1800, years relevant to this account of a youthful deportee.

Captain Phillip, as Commandant, had urged the government to take strong health measures for the care of all the passengers of the First Fleet, and indeed for all following transports. He wrote to Under Secretary Nepean on 17 March 1787 concerning the ships lying at anchor at Portsmouth:

> 'the giving of cloaths to those convicts who have been embarked at Plymouth is so very necessary. I have ordered it to be done . . . but . . . unless orders are being given for their [i.e. the still-to-come convicts] being washed and cloathed on their leaving the prison or the hulks, all that we may do will be to no purpose.'[127]

Phillip feared 'a fatal distemper' might spread aboard the ships and thus prevent entrance and hospitality in foreign ports, a necessary exercise for ships needing water, greens and fresh meat. He continues:

> 'The situation in which the magistrate sent the women on board the Lady Penrhyn [a First Fleet transport] stamps them [the magistrates] with infamy — tho' almost naked and so very filthy, that nothing but cloathing them could have prevented them [women convicts] from perishing [and did not] prevent a fever which is still on board that ship, and where there are many venereal complaints.'

Phillip's great care in maintaining exercise and fresh greens where possible, on the First Fleet transports, resulted in the safe arrival of nearly one thousand souls in January 1788. However the story of the Second Fleet, arriving in 1790, was not such a happy one. *Royal Admiral* was more fortunate.

Travellers' Tales of Other Ships.

In order to hoard provisions for later sale to settlers, many avaricious contractors sought to deprive convicts of their due food allowance — likewise paying little or no attention to the necessary care and cleanliness of the cramped unventilated quarters, they not being obliged at first to produce live bodies for a final bonus from the Government. The male convicts suffered greater hardships than the women; the latter were not shackled, and often they enjoyed the freedom of the decks.

Captain Hill, second Captain of the N.S.W. Corps, travelling on the *Surprize,* wrote one of the many letters (July 1790) which filtered through to England in 1791. He details the voyage 'on a bark unfit to be sent so great a distance' of the misery 'as rendered so by the villany, oppression and shameful peculation of the masters of two of the transports'. Hill reports the storm, when the sea water shipped on board the *Surprize,* of the Second Fleet:

> 'the convicts were considerably above their waists in water . . . they were obliged . . . to be pen'd down: but when the gales abated no means were used to purify the air by fumigations, no vinegar was applied to rectify

the nauseous steams issuing from their miserable dungeon. Humanity shudders to think that of 900 male convicts embarked in this [second] fleet, 370 are already dead and 450 are landed sick and so emaciated and helpless that very few, if any of them, can be saved . . . The irons [shackles] used upon these unhappy wretches were the same shackles used by them [the contractors] in the Guinea trade [slave trade — the contractors' usual trade] . . . made with a short bolt [bolts not more than three quarters of a foot in length] instead of chains that drop between the legs . . .

. . . as well as miserable pittance of provisions, altho' the allowance by Govt is ample . . .'[128]

The Reverend Richard Johnson in a private letter to a Mr. Thornton in England, written at the same time, 1790, tells of his horror on visiting these ships, the *Neptune, Scarborough* and *Surprize* on arrival in port, as he, Johnson

'went down amongst the convicts . . . a great no. of them laying, some . . . nearly quite naked without either bed or bedding, unable to turn or help themselves . . . smell so offensive . . . The landing of these people was . . . shocking . . . some were slung over the ship side . . . some fainted some died upon deck & others in the boat before reaching shore . . . on shore . . . some creeped [sic] upon their hands and knees — some were carried on the backs of others . . .'[129]

Even now, almost 200 years away, it is a truly terrible story. How frightening for convicts committed to transportation in 1791 to read or be told of these reports of such inhuman treatment during earlier voyages.

Over 2,000 convicts were transported from Britain during 1791 — not really so surprising then that such information would have filtered back into the 'Stafford holden gaol' by May 1792.

Extracts from George Barrington's letter to his wife, dated 2 March 1791 were published in the *Morning Chronicle* of 9 March 1791 giving a fairly vivid picture of his experience when being delivered to the *Mary Ann* transport at Plymouth:

'Our departure from Newgate was so sudden it was utterly impossible to leave you even a single word. We had not the least notice of it till 4 o'clock in the morning; and before we could well get the better of the shock 319 of us were conveyed to the river side.'[130]

Such a departure was as sudden and final as unpremeditated death.

Most of these unfortunate male prisoners were loaded with irons and chained together. Till the new century conditions were only slightly improved: some contractors were, after the Second Fleet, paid according to the number of the live bodies which they delivered safely to Sydney. But the situation seems to have been little different on the *Hillsborough* some seven years later in 1798, as described in a letter to his sister by William Noah; his death sentence had been commuted to transportation for life. This is his account, (his spelling and phrasing),

'& on Wednesday Evening the 17th October 1798 an Order Came to Newgate for me and 22 more Convicts to get ready to set off on the Next Morning when we were calld up at 5 & Irond two together & at 8 proceeded in 4 Coaches attend'd by the City Constables to Black fryers Bridge where we alightd and was put on board a Sand Lighter & Dropt down the Thames. On board [the *Hillsborough* laying at Upper Hope, Gravesend] . . . after being searched [by the officers] below in the Orlop Deck[131]

'. . . wretchedness passd discribig we was served with a Bed Blankets Pillow Night Cap Biscuit & small Beer the Deck was Dark but we found there was a kind of Barracks for our Beds and . . . on the proceeding morning I examined our New place of Imprisonment & found it to be the whole Deck fore & Aft with the 3 Hatchways Barrackaded roud with Quarter Timber of Oak Drove full of nails . . . 28 Barracks each side & hold 4 beds — room for 224 Convicts with 4 Easing Chairs instead of a necessary'[132]

On Christmas Day 1798 five days out from Portsmouth, Noah's ship suffered in a gale, very much as in earlier accounts of sufferings of these leaky transports. Continuing on Thursday 27th he writes with vivid detail:

'Blowing very hard . . . making a Deal of water . . . the Distress of the Convicts cannot be here Describ'd — every One thinking that every Moment the Ship would be swallow'd up the Bowell of the foaming Ocean which Came pouring down the Hatchways and the Convicts being Chaind two & two the Deck half full of Water, their Bed & ca all afloat in the hole they was in a sad helpless condition . . . the Quarter Gallery being Broke in by the Waves and the Sea pouring in among the women their Cries was Shocking to us that could not help one another in this Gale.'[133]

At St. Domingo, in the tropics, he writes how the

'convicts Bartered with them [bumboat merchants alongside] Jackets Shirts Handkerchief Blankets &ca for goats Hogs, Cocoa Nuts Money &ca . . . most of them little thought of what they would Suffer by Cold a going on the Voyage to the Bay'

One wonders how the convicts made communication with the indigenous boat bazaars — were they allowed on deck in this port of San Domingo? Noah also writes of the great heat at night on the Orlop Deck — 'so great was there Thirst that Water fetchd one a Monger another 2 shillg a Pint'. [sic]

This particular long sad journey was daily noted by Noah, telling of storms, of many sea and shore burials, and of sickness and short provisions. After leaving the Cape on 3 June 1799 Noah tells of a Captain's Passenger, Mr. Crossley, insisting on supervising the weighing of provisions:

'we found our plumb Pudding much bigger . . . owing to Mr Crossley . . . taking on himself to se our provissions weigh'd & gave to the Cook for after the Michief of starving & Close Confining we had lost a 100 men . . .'[134]

Despite Government intervention, as this diary shows, bad conditions continued during the last decade of the century. Governor Hunter in July 1799 reported to London of this ship:

> 'the *Hillsborough* transport, arriv'd yesterday in which had been embark'd three hundred convicts, but I am sorry to say that such had been the mortality on board that ship, two hundr'd and five only were landed.'[135]

There is well substantiated evidence of suffering on the *Active* of 350 tons and *Queen,* 380 tons, transports which arrived much earlier in September 1791. Collins wrote of the general horror and indignation aroused in the small colony when they saw 'the emaciated and feeble condition' of those convicts landed alive.[136]

Complaints and Petitions were made by the Public.

The *Pitt* was due to sail from Portsmouth in July 1791. In June 'J.W.' wrote anonymously to Lord Grenville begging some alleviation of the numbers already squashed into the bulging sides of the little ship:

> 'I allude . . . to the convicts on board the *Pitt,* now at Portsmouth, and destined to Botany Bay: they are about 500, besides the military corps and crew aboard. . . . [Knowing] the natural horror of screwing such a number of miserable objects within so small a compass [it] would be so evident to your Lordship that no further discussion would be necessary to obtain relief . . . I assert not a third of them can reach their destination alive. The present heat below decks is already almost suffocating [June in Portsmouth, England] and must accumulate . . . within the Tropics . . . the crew and soldiers cannot avoid the infection which must be generated among the convicts'[137]

Henry Dundas very smartly saw to it that urgent orders were sent to the Surgeon and Master Superintendent of "his Majesty's yard" to make an immediate strict and careful examination of the *Pitt.* J'n Evans, Rob't Read, and Ja's Marshall made such a required report on 30 June 1791 — finding:

> 'the number of male & female convicts on board amounts to 443 . . . Four Hundred and ten may be accommodated: and was the thirty three . . . excess . . . removed . . . by taking away the sick and diseased men from the prison . . . it would contribute to the health of the convicts . . . to that of the troops and ship's company also.'

So we find on the page is pencilled '22 removed'. Despite this when *Pitt* arrived at Port Jackson, one hundred and twenty out of three hundred and sixty convicts were on the sick list. During the passage forty-nine deaths had occurred.[138] The *Dublin Chronicle* 17 December 1792 reported that 'the convicts on board the *Pitt* . . . were attacked with the small pox . . . which went through the soldiers . . .[139]

These valid reports by crew, passengers and convicts concerning the cruelties and indignities inflicted, condemn contractors and the masters of these transports: masters who were both fearful of mutiny and revolt on board, hence the irons and confinement, and who, avariciously, were anxious to make a later profit by the sale of excess stores and goods when at the settlement. Trading did occur and high prices were paid. Captain Hill's words are apt, 'shameful peculation'.

The history of the mistakes, the tragedies, the high courage, and the greed of these adventurers, villain and victim alike, of the early transportation, paints a vivid picture of the experiences common to all including Molly Haydock. It is well to remember that Phillip, while a realist in his actual commission, before sailing wrote of ideal conditions and of his hoped-for intentions. The above horror-voyage accounts, together with even grimmer evidence, are well known and are now available in our State Archives. Evidence finally given in the enquiry into happenings aboard the *Queen* and the *Neptune*, reveal those appalling soulless greedy men who fiddled with lives as well as with weights and scales and with the allowances of flour and beef.

There were some instances of happier experiences: the aforesaid George Barrington writes in another letter sent in 1791 from the Cape of Good Hope, while on board the *Active* en route to Botany Bay — a breezy tale. It was reprinted in the *Western County Magazine* in 1792.[140] Barrington was a literate, cheerful, self-confessed pickpocket, much maligned according to his view; a convict who was apparently better treated than some on the transport *Active* — obviously well supplied with money for bribes. He was later to hold a good position at Parramatta.

Following a philosophical discussion upon the voyage of life and his own tranquillity of mind, Barrington continues:

> 'We have now been three months and two days at sea [since leaving Portsmouth] without putting into, or almost without seeing any land till we arrived here [the Cape]. . . . I find myself now . . . in much better health than when I left England . . . in as composed . . . spirits as ever I was in my life . . . I have had no illness of any sort since we sailed, not even . . . seasickness . . . Here we take in water, vegetables and every other refreshment so agreeable to people who have been a long time at sea and especially to those . . . used . . . to good living. There is tolerable beef . . . and . . . well fed mutton . . .'

Earlier, he has claimed his sole cash amounted to a dozen guineas, though he hoped for and expected a remittance. Yet at the Cape, Barrington acts as a gentleman convict "circumnavigator", spending lavishly, buying a sheep and good Cape wine for his mess, that is his group of convicts who were eating together. He was undoubtedly one of the well lined convicts who could buy their way to comfort. He wrote prophetically of the 'destined land where every man is to sit under the shade of his own vine and his own fig tree'. Barrington fulfilled that prophecy.

Barrington had his vanity: he adds a P.S. to his long philosophical report which is worth recording in full:

> 'PS I understand it was reported in the papers that when I came on board my hair was cut off, and my clothes taken away, but nothing of the kind happened to me. I was permitted to retain both, and continue to this hour to meet every indulgence that can soften my situation.'

In Britain public unrest fermented with the newspaper reprints of these private incriminating letters; and this unrest together with official censure by Phillip, caused Government unease. Questions were asked in the Commons.

Again the *Dublin Chronicle* — indefatigable reporter of Colonial affairs reports:

> 'The Botany Bay business is certainly to become the object of Parliamentary investigation. The return of the convicts, their treatment on the passage . . . their preclusion from . . . appeal to civil justice and humanity.'[141]

The public, hence the outgoing convicts and the shipping contractors were all well informed of the misery on board the transports during the long voyage to New South Wales.

This wretchedness needs to be well understood by us who flit from Heathrow to Mascot in a scanty twenty-five hours. Those grinding intolerable hours, days and weeks and finally months cooped up in those small vessels on the turbulent southern voyage to New South Wales, would test the hardiest of souls and of bodies too. In the 18th century Henry Dundas tried to improve matters. In May 1792 he told Phillip that he would 'take care . . . that justice be done', adding:

> 'It is proposed for the future to transport . . . the convicts . . . by ships in the service of the East India Company and I trust that by this means the evils which have subsisted will be put an end to.[142]

The *Royal Admiral* was one of the first ships sub-contracted by the Government from the East India Company. The story of the voyage now is the story of Molly, mustered as Mary Haddock (al Burrough), and her fellow passengers on board the *Royal Admiral,* a tale also of the recorded experiences of other women convicts.

Chapter 5
THE ROYAL ADMIRAL

The Ship and the Fairy Tale.

The facts must out! No matter how sad a blow it may be to the romantic at heart who hold to the popular belief that Mary met her future husband, Tom Raby (Reibey) on board that convict transport, the *Royal Admiral,* I must tell you it is simply just not true. The tale is merely an agreeable legend passed down the years, probably by the family, to be later elaborated by romantic novelists. The story is still presented as fact, as indeed by the *Australian Dictionary of Biography,* by novelists and tour operators. That young man was not a member of the *Royal Admiral's* ship's company. Perusal of the original ship's log book in the library of the India Office, and of the Pay Receipts Book of the *Royal Admiral* in which all the officers and crew signed for their pay, reveals no trace of a Thomas Reibey or Raby on that voyage from Gravesend 27 April 1792 arriving 7 October 1792. Frank Clune wryly commented upon this continuing fiction in 1964 in his review, *Bound for Botany Bay.*[143] Tom Raby (Reibey) was a young officer on board the store ship *Britannia,* under the command of his much admired Captain Raven, and this part of our history must stand aside for the moment. We are here concerned with the journey of Molly, now known as Mary HADDOCK on the ship's muster[144] and of her known companions on the journey south.

The *Royal Admiral,* under the command of Captain Essex Bond, was used by the British East India Company for forays in the lucrative trade with the Far East. Secretary Dundas, remember, had promised Governor Phillip that in future convicts would be transported in an orderly, supervised way on vessels of the East India Company in half-yearly batches.[145] In this way the Government administration hoped that public criticism would die down, that during transit to New South Wales conditions would be improved. The *Royal Admiral* was one of the first ships to be so organized, actually sailing just as Molly Haydock reached her fifteenth birthday.

On evidence vessels were pretty reliably roving the wide seas, depending for power solely upon man's age-old combination of sail and wind variations. (The power wheel has made a full turn, for in 1980, some cargo ships experimenting with rigid sails set according to computed calculations, with a view to fuel-saving, were in Sydney Harbour.[146]) Nor is it so astonishing to discover that many vessels were plying these long sea lanes.

Mary and others aboard were not with pioneering crews in the southern waters, as we may think, but were on ships fairly expertly handled by navigators experienced and steeped in the seafaring traditions of their island nation. Looking at the shipping lists of the late 18th century, one finds there 'slavers' carrying negroes, raw cotton and cotton goods on their triangular run, Liverpool — West Africa — Rio — and North America; there were the whalers which chased their prey in the Atlantic, the Pacific and the Indian Oceans, as so graphically told, later, by Melville's Captain Ahab; most importantly there were the many trading schooners which flaunted their sheets and sails in the further China Seas. These were employed by the East India Company in their successful dealings in tea and goods, busily trading with India, China, French Indo-China, and the Dutch Colonies in Java. Hence the flowering of the 18th century Chinoiserie in European homes, filled with exotic silks, muslins, furniture, ceramics and the scent of spices. The world's oceans had been mastered by these sailors who followed the earlier 15th and 16th century Portuguese navigators. Sailors and settlers from Portugal had left their fortified ports as far apart as Bahrain in the Persian Gulf and Malacca on the western Malay coast. Today the curious can still wander in the half buried desert ruins and in the old silted harbour.[147]

The Dutch traders of the late 18th century were crafty merchants bargaining with equally shrewed European shipping agents, although the Sumatran Straits were bedevilled with pirates as are some of those same seas today. But the long Eastern coast of New Holland, (or New South Wales according to Captain Cook), extending from Cape York to Van Diemen's Land, had not been exploited by the traders. (Indeed the whole hazy contingent had been spurned, our primitive shores had offered no sophisticated culture or trade; and the unlucky sailors driven ashore on the barren north west had made sour reports of the waterless terrain. In the Port Hedland district, Broome area, there are ruins of a well built town, Roebourne, abandoned for lack of water during the 19th century.) The advent of a British Colony at Port Jackson, though a penal settlement and only a little town of huts, meant a busy port in 1792, comparatively speaking. American speculating traders called, as did the whalers and sealers.

In a letter dated 24 November 1791 a passenger on the *Admiral Barrington* expresses surprise at finding 'the *Gorgon* and the *Supply* and ten sail of transports in the harbour'.[148] The highly successful shipping trade monopoly of the East India Company was jealously guarded.[149] Officers of the newly arrived N.S.W. Corps were to test this monopoly in 1792.

Mary Haydock's transport, although chartered by the East India Company, was privately owned by Thomas Larkins, Esquire. An agent, George Brown, was responsible to the British Administration for all the contracting. Some money was paid over in Portsmouth, while the *Royal Admiral* was at anchor, being fitted and loaded for her new role; and Two Thousand Seven Hundred and Fifty-four Pounds Twelve Shillings and Four Pence — a very exactly calculated amount surely! — was to be disbursed by the Governor of New South Wales upon discharge in Port Jackson.[150] The contract required clothing, slops, bedding, sufficient victualling for the voyage; moreover, the ship was to be supplied with a guard both prior to and during the trip. It is interesting to note that English carpenters would not remain on board while working in a British port, for fear of being trapped by the press gang, the soldiery given the unpleasant task of seizing likely looking citizens and impressing them into the lower ranks of the militia. No wonder Grose and Phillip came to complain of the atrocious types they found among the members of the guards. Extra supplies for the settlement were carried on board the *Royal Admiral*; flour, pork and beef.[151] The settlement, only four years old — a mere four years removed from the bare primitive, uncultivated land of the itinerant Aboriginal tribes, had become, at Rose Hill, a minimal producer of Indian Corn, much to Phillip's delight.[152] Yet food was still rationed and stores were needed if they were to avoid the great suffering of near starvation as in the first two years. The *Royal Admiral* had also been given permission to ship saleable goods for the makeshift stores — shops — in the Colony; goods included wine, essence of malt, and, it seems, some spirits. Her return voyage was scheduled via Whampo, China, India and the Cape. Many convicts firmly believed that China was nearby, somewhere North of Sydney Cove — leading some to make desperate escape attempts into a hostile bushland, only to find death there by spear or starvation. Some returned, to suffer the punishing lash as a reward for their adventure.

The Prisoners.

The clothing doled out to the women was pitifully scanty both in quality and in quantity. Unless Mary had a personal supply, which in any case would have been put in store for her, she must have been very miserable with the allowance of one cloth petticoat, one coarse shift, all made of an unsubstantial light linen known as Osnaburgh (originally made in German Osnabruck). To these were added one pair of stockings, one pound of soap, one quarter pound of thread (it must have been pretty coarse to weigh so heavily!), two ounces of pins, six needles, one thimble, and a pair of scissors. They were to be given cloth on arrival, for sewing garments.[153] Phillip earlier from Rio had complained 'that the women's cloathing [sic] [was] made of very slight material, was most too small and came to pieces in a few weeks'.[154]

Surprisingly the male prisoners received a hat, but none seemed to have been issued to the women. The reason seems to stem from this amusing (to us) order made by Secretary Nepean. It reads:

> 'a number of worsted nightcaps be also issued as maybe requisite for the supply of such convicts whose hair it may be necessary to cut off.'[155]

The order was made to please Phillip who was kindly anxious to care for the bald heads of the males who had to submit to prophylactic barbering. Sympathy is a must for these unfortunate gentry setting out on their long, uncomfortable journey across the seas to, willy nilly, lay the footings for a great city.

Minutiae like this order for caps for men made up a vast part of the organization of such an undertaking as sending these souls to a place where no single source of the most elementary needs was to be found in 1792.

The Ship's Complement — Passengers, Crew, et al.

On board was a gathering of forty-six other female prisoners kept most rigorously apart from the 289 male convicts. The men for the early part of this voyage suffered the cramped conditions of the Orlop deck, wearing, for part of their time, chains hung around their waists from which hung tethering chains to their ankles. Doubling ironing referred to the fiendish practice of hobbling each foot to the other with the barbarous short loop used on the slave ships. Chaining was customary, as Captains feared mutiny; hence also the rather limited use of the decks by male convicts, though such was very necessary in the interests of hygiene. Women convicts, allowed the freedom of the deck, consequently had contact with the crew and those passengers disposed to friendliness. There are scanty references to transport life in those early years; Mary Talbot, convict on board the *Mary Ann,* had written in March 1791 of a most frightening experience during a sea-storm, but found she could add 'we are much better off than we expected and have as much liberty as our unhappy situation possibly allows'.[156]

This was not always the picture as is only too well known; however the available records relating to the *Royal Admiral* show a similar milder treatment of the prisoners. Mary Haydock, according to the information we can deduce from all her previous experiences, probably went on board as a shortish, flat chestered, cropped haired, unbecoming type of girl, looking far more like a thirteen year old lass than the fifteen years she had just notched. I wonder if she still retained her own counsel, rejecting overtures of friendship. The transports were accustomed to dropping down to Spit Head, picking up convicts as they came from the holding gaols — picking up the various gangs from Plymouth and Portsmouth, as the ships were fully loaded and finally checked. Stafford prisoners were said to be staged through the early Millbank prison. Mary was probably moved by coach to 'Black fryers [sic] bridge'[157] and from there rowed to the transports. These vessels, ruefully quitting the Motherbank, sailed south well protected by the Navy in the European danger zones.

The *Royal Admiral* sailed from Gravesend on 27 April 1792, according to official East India Company records — she bore south to Teneriffe, west and south to Rio, to refresh, then east and south to The Cape, to False Bay at Capetown for water and fresh food. Pushed by the roaring forties due east on that last long leg for Port Jackson via Van Diemen's Land, she made landfall on the 7 October 1792 in Sydney Harbour after a fast five weeks in the southern reaches of the Indian Ocean.

Certain Passengers and Crew.

Some of the free passengers were sailing south to take up appointments, contracts for which had been signed before embarkation. Thomas Allen was with his family, journeying to practise as a master miller, a very necessary technician now the Colony was producing Indian Corn and grain. On the day of his arrival he is recorded as a master miller employed at His Majesty's settlement at Parramatta. Phillip liked to revert to the Aboriginal name Parramatta for the district of Rose Hill. Tom Allen was still recorded in that job in the 1795 returns.[158] William Peat with his Phebe, both free, came out to take up his contract at Norfolk Island as a master carpenter.[159] Phebe was about four months pregnant on sailing, as she gave birth to a boy, William, on the 10th October, three days after the *Royal Admiral* dropped anchor in the Harbour. The poor little babe lasted a bare three weeks, as the announcements stated that Wm Peat, 'an infant free' was buried on 3 November 1792. As if that was not tragedy enough, a notice told how Phebe herself was buried at Parramatta on Saturday 8 December 1792.[160] Maybe funerals were only attended to on certain days, as curiously we find that William Peat the father and widower, sailed on the American ship the *Philadelphia* on the day before the burial of his wife.[161] I include these stark details of various personnel on board that small ship, the *Royal Admiral,* to raise questions as to whom Mary may have known, mixed with or observed from her quiet distance. There would be talk, gossip between the members of that little microcosm both ashore and on board. There just HAD to be. So William Peat, widower, went off to Norfolk Island to take up his position.

The question arises as to why William and Phebe were at Parramatta. True, Governor Phillip ordered the healthy convicts, but not the free settlers, to be sent to Parramatta 'at once . . . to do away with any attachment to the port . . .' Convicts were to be sent from the ship to the place of their future residence and employment without stepping ashore at Sydney, 'which town possessed all the allurements and evils of a seaport of some standing . . .'[162] Really, how could one think of say the allure of Marseilles and London docks and think the same of Port Jackson in 1792? Phillip had a difficult job indeed! Still, there was a new hospital nearing completion at Parramatta, and a hundred and more huts had recently been built. Phebe, heavy with child, at all events found herself there, giving birth and dying while awaiting transportation to Norfolk Island to Will's job. Also travelling on board the *Royal Admiral* were the Jamiesons, likewise bound for Norfolk Island. John accompanied by his wife and child[163] had been appointed as Superintendent of Convicts on Norfolk Island on the day of arrival, 7 October 1792. They too took passage on the *Philadelphia,* no doubt helping William Peat in some way, who was himself to be recorded by 1795 as dead. Poor Peat family!

Two people from the crew have recorded interesting experiences for us; Richard Alley, surgeon, and Gunner George Thompson. James Lacy, convict, had some contact with Thompson and has also given us his account of shipboard happenings. Richard Alley had been appointed Assistant Surgeon and charged with the care of the convicts. He had already spent a very interesting time travelling with convicts and resting in the Colony. He seems to be a possible prototype of the professional officers of the ships, their only concern being their present duty, observant and competent, and caring for the general health of their charges. It would be fascinating to know if the naval surgeon had much contact with the future business lady when she was aboard as a slight teenaged girl; however, we must deplore the apparent loss of Surgeon Alley's reports on his activities and patients. He knew the Sydney sailing run, knew the brutalities of the system, he having accepted appointment on two such convict transports.

Previously, on 29 July 1789 Dr. Alley had sailed as Surgeon on board the *Lady Juliana.* In due course the indefatigable *Dublin Chronicle* published an interesting letter from Richard Alley sent from The Cape, dated 22 March 1790, written after a safe, slow seven month journey from England.

It is a thoughtful and lively account of Rio, of the care taken to refresh the convicts at Rio, Alley writing 'At present we are remarkably healthy; how long we remain so God knows, as the worst of our passage will be to New Holland'.[164] Some two years later on the same route, though travelling infinitely faster, it is a safe bet I think to see the experienced and confident young surgeon caring for the *Royal Admiral* convicts with equal care, if not wholly attended with success. He remains one of the rounded characters in the overall shadowy picture of the people surrounding Mary Haydock. Richard Alley had already been given a fair testimony by one of his female convicts from the *Lady Juliana.* Again we are indebted to the ubiquitous *Dublin Chronicle,* this time published on 4 August 1791, and possibly avidly read if obtainable, by the literate prisoners in Stafford gaol. The lady wrote from Port Jackson, on arrival, when she must have known that three women and one child had died on the trip:

> 'We arrived safe after a long voyage, in very good health . . . we had everything we could expect . . . and all our provisions were good . . . Five or six children were born on board . . . they had great care taken of them, baby linen and every necessary was ready . . .'[165]

On this earlier voyage, whilst in Sydney, Richard Alley, after the arduous duties on board the *Lady Juliana* had exercised his opportune and colonial right, maintaining a liaison with one lady convict Ann Marsh, living with her as his concubine until departing on the *Waaksaamheyd* (a snow, a type of cargo ship) on 22 March 1791. At this time, as might be expected, Ann was some six months pregnant, and was left sharing a hut with another female convict, complete with baby linen and sundry goods, sugar/coffee/tea/cotton. Alley's not to reason why, it was all part of his job! A daughter was born on 5 June 1791, faithfully acknowledged at christening as Charlotte Maria (H)Alley, daughter of Richard Alley, surgeon and convict Ann Marsh.[166] This little currency lass didn't make it either, and is recorded as having been buried some five days later on 10 June. Childless Ann Marsh then staged on 22 July 1791 a real convict's brawl with her hut mate Ann Flavelle, over missing goods and baby linen, ending in Ann Marsh's evidence sending Ann Flavelle to the Cart Wheel. She received 25, *repeat* 25, lashes.[167] Life was cruel, bitter, when it came to the priorities, and goods were the most precious things in the sparse, lonely life of the convict huts. This was the implacable woman whom Richard Alley had sought for a companion.

Well, while his concubine was living out her penal life, Alley was enduring the long thirteen month voyage back to England on the *Waaksaamheyd.* Immediately on arrival he was appointed as 'surgeon to superintend the convicts and assist the surgeon on board *Royal Admiral*[168] so, after a bare four weeks back 'home' Surgeon Alley took off on the *Royal Admiral* in May 1792. And this was the young medico who, together with Gunner George Thompson, cared for those convict men and women on board.

By contrast with the voyage of the *Lady Juliana,* the *Royal Admiral* was to make a very fast trip, a mere four months and ten days. It is good to read one report which claims, according to Collins, that the surgeons and

Captain Bond took extreme care with the cleanliness of the convicts. So much the better for the young girls and boys travelling as convicts.

George Thompson, gunner and assistant to Richard Alley, adds a further touch of colour to the picture. One supposes that a gunner would not be concerned with his weapons once the travellers had left the European waterways. At any rate he has left for our benefit a book based upon his observations, both on the journey and upon his survey of the settlement, according to the bias of his own perceptions.[169] He was yet another person on the *Royal Admiral* who was thoughtful, observant and helpful to the three hundred odd prisoners. Keep viewing their predicament within the overcrowded confines of the small four hundred ton sailing ship; people crammed alongside stores, galleys, masts, shipping gear, boats, quarters for crew and passengers; all in spray, sunshine and storming gales; that is, if the whole drama is to be fully comprehended! George Thompson appears to have been right in the middle of that little world. A convict on board, James Lacey, from The Cape, wrote of Thompson. As noted, The Cape, then a Dutch possession, was a great place for shipping to mingle, being on the crossroads between the Far East and Europe; many letters were sent 'home' by outgoing passengers, or East bound people, through the good offices of homeward bound vessel personnel. So on 19 August 1792, Lacey wrote to an unidentified friend in a high position, of the experiences on board the *Royal Admiral* during the leg from England to Cape Town. He mentions George Thompson, gunner and surgeon's assistant, writing:

> 'of Mr Thomson [sic] who fills the joint offices of gunner and inspector of the convicts . . . the greatest praise falls short of what this gentl'n [sic] deserves for his unremitted attention to the health and comfort of the unhappy men under his care, his own stock, purchased at his own expense, being at all times dedicated to the use of them whose situation seemed to require it . . . I have been [so explicit] at the particular desire of a number of convicts, who, from gratitude wish that his treatment be made as public as possible.'[170]

James Lacey's letter was written after the fifty-one days from Portsmouth via Rio to The Cape, and there were yet to be endured the five weeks ahead, of a positive race to Port Jackson. After Gunner Thompson recovered from his own sickness, suffered in that port False Bay, no doubt he continued his sympathetic ministrations. George Thompson writes in his own account of some of his own charges, the very young convicts; the boys Alexander Dempster, Thomas Galloway, William Collins, each only fifteen years of age, and each facing a seven year sentence. Of the girls there are named Ann Wilson, eighteen years, Ann Holms a sixteen year old who had been transported for life, and a partially identified girl, one . . . Scott who could, possibly, be Mary Haydock. On the ship's muster she is listed as Mary Haddock, which could be a London clerk's spelling of the Lancashire pronunciation of Haydock. After all the document rejecting the Petition spells the name very precisely as Haydock, so the broad Northern accent seems a reasonable explanation for the misspelling on the muster. It is but a step for the girl to be thought of as a Northerner, even considered a Scot by London ears. Maybe she was nicknamed Scot. Possibly George

Thompson's touching comment refers to Mary Haydock. She had already passed as a young, very young boy. The sensitive kindly gunner wrote of this young convict girl:

> 'Finally, there is Scott, only thirteen years of age (Quis talia fando temperet e lachrymis) [who saying such things could refrain from tears — Virgil] . . . Scott was transported for life.' [From Aeneid. Bk II][171]

Certainly the age is understated, but she was small; certainly her sentence was for seven years, but that really does not negate the assumption that this was indeed Mary. From this very painful reflection of Gunner Thompson it seems that the little girl referred to might have been overcome with all the happenings around her, and have sadly lived out those four and a half months on board in as private and secluded a way as she could. One thing is certain; the assumption that she was sent out under the pseudonym of Scott is just airy nonsense; the Muster is definite enough — Mary Haddock. One thing more comes from Thompson's grouping of his young convicts together; she would have to have been mentioned among those six youngsters, and another likely consideration is the possibility that Gunner Thompson was able to segregate these young people from amongst the older, wilder, experienced men.

James Lacey, the very literate convict, who has spoken so well of Thompson, has more to add. He, Lacey, is a shining exception to the majority of exiles — which majority as research has shown[172] were 'in fact mainly the sweepings of the provincial cities and that they were people who had chosen a life of crime in preference to any other'.[173] But there were a number in the minority who were of Lacey's literate educated group. Yet he was a criminal as were the others. I wonder if his wife had talked with Mary both on the ship and after landing. His letter from The Cape reads that he records 'the most material occurrences that has happened . . . since our arrival on board' after leaving land their particularly severe confinement was 'in a great measure abated, our treatment in every respect far superior to what from the outset we were led to expect.[174] He hints at Jew baiting, maybe after provocation, amongst the prisoners, telling of a Jew who fabricated (to the Captain) a story of threatened mutiny. (This violence was always feared by ship's officers. There had occurred the successful mutiny on the *Bounty*.) Lacey tells how Gunner Thompson spiked that rumour and endeavoured to eradicate the harm done. Significantly Lacey adds:

> 'of the captain and officers I shall speak in general terms. They are very human, good men; but not having tasted the bitter cup of affliction themselves, they are apt to view us wretched beings with more contempt than is necessary or than their services deserved, being at all times employed in the most slavish part of the ship's duty.'

While these remarks are given in a conciliatory manner it puts the spotlight on the relationship between officers and convicts. He tells of the deaths of six male convicts happening between Gravesend and The Cape. The writer had a wife travelling as a free woman and he was angry that the women convicts had the same liberties as did these passengers. He writes:

> 'None of the women [convicts are] deceased, which may be in a great measure imputed to their being under no restraint or confinement, their

> situation being not only superior to the men convicts, but likewise to those denominated [sic] passengers . . . women accompanying their husbands, a circumstance that strikes me as not exactly to y'r Honour's intentions.'

His wife had been one of those loyal women who followed their men to the 'lands beyond the seas'. In this case their child had been left in the care of the addressee of this letter. Lacey adds 'I thank Heaven for restoring my wife to her health, which has been greatly impaired thro' extreme anxiety for her child.' Lacey also tells how the provisions for the convicts are being tampered with but 'the excellent purser, Mr Halliday, by his strict attention prevented many frauds being practised on the provisions of the convicts by those employ'd to deliver it.'

Thomas Watling joined the *Royal Admiral* at the Cape, previously having escaped from the *Pitt.* As a member from the convict Push of the *Royal Admiral* had escaped from the False Bay (Cape) hospital during this stop-over, Captain Bond had agreed with the Dutch authorities to accept as a substitute Thomas Watling, sentenced for forgery to serve in Port Jackson. His was still another articulate voice among the convicts on board. Watling was reported as being back in Europe by 1800. He has left us a heritage of pictures of scenes of the early settlement, sketched with his forger's skill.

Amongst the women convicts who mingled with Mr. Lacy's wife and young Mary Haydock, was Mary Springate suffering all the inconveniences of a pregnancy while sailing the Southern Seas. She gave birth to a daughter, while still on board in the Harbour of Port Jackson, three days after arrival on 10 October.[175] Mary Springate did not survive and her little girl, Eleanor, died a day later. (A few years later Mary Haydock was to give birth under fairly primitive conditions on the Hawkesbury farm.) Now, aged fifteen and a half years, she, who had witnessed so much suffering, so many different reactions to gaoling, birthing, dying, quarrelling, punishing and just sheer stubborn tenancious surviving, must have stored a great fund of experience which helped her on final arrival at the settlement.

Presumably Mary landed in a healthy condition, physically at any rate. Thompson's comment about the pitiful little 'Scot' which I accept as referring to Mary Haydock, seems to indicate some private understandable grieving by the girl. Since all healthy convicts were rowed straight to Parramatta (see ante), the immediate disposition of Mary remains guesswork. Legend has it that she was immediately employed by the Lieutenant Governor, Francis Grose, and his wife, as a nurse maid. Here again the great lacunae in the Grose papers leave us guessing, except for one scrap of evidence reported in 1806. In this Muster she was listed as being a housekeeper. It seems possible that she could have been employed by Grose and his family in Parramatta while the Lieutenant was impatiently waiting to take over from the incapacitated Governor Phillip. Later she would be brought to Sydney where she was eventually to meet Tom Raby. Collins records that three hundred and thirty-six convicts arrived finally — there are discrepancies — yet the women survived the journey better than the men.[176] Phillip, reporting to Henry Dundas wrote:

> 'Of the convicts embarked on that ship [*Royal Admiral*], ten men and two women died on the passage, and four children were born, one of whom died . . . seventy two men, eleven women and five children have been landed sick. I have no doubt but that strict justice has been done them . . . but sir, if I was to give an opinion I think the people have been too much crowded on this ship.'[177]

Phillip's guarded report on this first venture with a seconded East India Company ship does raise some doubts as to the administration by Captain Bond. Undoubtedly he was a fine seaman, and an able navigator, yet there is that disturbing fact concerning the quarter master and six sailors who 'jumped ship' while the *Royal Admiral* was preparing to return, once discharged by Governor Phillip, via China to England. Why Sydney, of all places, in 1792? What could those men be looking for? Employment on an itinerant American whaler? Looking for a South Sea holiday on Norfolk Island after the fashion of Bligh's Bounty Boys? The quarter master knew Norfolk Island, having been shipwrecked there from the *Sirius* on which he had served, in 1790. Yet these men didn't want to serve with Captain Bond any more, to travel via Whampo, China, India, to their home. The Quarter Master knew Dr. Richard Alley well, having shared that long thirteen month voyage with him on the *Waaksaamheyd,* when returning to London. So? Captain Bond who had signed on that Quarter Master in London for the complete round trip, had to leave Sydney without him, together with the six absconding men; they were helped by the settlers and he 'concealed himself in the woods.'[178] Collins reveals that the Quarter Master came out of hiding later and attempted to sign on with the *Atlantic.*

As to the motives of the sailors one can only hazard conjecture, and then add together the tangled happenings on board the *Royal Admiral,* making the rather lively picture which emerges from our fairly scanty resources. I guess Mary and her fellows would remember how they sailed away from Portsmouth with nearly four hundred souls on board, male prisoners crammed into the Orlop deck, women apart, with free passengers making do in their shared quarters. By The Cape, the scandal and subsequent punishment for the threatened mutiny would have been food for gossip; far more important would have been the memory of the steward's intervention in their interests in the dispersal of food. The deaths of the six prisoners from the gaol fever would have become a memory, a happily passed danger. On the voyage certain persons must have been fairly prominent, such as Watling, Gunner Thompson, convict Lacey with his free wife, and those six young people so sensitively discussed by Thompson.

The question is, once they were all landed, within the now four thousand strong colony, how many of these last arrivals met each other, whether at Parramatta, at the Port, or on Norfolk Island; how many claimed each other as an old acquaintance with a recently shared experience? Or were some of them, as Mary Haydock undoubtedly was, anxious to retreat away from it all? The voyage on this ship must have left quite a mark on most of those carried by her to this far new settlement.

'Emigration in search of a husband'

National Library of Australia

National Library of Australia

Augustus Earle National Library of Australia

The Annual Meeting of the Native Tribes at Parramatta, NSW.—The Governor meeting them.

Thomas Whitcombe

National Library of Australia

Departure of Whaler *Britannia* [on left] from Sydney Cove, 1798.'

Chapter 6
SYDNEY TOWN AND THE BRITANNIA

Arrival Chaos.

It was a great day — a boat day — on Sunday 7 October 1792, for Sydney Town. Atkins recorded

> 'Hot weather, Wind East, about 12 heard distinctly 15 guns, so that we hourly may expect an account of a ship's arrival.'[179]

And it was a ship. For there, sailing safely up the harbour on that easterly breeze, was thankful, weatherworn *Royal Admiral,* a record five weeks behind her from the Cape, and she passed, down harbour, the *Britannia* at anchor. On the hot Spring day over the rail of the *Royal Admiral* probably peered the small young Haydock lass, whilst undoubtedly Captain Raven's duty officer, twenty year old Tom Reibey, would have scanned this latest arrival from England, the transport, looking for fellow officers in the East India ships. This is surely an allowable romantic possibility, of an unheeding, unknowing glance between our two people. Sadly history is blank and it looks as if the pair could not really have met during those fourteen days while both ships were at anchor in the port.

The available facts of the drama caused by the early arrival of the *Royal Admiral* points to great turmoil, to disordered order on board, in the port and at Parramatta, which tends to rule out an October 1792 meeting. There waited the *Britannia,* busy making ready for her much contested chartered voyage to the Cape. Thomas Reibey was indeed a member of the *Britannia's* complement . . . his 1811 burial notice plainly shows that he first reached the Colony on *Britannia,* July 1792.[180]

The *Britannia's* Charter.

This store ship, part owned by the Captain, William Raven, was delayed in Sydney's port by a pretty to-do — a serious difference between Phillip, the about to retire pain-ridden governor and his imminent successor, Major Francis Grose. The persistent officers of the N.S.W. Corps had strongly argued their case for their hiring of the *Britannia* for a journey to the Cape to:

> 'return with a freight of cattle and such articles as would tend to the comforts of themselves and the soldiers of the Corps which [articles] were not to be found in the public stores.'[181]

Grose quite vehemently presented their case to Phillip; with hindsight one has some latent sympathy with the Major. Phillip, in accordance with his own strict code, had sternly insisted that, when rationing was an essential necessity, all portions would be equal. This in order to eke out the meagre stores, and the Vice-Regal share was no exception. Grose, reporting that the bargaining with the *Britannia* had been completed and the ship was ready to sail, appealed to his superior, writing:

'I have now to request you will interest yourself in our [officers'] favour, that you will . . . protect this ship from interruption as much as you can, and that you will assist us to escape the miseries of that precarious existence we have hitherto been so constantly exposed to'

and he spoke of

'the situation of the soldiers under my command, who at this time have scarcely shoes to their feet, and who have no other comforts than the reduced and unwholesome rations serviced from the stores.[182]

Phillip unwillingly acceded, but wrote to Secretary Dundas indicating he felt that his duty lay in the protection of the Government backed monopoly of the East India Company from

'the opening a door to a contrabande [sic] trade; at the same time I beg leave to say that I do not think His Majesty's service will suffer.'[183]

Phillip was so right — it was the beginning of independent trading by the officers and others.

Captain Raven, of the *Britannia,* held a fishing license for three years, allowing him to dally in the Southern waters, seeking whales and seals. Evidently sensing a more profitable exercise he agreed to the charter by the military officers for the very considerable sum, in 1792, of Two Thousand Pounds. Still the voyage meant considerable rearrangement of the ship's decks for cattle carrying and a fresh victualling of the ship for the long landless sea voyage. Collins wrote:

'that the ship was well calculated for bringing cattle, having a very good between-decks; and artificers . . . were immediately employed.'[184]

The *Britannia* had come to Sydney on 26 July of that year, twenty-three weeks out from Falmouth, with a full load 'of clothing for convicts, beef and pork for a full allowance calculating their numbers at four thousand six hundred and thirty nine'.[185] Unloaded and discharged by the local authorities Captain Raven and his officers had been free to enjoy Sydney hospitality, attend to the necessary careening and repairs after the long sea journey, preparatory to the planned fishing foray to New Zealand. Captain Raven occupied a hut on shore, as we know from the excellent Collins writing of a daring burglary committed on 10th October as he [Raven] was lying asleep. (He lost his knee buckles and a rather tinny watch, to the disappointment of the thief.)[186] The ship had anchored down harbour in September preparing for the New Zealand voyage, but now in early October all orders were changed because of the lucrative charter to the Cape; all was very busy. So where do we find young Thomas? When not on duty no doubt being lavishly entertained by news-starved settlers and civil and military personnel, all anxious to enjoy the company of a young gentleman, a ship's officer fresh from England with the latest military and political gossip, considering the rumours of war. Again Collins paints in the details as, with much restiveness, he comments:

'It was impossible that a ship could ever reach this distant part of His Majesty's dominions, from England or any other part of the world, without bringing a change to our ideas, and a variety to our amusements. The introduction of a stranger among us had ever been an object of some moment; for every civility was considered to be due to him who had left the civilized world to visit us.'[187]

Seamen, of course, were not encouraged ashore at night; jealous male convicts understandably resented any attentions to the female minority in which they had a proprietory right. It is obvious that Tom Reibey would be fully occupied implementing the necessary new orders for the projected Cape venture, as well as being involved socially, one imagines. The *Britannia* left the harbour on 25 October 1792.

The *Royal Admiral*'s Passengers.

The *Royal Admiral,* after her fast dash south-east across the icy Indian Ocean, would have sent shock waves through the lonely little seaport of 'a huddle of buildings near the waterfront'.[188] To the Colony she brought stores, food, people and that most eagerly sought after commodity, news; hopefully newspapers, even though so out of date. She brought people who had to be accounted for, accommodated and attended to; the sick and the healthy, the free and the bond, and Major Johnston's last group of the N.S.W. Corps; she brought old friends, as Dr. Alley and the Quartermaster; moreover, she brought goods for sale on the primitive markets.

Also, the *Royal Admiral,* alas, 'brought in with her a fever . . . the sick to the number of eighty were all immediately disembarked'.[189] We already know that poor Mary Springate died on board the *Royal Admiral,* in harbour, on Wednesday 10 October. Some people were still on board, evidently, three days after reaching port. The incoming men and women, as per custom and health regulation, were washed, thus removing any clinging germs it was hoped, after which the convicts were possibly paraded at Parramatta and allocated as workmen or women for settlers and Government, and the women who were unattached mostly chosen as 'wives'. There is plenty of recorded evidence for all these regulations being carried out. Collins, a most faithful and indefatigable chronicler tells:

'the remainder of her [*Royal Admiral's*] convicts were sent up to be employed at Parramatta and the adjoining settlement . . . without permitting them to disembark at Sydney, which town . . . the only place where shipping anchored possessed all the evils and allurements of a sea port . . . to do away . . . the possibility of any attachment to this part of the colony . . . their being immediately sent from the ship to the place of their future residence . . . and . . . they went with cheerfulness.'[190]

The immediate placement of Mary Haydock was debated in Chapter 5, that is, was young Mary sent immediately to Parramatta? Some of the free settlers, such as the unfortunate Peats, as well as healthy convicts, went to Parramatta, acclaimed by George Thompson as the important settlement. There would be much confusion and coming and going between ship and shore, long boats and Parramatta. For example the sailors who refused to return with Captain Bond in the *Royal Admiral,* when found were kept manning the longboats to Parramatta. Some of them were hidden by settlers in 'the woods'; this to gain extra hands on the stony farm holdings. Obviously this could only happen within confused crowds and there were some four thousand souls scattered between the two settlements. Moreover, the ship was busy unloading stores including 9,287 gallons of rancid oil, originally destined for use as butter for the hungry settlers.

The Lucrative Market.

At Sydney and Parramatta shops were opened for 'the sale, private, of articles especially brought out for this purpose'.[191] Illicitly spirits were also sold alongside the legal 'porter'. Lovely unaccustomed intoxication followed; great were the riots, the wife-beatings, the destruction of unwilling crops, and all! Collins speaks most unsympathetically of the scandalous profits made by the business minded among the mob who resold their goods, of the huts becoming nothing else than porter houses. Captain Bond was no piker in these deals; having reaped Three Thousand Six Hundred Pounds from his sales he was still obliged to set sail for Canton a month later, on 13 November, leaving articles to be sold on commission to the amount of Seven Hundred and Fifty Pounds.[192]

George Thompson speaks of many things, happenings, social differences which were new to the eyes of the incoming passengers. Parramatta was to him the grand settlement, so he too was among the group of visitors who made their way to the top of the river arm of the harbour. He is quite horrified at the tenuous food position, reporting:

> 'those that are now living chiefly owe their lives to those that are dead, the provisions being so scarce that had they not died all must have perished. When our ship [*Royal Admiral*] arrived, which was quite unexpected, there was no more than one week's salt provision in the store at the full allowance.'[193]

He did not share Governor Phillip's optimism, caused by the ripening corn at Parramatta/Rosehill.

The Prospects for the Women Passengers on Arrival.

Thompson is quite definite about the distribution of the women:

> 'The women have a more comfortable life than the men. Those who are not fortunate enough to be selected for 'wives', which every officer, settler and soldier is entitled to, and few are without, are made hut keepers; those who are not dignified with this office are set to make shirts, frocks, trousers etc. for the men at a certain number per day; occasionally to pick grass in the fields, and for a very slight offence are kept constantly at work the same as the men.'[194]

Similar reports come from other sources, both earlier and later. For example, T. W. Plummer complained to Governor Macquarie in a 'welcome letter' in 1809:

> 'It will perhaps scarcely be believed that on the arrival of a female convict ship, the custom has been to suffer the inhabitants of the Colony each to

select one at his pleasure . . . rendering the colony little better than an extensive brothel.'[195]

I prefer the happier tone of the anonymous writer who factually reported:

'The female convicts on their arrival are treated in the same manner as the males . . . being well washed and furnished with a change of suitable apparel. The commissioned officers then come on board, and as they stand on deck, select such females as are most agreeable in their person who generally upon such occasions endeavour to set themselves off to the best advantage.'[196]

Both Lieutenant Bowes and Captain Watkin Tench of the First Fleet spoke of natural consequences when the convict men and women were united once on shore; I have no doubt that this was a frightening happening for some sensitive women; even hardened pro's might be a little unnerved considering that appalling ratio of men to women. Bowes writes:

'Women landed after being searched. They were dressed in general very clean and many of them well dressed. [They would have had their own goods handed back to them on arrival.] The convicts got to them very soon after their landing . . . the scene of debauchery and riot . . . may be better conceived than expressed.'[197]

Tench is more sympathetic, arguing:

'nor will a candid and humane mind fail to consider and allow for the situation these unfortunate beings so peculiarly stood in. While they were on board ship the two sexes had been most rigorously kept apart, but, when landed their separation became impracticable and would have been, perhaps, wrong. Licentiousness was the unavoidable consequence and their old habits of depravity were beginning to recur . . . To prevent their intercourse was impossible; and to palliate its evils only remained. Marriage was recommended.'[198]

It is interesting that many cheerfully became bigamists, conveniently forgetting the partner left behind, accepting the situation, becoming good settlers with the incentives offered by Phillip. Possibly many married in haste to survive the system of unequal percentages of the sexes.

An anonymous writer had suggested to Sir Joseph Banks that

'the recruiting of the gorgeous women of the Pacific Islands might solve the problem and from such a union of physically perfect women with convicts a nation of people would arise at Botany Bay which would be 'an ornament to human nature'.[199]

One woman's point of view of her 'disconsolate situation in this solitary waste of creation' has been preserved with all its vivid account of the times:

'As for the distresses of the women, they are past description . . . As they are deprived [on arrival] of tea and other things they were indulged in on the voyage by the seamen . . . though a number of marriages have taken place, several women, who became pregnant on the voyage and are since left by their partners who have returned to England are not likely even here to form any fresh connections.'[200]

The *Lady Juliana* had arrived in 1790 with some 222 relatively healthy females, under the care of Dr. Alley, medico on the *Royal Admiral.* This supply of the much needed female balance was too much for Collins, perhaps a misogynist; he was both hungry and angry as he complained:

> 'in the distressed situation of the Colony it was not a little mortifying to find on board . . . a cargo so unnecessary and unprofitable as 222 females instead of a cargo of provisions . . . when the women were landed many of them appeared to be loaded with infirmities incident to old age and to be very improper subjects for any purpose of an infant colony.'[201]

However, a female passenger convict, on the *Lady Juliana,* wrote privately home 'safe after a long voyage, in very good health . . . the greater part of the women were immediately sent to Norfolk Island.'[202]

When Mary arrived there were convict women scattered in all the settlements, and allegedly, many were much healthier and more were pregnant than was normally expected at their mature age.

What of Mary Haydock?

The reiterated statement in various novels and newspaper accounts of this young fifteen year old convict girl, that upon landing she became nursemaid to the Grose household, cannot be substantiated by any presently available source. True, in the 1806 Muster the word 'Housekeeper' is used. There is also no evidence of any child being born to her following the voyage. It seems fair to assume that her small stature, boyishness and apparently most unfriendly attitude to her companions, or if that is too hard, her reserved nature as in prison and perhaps on ship, preserved her from forced marriage. I tend to accept two practical possibilities on the evidence re the convicts from the *Royal Admiral*: one, she was sent with healthy convicts to Parramatta, escaped hungry bridegrooms and became nursemaid or servant to one of the settlers or civil officers' families; in this case it would be very surprising if young Tom Reibey should have met her in those two weeks; secondly, if she had been among the sick then she would be either in the small Sydney hospital or up in the spanking new wards of the brick Parramatta Hospital. At all events, so far as reliable sources show, Mary Haydock disappears from our view until her marriage with Thomas in September 1794.

What of Thomas Reibey?

However the settlement is there for us to see and the interesting voyages of the *Britannia* are well documented. There is no evidence of Tom Reibey's origins, family, education or whatever, other than that he reached Sydney in 1792, July, on board the *Britannia.* Still his picture comes across by extrapolation from the snippets. He was young, but old in experience; though a mere twenty years he was Junior Officer for Captain Raven of the *Britannia,* evidently being very fond of his Commander. Later he christened his sloop the *Raven,* and quite coincidently, Raven was in 1795 granted 100 acres at Eastern Farms in the Colony. The voyages on the ship must have acted as a catalyst for the young man as he passed that shadowy line of Conrad's[203] from a callow youth to a sea seasoned commander after trial in sailing ships. For Tom Reibey was always at home at sea.

The *Britannia* left Sydney on 24 October 1792 en route for the Cape to speculate for the officers in cattle and horses. Maybe Thomas here did some early enquiry into farm animals, as did so many officers. Collins commented:

> 'The ship was well calculated for bringing cattle, having a very good between-decks . . . artificers from the Corps [N.S.W.?] were immediately employed to fit her with stalls proper for the reception and accommodation of cows, horses etc. . . . A quantity of hay was put on board sufficient to lessen considerably the expence of that article at the Cape.'[204]

(Certainly the charting officers were business men.) The ship collected seals from New Zealand, rounded Cape Horn 'in very favourable weather', paused for eighteen hospital days at the Portuguese island Santa Catherina on the Brazil coast — then 'he stood over to the African Continent'. My late twentieth century eyes still pop, figuratively, contemplating that long southern sea run, pushed by westerlies in the late Spring. Loaded with thirty cows, three mares, twelve goats, flour, sugar, tobacco, and spirits, the *Britannia* continued her easterly way from the Cape to Sydney's Port — pounded by huge seas in gale winds, dodging islands of ice — Captain Raven reported skirting Van Diemen's Land without seeing land — arriving back in port with twenty-nine cows and three goats dead. The journey took eight months.[205]

All that money invested by the officers for such a poor return. At the Cape Captain Raven and his crew had learned of warlike preparations going on in England. He'd also learned that the *Royal Admiral* had reached the Tigris in a record thirty-seven days after leaving Sydney on 13 November 1792 — similarly she'd been seen to be a 'flyer' when bringing out that group of people in October.

The *Britannia* was back in harbour in June 1793 and remained there till August. Maybe in that time Mary met Tom. The ship was being repaired by Colony artificers, Captain Raven meanwhile offering the now Lieutenant Governor Francis Grose the use of the ship, at, of course, a reasonable fee. Raven is spoken of very highly by various authorities. He had become a Master in the Royal Navy at the age of twenty-three after having served in merchant ships. He sounds the right sort of Captain to have won Tom Reibey's regard. The vessel remained in Sydney port from June to 26 August 1793. There were nearly ten weeks of dalliance in the port. Were indeed Mary Haydock to be in service in Lieutenant Grose's household or in a similar home, she would have been relatively safe from the prostitution practically forced upon many of the women convicts. Now turned sixteen years, maybe the girl has blossomed, her dreadful experiences since leaving Blackburn having faded somewhat.

Nevertheless Tom Reibey sailed once more with Captain Raven en route to Bengal to gather food for the Colony, and this time the *Britannia* met a really terrifying experience — pirates and all. The *Britannia* went to Norfolk Island, collected fresh provisions, vegetables and water, and took on board Lieutenant King, the Commandant, and two New Zealand men for a return trip, Norfolk Island to Dusky Bay, New Zealand. Leaving Norfolk to the south, Captain Raven took the *Britannia* through the passage of Mindanao or Borneo, making for Bengal — through the Straits of Malacca — but as told in Raven's own graphic but restrained words:

> 'was there engaged for six hours by a fleet of proas armed and full of men, when, after having expended all our powder, the pirate obliged me to relinquish that passage . . .'[206]

For six long hours, mark you, the wild men, *despite* the guns of the *Britannia,* continued to attack the ship, finally forcing her withdrawal. And young Tom Raby was there fighting, helping to keep the sails trimmed at the same time to get movement away from those many piratical proas.

With the fear of further involvement with the numerous French privateers known to be swarming in the Indian Ocean, the journey to Calcutta was abandoned, with the *Britannia* retreating to the Dutch port of Batavia. The Dutch East India Company's stores came to the rescue, for a price, and the *Britannia* returned to Port Jackson with the desired cargo in June 1794.

The Marriage.

Whether wearied with the sea, for the time being, or charmed by Mary Haydock, Thomas Reibey had decided to leave the vessel, had applied for a grant of land and had applied for permission to marry the young convict. So the prince found his princess, even if it was to take her to a tough life on the banks of the Hawkesbury River — it would still indeed, after all her troubles, be a private haven of joy for the now seventeen year old lass. Thomas Reibey had left his ship, and incidentally never returned to England. (It is interesting to note that in 1820 Mary Reibey made no visit to any Reibey families when visiting England and Scotland, at least none was noted in her daily record.)

It is also interesting to note that these two appear, from this distance, 1981, to have made a very solid, loyal working partnership. What a splendid happening this was, that a free, eligible young maritime officer should recognise in this hardy small young lady, this convict lass serving her time in New South Wales, a young woman who had all the strengths, loyalties, refinement, to make him a first rate wife. So on 1 September 1794, Mary Haydock became Mary Reibey. A very private affair, I think, since the witnesses were two people unable to sign their names, and we find, in the presence of the Reverend Richard Johnson, signatures by

"Thomas Raby [sic]
Mary Haydock
Witnesses: Sarah Higginson (her mark) X
William Denman (his X"[207]

The Reibey name became very important to this country from this day when Thomas took Mary Haydock to wife.

PART II
MARY REIBEY — WOMAN AS BUSINESS MAN

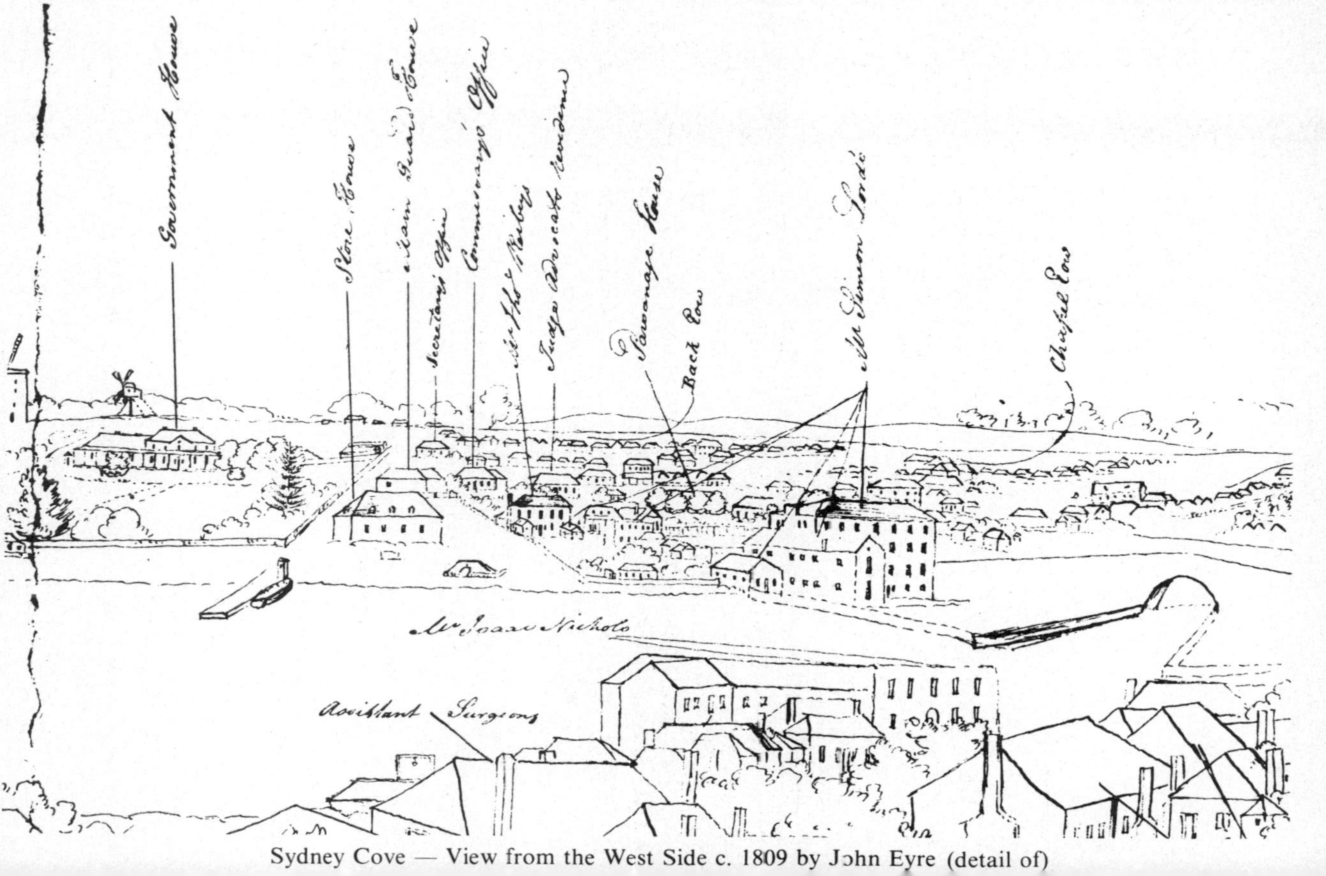

Sydney Cove — View from the West Side c. 1809 by John Eyre (detail of)

Chapter 7
THE HAWKESBURY

The Gentleman Tom Reibey

After all it was Thomas who gave to her the name which now rates high in our legends, our folk lore, mishmash though it may be of jellied myth and history. Reibey is the name which jerks these historical puppets to life when today's interested Australians and tourist travellers make enquiries around the Sydney Rocks area or when at Entally House, Hadspen, Tasmania. So what of Tom Reibey? This man with no recorded birth place or family, presumably English in origin, was a most energetic, able person, brave and adventurous. It is his activities which largely dominate these seventeen years of the Reibey couple's story. Yet at his untimely death in 1811, there is barely a whimper of an obituary in George Howe's *Sydney Gazette*; only a few quiet lines mark the end of these hectic years of private commerce and trading.

Thomas Reibey, maybe, was a Romantic; certainly a man with a tremendous faith in his future, away ahead of the neatly organised, classical 18th century contemporaries. Denholm suggests that colonists were romantic fellows at heart, arguing that 'the Romantic Age dawned in the late 18th century when Sydney was a straggling village.[208] Captain Tench, a Georgian gentleman, when viewing the Hawkesbury area from an eminence perceived it only a vast rocky, unruly inimical area. He wrote:

> 'I record with regret that this extended view presented not a single gleam of change, which could encourage hope or stimulate industry, to attempt its culture.'[209]

Tench was a pleasant person, who thankfully returned home after faithfully serving the Government for the Colony's first four years. Alas classical gentlemen are often tunnel-visioned. Luckily for Tom Reibey, the Lieutenant Governor, Frank Grose, a bucolic man with a practical viewpoint had encouraged officers of the Corps (and ipso facto free settlers with any substance) to engage in interdependent trade and agriculture. For any officer there were 100 acres for the asking. Grose meant to improve the quantity of food and goods for the Colonists. Therefore Thomas Reibey was in line for a grant.

The Settlements.

George Thompson, the Gunner and Supervisor of the *Royal Admiral* recorded his impressions about Sydney as:

> 'the spot where the first settlement was formed merely for the advantage of good water and the conveniency of the Harbour . . . only gardens sufficient to supply the inhabitants with vegetables etc. The Governor and principal officers chiefly reside here . . . [with] convicts . . . to attend the storehouses . . . fishing boats and officers . . . two miles from the place are the brickfields [Brickfield Hill] . . . not such a thing in the

> Colony as a set of stairs except in the Governor's house of only one story . . . Parramatta is the grand settlement about sixteen miles from Sydney by land . . . forming one large street nearly one mile long . . . [where are] a large hospital, church, store houses . . . The Governor has a house at Rose Hill, a most delightful spot . . .'[210]

Thompson was kinder about the birds than some chroniclers and later poets:

> 'the birds in general are very beautiful, a great variety of different sorts of parrots [are here] many other birds unknown in England . . . Insects [are] very troublesome and destructive . . . musquittoes [sic] and flies are in great quantities: the latter will infect fresh meat in such a manner that it is sometimes difficult to keep it free from maggots even one hour after it is killed.'

Small wonder early colonists invented the wonderful 'cooler' safe, complete with hessian sides dripping in water and stood upon ant-proof saucers.

Thompson continues:

> 'The trees in which the whole country abounds are found to be of little use . . . not fit either for building houses or boats . . . some distance up the country the trees grow very strait (sic) and to a great height, though not one in a hundred are sound.'

Thompson was not to know of our lovely cedar, discovered and madly and happily exploited to decorate with great beauty the 19th century homes. The early cedar cutters scrounged it all, including the savage clearing of the Hunter Valley's rich lush acres. In the early years of the century Reibey boats carried cedar to Sydney.

At Parramatta, John Macarthur had been granted his first 100 acres together with the labour and keep of ten convicts. He was not alone. Even Grose's 'man of most troublesome character,[211] the Reverend Richard Johnson, found himself able to accept one hundred acres which the reverend gentleman, incidentally, farmed with great skill. Each settler was supplied with available tools and seed from the public store, supplies for two years and free convict labour. Grose was seen to be and was in fact encouraging the implementation of his stated policy of lifting the Colony out of its dread dependence on unpredictable overseas supplies. His officers were in an enviable position, free to trade with ships' captains from India, America, Java, as well as from Britain.

Success Stories.

Tom Reibey would certainly have known in August or September 1794 that the N.S.W. Superintendent of Public Works and Paymaster, John Macarthur, had become a most successful farmer at Parramatta. Mrs. Macarthur in 1794, writing happily to her family, records Macarthur's own letter to his brother:

> 'The changes we have undergone since the departure of Governor Phillip [December 1792] are great and extraordinary . . . scarcely credible . . .

Our own house [Elizabeth Farm] a very excellent brick building 68 feet in length and 18 feet wide, independent of kitchen and servants apartments . . . I have a farm containing 250 acres . . . 100 under cultivation . . . of produce I have sold Four Hundred Pounds worth . . . now . . . in my granaries . . . [are] upwards of 1800 bushells of corn . . . at this moment 20 acres of very fine wheat growing . . . 80 acres prepared for Indian corn and potatoes . . . My stock consists of a horse, two mares, 2 cows, 130 goats and upwards of 100 hogs . . . I have received no stock from Govt but 1 cow; the rest . . . purchased or bred . . . my table . . . supplied with wild duck and kangaroos . . . the house is surrounded by a vineyard & garden . . . The farm being near the Barracks, I can without difficulty attend to the duties of my profession.'[212]

Well bully for Macarthur! Maybe he was a lucky man; with his military office he was influential and fairly 'well-heeled': nevertheless he was a hard worker, a clever organiser of labour and intensive agriculture having

'frequently in his employment thirty or forty people, whom we pay weekly for their labour . . . these we both feed and clothe, . . . We have but two men fed at the expense of the Crown . . .'[213]

Another letter written in December 1794 by a member of the N.S.W. Corps mentions happily, but critically, the rising settlement — now 3,500 souls:

'I have many great friends here, and live much better than might have been expected in my station — in a military life . . . Major Grose has made great improvements. Sydney contains 700 good comfortable huts, exclusive of numerous brick buildings, the property of Government . . . We have many pigs and goats, but they are chiefly in the hands of gentlemen . . . Spirits being now plentiful, a number of persons retail the same, but the price as well as the quality varies much . . . the gentlemen always purchase the cargoes, and this watery mixture is sold at 16^{s} per gallon.'[214]

This anonymous soldier speaks admiringly, as did Mrs. Macarthur, of Phillip's Parramatta garden 'abounding in the season with grapes, melons, pumpkins and every other fruit and vegetable'. Delightfully, this same romantic chap adds:

'The Governor's garden at Parramatta is so situated by nature that, in my opinion, it is impossible for art to form so rural a scene'

A true 19th century romantic! Nice to think he remained to try his luck in the Colony, for he concludes:

'My commanding officer [Grose] prior to his departure [by the *Daedalus,* December 1794] was pleased to give me a grant of twenty-five acres of good rich land for ever, so that in a short time I hope to be a respectable farmer, having besides with me a hut of three comfortable rooms, a good garden of half an acre of land, where I have every production of this place in profusion. My live stock at present are two pigs, twelve fowls, three pigeons, a dog and a cat, which with my station [in the Corps], stock, garden, and farm, give sufficient employ.'

Something we can never know is whether this soldier settler finally 'made it', alongside an agreeable female companion and a corresponding expanding family. Reports of such moderate contentment do sparkle in the history of our early settlers, and Australia is the product of their balanced approach to work. Tom Reibey may well have asked himself might he not similarly make his fortune, since Macarthur and others had generated such success in only four years.

The Hawkesbury Venture.

It would be of little moment to the two young people to leave Sydney and Parramatta behind, even though those places had greater opportunities for Mrs. Macarthur's civilized conversation and music. Mary had lived in Sydney/Parramatta since October 1792 and Thomas had been a visiting Sailor-Officer since early 1792. Phillip had written of the scarcity of agricultural tools and the difficulties of attempting distant settlements. Yet Grose had successfully settled seventy families by January 1794 who 'are doing exceedingly well'.[215]

Nine months later the Lieutenant Governor was organising another group, in which were Mr. and Mrs. Reibey. According to the Bonwick Transcripts, Box 88 page 35, the appendix to the 1802 Muster, Thomas Reibey appears in the 'List of Free Settlers from England who have been left by different ships without any order from Government.' Tom was a free settler and a marine officer, yet the original grant was only for the customary thirty acres at Mulgrave Place (Hawkesbury River). It reads:

> 'Land Grant No 310
> 19th November, 1794 in the district of Mulgrave Place to Thomas RAIBY [sic] Block J
> 30 acres for fourteen years, Annual Quit rent commencing after 5 years'[216]

Larger grants, as mentioned, were made to wealthy settlers and Officers of the N.S.W. Corps — this Reibey grant lay next to William Cobcroft's grant, on the bank of the river. By comparing old maps and noting Mary Reibey's later advertisement in the *Sydney Gazette* re letting their

> 'two adjoining Farms down the River at Hawkesbury . . . Reibey's Farms . . . situate between Cobcrafts [sic] and Roberts'

it seems that Thomas could possibly have eventually taken over Williams' grant, although Lieutenant Grose's Plan of the River Settlements[217] shows the land of J. Roberts as No. 18 as at 29th April 1794. D. G. Bowd[218] (who doesn't include Reibey as a settler of 1794) shows John Cobcroft 1795 at Block 6, No. 6 was issued to J. Rous in 1794 according to Grose's map.

The Reibeys did take over, by lease, grants surrendered by failing settlers, and Rous did fail, yet again!

In all probability the journey, alongside other Hawkesbury pioneers, would have been made by a small 14 foot sloop, out of the Heads and up the coast to Broken Bay. For although Grose had caused a road to be made from Sydney to the banks of the Hawkesbury, there were no bullocks and drays as early as 1794. I like to think that the providential Thomas, having travelled twice with Captain Raven in the *Britannia* to purchase goods and cattle for the trader-farmer officers of the N.S.W. Corps had made his own purchases at the Cape and at Batavia. There he was, a sailor-farmer daring Tench's dictum 'It is not often that sailors make good farmers',[219] having no doubt about his ability to fulfil his plans. That Mary became part of that plan is charming and splendid. He knew all about convicts, their woes, trials, experiences, their place at the bottom of the Colony's hierarchy, and with her he turned his back upon the past and Sydney — romantic Thomas and his indomitable young seventeen year old bride.

He would have been granted an extra twenty acres as a married man, with the right to hire convict and emancipist labour. Their cottage on the river bank, once built, was probably initially two rooms of clay plastered wattle, with a bare earth floor and a thatched roof, attached to a separated kitchen. Similarly built old cottages with a skillion kitchen (or one separated by a covered way) are still to be seen in the west of New South Wales. The Reibeys' animals would be pigs, and their crops would be fresh vegetables and maize and wheat.

The River.

Records of the river are rather forbidding; it was a very young eight months old settlement in October 1794. The fertile fields of rich flood mud were of course a joy after the sterility of Sydney's rocky soil — the Hawkesbury area was to be a granary for Sydney for some years. But there were the floods, the infighting between some of the settlers, and most alarmingly, the attacks by the displaced Aborigines. All this had to be faced.

The floods on the Hawkesbury in a very few hours still reach up to a startling thirty feet above the normal river level. Then as now, floods berserk at their peak are terrifying as they race along the current dragging their troublesome trees, bursting the banks, destroying cottages and fences which may stand in the water's path. Hawkesbury floods are fast, high and devastating. Horror stories of lives lost were many; the 1795 floods drove many settlers back to Sydney.

The Aboriginal Troubles.

There was continuing attrition between the Aborigines and the settlers. With hindsight it is fairly obvious that the Aborigines were filled with fear and resentment at the unwanted intrusion into their historic hunting grounds by these ubiquitous white settlers — the intimidated 'whites' must have endured agonies of terror under continuous threat by those deadly spears. Moreover these settlers were not united amongst themselves — there was a quarrelsome atmosphere. A high percentage were ticket-of-leave men, unskilled emancipists and many assigned convict labourers. There were parochial troubles without the menace of floods and unfriendly Aborigines. As well as their intermittent harassment by the 'Indians', moreover, it was all so strange, so weird, so different in the bush. Perry, in

Australia's First Frontier, makes a valid comment concerning the extreme differences in this new land as compared with what British Colonists found in North America — there the English, Irish and Scots found very similar trees and identical climatic seasons, whereas the newcomers to the Antipodes found

> 'themselves in an up-side-down land. January was hot and July cold . . . Kangarros [sic] hopping through the scantily-leaved forests: emus running awkwardly and unable to fly . . . natives were scrawny, ill kempt, and ignorant of all but the most primitive arts and skills.'[220]

The Aborigines had learned to covet the provisions, the bread, the corn and some of the possessions of the white men. In September 1794, the very month that Tom and Mary married, Collins reported

> 'At the Hawkesbury they [the natives] were not so friendly [as at Sydney]. A settler there and his servant were nearly murdered in their hut by some natives from the woods, who stole upon them with such secrecy, as to wound and overpower them . . . A few days after . . . a body of natives having attacked the settlers, and carried off their clothes, provisions and whatever else they could lay their hands on, the sufferers collected what arms they could . . . followed them seven or eight of the plunderers were killed on the spot.'[221]

but he adds that the settlers had often provoked the Aborigines by wantonly firing upon them and then forcibly detaining abandoned children. A fight for survival was being waged between the two groups. Six months later, in May 1795, Collins further reports:

> 'At that settlement [Hawkesbury River] an open war seemed . . . to have commenced between the natives and the settlers . . . The natives appeared in large bodies, men, women and children, provided with blankets and nets to carry off the corn, of which they appeared . . . fond . . . In their attacks they . . . made use of their spears and clubs . . . Captn. Paterson directed a party of the [N.S.W.] Corps to be sent from P'matta with instructions to destroy as many as they could of the 'wood' tribe (Be-dia-gal) . . . to erect gibbets [as a warning].'[222]

Professor Bernard Smith speaking of the complete lack of understanding and communication between Aborigines and equally uninformed settlers, when they chanced to meet, asks 'Did they laugh as they teetered on the edge of violence?'[223] That, to me, succinctly sums the atmosphere of fear infusing the early situation.

Collins again reports that as the troops withdrew, on one occasion:

> 'the natives attacked a farm nearly opposite Richmond Hill, belonging to one William Rowe and put him and a very fine child to death . . . the wife after receiving several wounds, crawled down the bank, concealed among the reeds.'[224]

This is only one of the many instances of this fierce unhappy strife along the River during the years 1794 onwards into the new century. But Mary had weathered the horrors of prison and transportation and Tom had survived wild voyages with piratical attacks in Sumatran Waters so maybe they approached the Hawkesbury venture with a fair amount of cynicism, as well as faith in themselves.

In January 1795 Lieutenant Governor Paterson had sent a military guard on a Colonial schooner to the River —

> 'the sloop also having on board a mill, provisions for the settlers here . . . the commanding officer of which [guard] was to introduce some regulations amongst the settlers and to prevent . . . the commission of those enormities which disgraced that [River] settlement.'[225]

The enormities continued and included such offences as the pack rape of a Dublin convict, Mary Hartley, by four convicts, English and Irish, all labourers of the River. There were the laxities of some of the settler farmers who, as Collins complained

> 'scarcely made any preparations (as putting wheat in the ground) consuming their time and substance in drinking and rioting . . . trusting to the extreme felicity of the soil.'[226]

It was with such unhappy, unfortunate people that the more resilient settlers (as Andrew Thompson, Rous, Arndell, and the Reibeys) endeavoured to tame the luxuriant flood-prone river banks, to fight off the Aboriginal menace and to create a surviving ordered settlement.

But 'to make a fortune' was just a hazy dream in 1794. In 1796 the river tribes, as yet undeterred, attacked a carrier boat plying between the port of Sydney and the River, mortally wounding one of the crew. Collins speaks of the apathetic attitude of the farmers, in February of that year:

> 'The frequent attacks and depredations to which the settlers situated on the banks of the Hawkesbury were exposed from the natives called upon them for the protection of their families and the preservation of their crops, mutually to afford each other their assistance . . . by assembling without delay whenever any numerous bodies of natives were reported to be lurking about their grounds; but they seldom or never showed the smallest disposition to assist each other. Indolent and impoverished even for their own safety and interest, they in general neglected the means by which either could be secured . . .'[227]

Is this criticism by Collins a little too severe? Too savage? Apparently not, as Lieutenant Governor Paterson positively proclaimed that persons who kept back their assistance from those threatened would be punished as persons disobeying the orders of the settlement. Also the taking of the lives of Aborigines by wanton firing would be considered as deliberate murder. There were strange bedfellows on those banks. Two emancipists, Wilson and Knight, actually had made contact with the Aborigines living with them as tribesmen. (This was apparently acceptable until the whites coveted a lubra belonging to a fierce black hero!) These two men

> 'preferred a vagrant life with the natives . . . [and] led them on to every kind of mischief. They demonstrated to the natives of how little use a musket was when once discharged.'[228]

The Reibey Family

Into all this little world of violence was born young Thomas Reibey the second. We opted, way back in Chapter 2, 'for a plucky hearted character; (Molly Haydock) 'a cool determined young girl who took a daring, calculated plunge into an unsheltered life on the roads'. Five years later this assessment still holds good for Mary Reibey née Haydock who gave birth in that troubled raw bush settlement. In June 1795 the State of the Settlement[229] shows that, at the Hawkesbury River there were nine free men and nine free women, possibly army people, 'of settlers, 4 free men and 138 convicts'. Tom was certainly one of those four free people. Was Mary one of those 138 convicts? Her sentence ran till 1798. One emancipated woman, is recorded on that list. Counting those listed as above, together with all the children and the 170 men and 55 women servants/labourers, gives a total of 546 for the Hawkesbury settlement. The little family was not exactly isolated in the bush, even if the neighbours were varied and they all came from the United Kingdom. Thomas was born on 6 May 1796, nine days before his mother's nineteenth birthday. James followed on 2 October 1798 and George was born on 2 February 1801. These children and the later four siblings were all baptised at the old St. Phillip's Church, Sydney. These christenings were possibly in person. The Mutch Papers[230] show that each was baptised some six weeks after birth, indicating perhaps that the little family made its way with each baby to the Metropolis, to that early wattle-and-daub church built by Reverend Johnson himself. Records show that Thomas born 6 May 1796 was christened on 20 June 1796. Similarly the second son James, born 2 October 1798, was baptised on 10 November 1798 at St. Phillip's.

Commerce and Chartering.

Thomas, using his sloop, the *Raven,* with six men, was running a cargo business between the Port of Sydney and the Hawkesbury. Evidence shows that he gradually transferred his base from the River to the Port, although for many years he was involved with the Hawkesbury. He had, however, a weatherboard house on The Rocks. He used the Government Wharf. In 1803 he received from Governor Philip Gidley King a grant on the Hawkesbury River, to 'Thomas Raby [sic] and his heirs and assigns forever of 100 acres . . . situate in the district of Mulgrave Place to be called 'Raby Farm'. This area is now known as Freemans Reach; the property became known as *Reibeycroft.* Then in 1804 there was the very favourable grant to Thomas, of Block 70 at the Harbour's edge, on the eastern bank of the Tank Stream, reaching back to the present Macquarie Place. The young Reibeys had done well to prosper with their Hakesbury venture, farming and shipping goods to and from Sydney and the Hawkesbury. Hunter, in 1796, reported that over 1,000 acres were under cultivation on the river, with the Vice-Regal comment about the general situation: 'The settlers on the Hawkesbury are more in debt than in any other settlement.[231] There were extenuating circumstances, as we have noted; also, these settlers were a long, long way from the City market, where, in any case, the Corps Officers had the monopoly. Thomas had shrewdly assessed that the carriage of goods would be good business; who better to handle this navigation down the coast than ex-officer (naval) Reibey? He had entered the fur and skin trade as well as undertaking the carriage of coal from Newcastle. Paterson had established a store for trading on the River at Mulgrave Place in 1795 when there were some 400 customers around, but the tremendous floods of 1796 had swept away everything.

As to when the family actually transferred residence from the River to the Port is not easily pinpointed. However Reibey did own a weatherboard two-rooms plus kitchen cottage situated on The Rocks, far enough along the point to be able to see down the Harbour as far as the South Head.

The advertisement appeared in the *Sydney Gazette of* 1 April 1804 (when, presumably the new stone house was completed) offering this cottage for sale:

> 'Thomas Raby [sic] offers a commodious DWELLING HOUSE for sale . . . newly weather boarded, shingled throughout and glazed . . .'

Baking facilities, the three rooms including the kitchen and the fruit garden were specified, and then

> '. . . the whole admirably and deservedly situate on the Rocks with a delightful and extensive command of prospect to South Head. The property of and formerly occupied by Thomas Raby on the Rocks.'

This then may be seen to be the first dwelling place for Mary and the little boys in Sydney.

Extraordinary things were happening. The extension, the exploration, the building, the trading, all made for a great jumble in the Port of Sydney. Society per se was ensuing division as ever, according to rank and free man. But this little settlement was to be the product of hard won money and clever trading. Success came only after much trial.

N°	To whom leased	N°	To whom leased	N°	To whom leased
1.1	Robert Campbell Esq.	34	Jno Bolger	67	Sim Lord
2	Do	35	Chas Whelan	68	Thos Randall
3	Wm Balmain, now belongs to Government	36	Serjt — Ricketts	69	Wm Chapman
4	Mr White	37	John Fleming	70	Thos Reibie
5	Capt Wm Raven	38	Geo Pitt	71	Wm Blake
6	Sam Thorley	39	John Fleming	72	Thos Jameson
7	Henry Kable	40	Richd Clarke	73	Isaac Nichols
8	Major Geo Johnston	41	Thos & Mrs Hobby	74	Danl Mc Kay
9	Richd Chears	42	Capt Nichols	75	Chas Griffin
10	Thos Prior	43	Jonas Bradley	76	Thos Saunders
11	Capt Waterhouse	44	Anne Robinson	77	Jno Mc Arthur
12	Edwd Laing	45	Willm Roberts	78	Robt Sidaway
13	Jas Underwood	46	John Driver	79	John Harris
14	Grant to Orphans	47	Thos O Neale	80	John Palmer
15	Col. Wm Paterson	48	Mat Kearns	81	Nat. Lucus
16	Garnham Blaxcell	49	Jno Jas Grant	82	Wm Bennett
17	Mr Thos Laycock	50	Joseph Smith	83	Wm Day
18	Mr Jno Harris	51	Capt Jno Houstoun	84	Edwd Luttrell
19	Richd Chears	52	Mary Newton	85	James Thomson
20	Robt Turnbull	53	Neil Mc Kellar	86	James Wilshire
21	Jno Black	54	Thos Whittle	87	John Tucker
22	Wm Jameson	55	Jas Bloodsworth	88	Richd Palmer
23	Edwd Haven	56	John Gowen	89	Joseph Sherrard
24	Lieut Wm Moore	57	Geo Howe	90	Capt Thos Prentice
25	G. Blaxcell	58	Serjt Richardson	91	John Redmond
26	Richd Atkins	59	Jno Aicken	92	Thos Alford
27	Edwd Johnson	60	Capt W Wilkinson	93	Nat Lucus
28	Capt A F Kemp	61	Thos Storer	94	Shad Shaw
29	Wm Hudson	62	David Bevan	95	Nichs Divine
30	Revd Johnson	63	James Petty	96	Nat. Franklin
31	Sam Skinner	64	Danl Mc Collom	97	Fred Markett
32	Rosella Marsh	65	Wm Bennett	98	Jas Callam
33	Robt Cummings	66	D D Mann	99	Alexr Mc Donald

References to Map on page 64

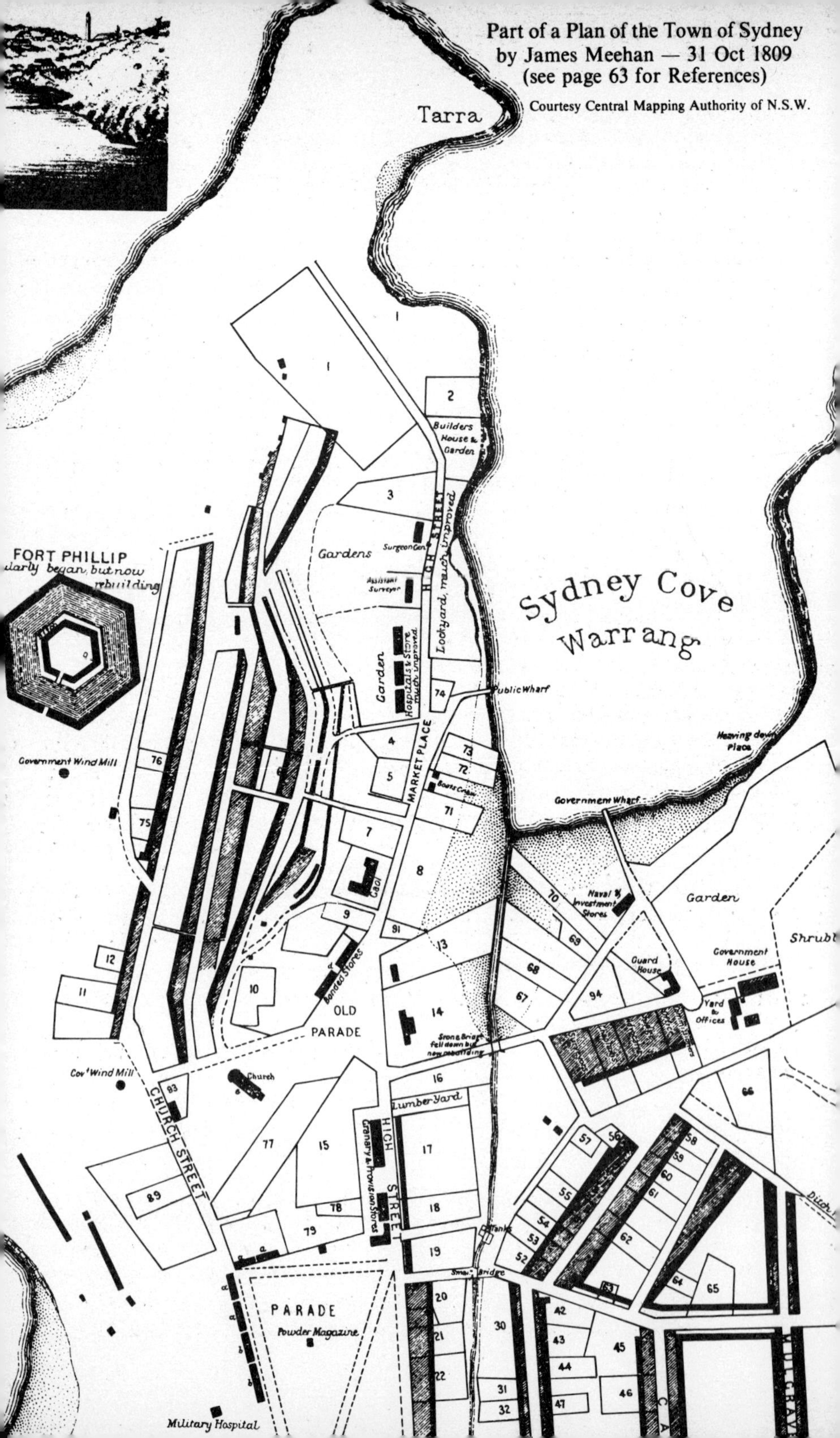

Part of a Plan of the Town of Sydney by James Meehan — 31 Oct 1809
(see page 63 for References)
Courtesy Central Mapping Authority of N.S.W.

Chapter 8
SYDNEY AND THE SEA

Sydney.

Mary was not to know that the trading store now established in her house, the timber yard on the foreshore of Block 70, together with the boat building sheds, were virtually a Froebel school of preparation for her — a preparation for her future management of what was becoming a big business. Thomas Reibey, with his partner, was extending his activities from the Hunter to Bass Strait, from Sydney to Otaheitie and the 'Feejees', whilst still retaining the early lucrative business on the Hawkesbury, and leaving much of the oversight of the business to the care of Mary.

Despite the Penal Establishment, the genesis of the Port, the over-riding official Government, Army and Civil Administration, the place was humming with new development. The Rocks were hugged by the lonely ticket-of-leave and convict brethren, while the exclusives were moving towards the East Sydney heights and Harbour front leases. Sydney's area was at that time bounded by Cockle Bay (the present Darling Harbour), Brickfield Hill (then some metres higher — indeed a real hill), and Wolloomooloo, with outstations towards the East Coast to Botany Bay. There was 'a fine road to Parramatta' and a rough track to the Hawkesbury. To the North was the near North Shore, mostly still the abode of the local Aborigines. There was a spirit of unrest, not unusual in time of growth; the Colonists were uneasily aware of the dominance of the Corps by Macarthur and of his studied disagreements with the Governor — indeed, Governors.

Society was sharply divided between the free and the emancipists; that is the free exclusives and the ticket-of-leave emancipists. Some of these latter, of course, were talented, educated people rapidly rising as the business power in the Colony; what was more to be feared, the emancipists, by passing of time, were in the majority. So, where was slotted Mary Reibey, *emancipist* wife of a successful *freeman*, trader and farmer and a former naval officer to boot? She was busy with a rapidly extending family, finally totalling seven children. She was busy listening to and working with Tom and such men as Robert Campbell, the free and successful Scottish trader who lent money to Thomas for the latter to extend his business; with emancipists Simeon Lord and the French Jew James Larra; with Underwood, and Kable, who like Tom were ship-builders; and with Edward Wills, Tom's partner and a former convict. All very able business men, all advertising largely in the *Sydney Gazette,* and all purveyors to the Exclusives.

Up on The Rocks, which then reached to the Shore and the Hospital Wharf, the ticket-of-leave holders, the labourers and some of the indentured convicts all clung together, carefully copying their old City haunts of the United Kingdom. Olaf Ruhen wittily sums up the Sydney-side situation: 'Noll' noted with approval that his predecessors (earlier transportees) had hastened to set up a reasonable facsimile of London living with dwellings crowded close and 'bothies [sic] selling grog and raucous company and narrow lanes and tiny yards and crowded living room'.[232] The convicts were arriving in large numbers to serve their sentences 'beyond the seas', as convicts would until half way through the century, here to suffer certain 'hiving off' in locale, employment and no doubt 'treatment as deserved by wicked felons'. The chain gangs were around for all to see, the convicts who were used by the Government for civil works, for roads, farming and buildings. The stocks still had their unwilling occupants. Really heinous crimes required the evil doer to publicly expiate his deed upon the gibbet. So much for the penal settlement.

Tom's business affairs seem to have been rather daringly volatile at the beginning of his Sydney career. To carry on the Reibey business there was indebtedness to Robert Campbell[233] for One Hundred and Sixty Pounds Ten Shillings, in 1801, and again with the same man a mortgage using Tom's collateral of three Hawkesbury farms in all comprising 260 acres, for a further loan of One Hundred and Fifty Pounds. High finance was already a feature of Sydney business and located, it appears, not so far away from today's Stock Exchange, right at the old Bridge, (Bridge and Pitt Streets, 1981).

The Sea.

Reibey and Wills owned the small sloops *Raven, Edwin* and *James,* and had laid down an ambitious keel of forty feet to eventually become a seagoing vessel, maybe the *Mercury*. News of the sloops and the *Mercury* recur in every couple of editions of the *Sydney Gazette*; their share of adventures shows how very close to an unruly frontier of sea exploits were those early sailors. There were many ships looking for trade, selling goods brought from China and the American continent, looking for seal skins to take home with them; there were pirates around the North of the Continent. Once the *Raven* returning from Kent's Bay (Bass Strait) had picked up a lonely marooned man, or so he thought himself, left alone on a distant Bass Strait isle to guard food stores by the unfeeling *Ceres* commander; the *Raven* bringing him safely home along with its load of skins. Reibey and Wills boats were regularly reported as travelling to Kingstown (Newcastle). They brought back cedar logs and coal. They took back stock, food, clothing and tools. On Sunday 2 September 1805 their load included prisoners, transferring them from the Derwent to the Hunter River Penal Settlement. Ironic that Mary's subsistence might in part have been paid for by money earned by the transportation of convicts. Tom repeatedly advertised for cedar cutters, as in May 1804, requiring cedar cutters and a handy carpenter who understood boat building, 'persons capable of entering into an agreement'; plus a couple of greyhounds to go to Newcastle, adding 'They must be warranted to Kill and Show . . . and will be treated for liberally — signed Thomas Raby [sic].' In their efforts to field a crew for the 'fur and oil' (seal and whale) trade they were reported as signing on a very willing and well known Aborigine.

Already the Colony was shipping coal to China and possibly the United Kingdom. In August the *Raven,* 'Raby master', brought ten tons of coal from Newcastle, her cargo then transferred to H.M. vessel *Experiment.* The sloop *James* was lost in April 1804, near Broken Bay, the crew, five in number, all saved. The friendly *Sydney Gazette* adds:

> 'She sailed from Newcastle on Monday morning, very leaky, and shortly encountered a gale ... the contrary wind continuing, baffled every exertion ... pumps choked, seas running very high, ... baling with buckets ... stood onto a sand beach ... where she was dashed to pieces by a tremendous surf ...'

In August 1807 Edward Wills and Thomas Reibie (sic) were advertising for two or three shipwrights to complete the building of the vessel now standing in their yard. Maybe this vessel became the new *Mercury* which belonged to the two and begins to figure very prominently in all the shipping news, carrying goods including salted pork imported from Otahetie (sic) as in July 1808. The opening sentence of the *Sydney Gazette*'s shipping report is mildly deceiving as to the real adventure. Such tales (here repeated in brief snippets) must have filled the young Reibey boys, Thomas, James and George, with a wild longing to go to sea. And what a heritage of adventure stories to pass on to their own young!

This particular tale tells that 'The *Mercury,* Captain Raby, arrived with a cargo of pork, the whole in high preservation' (and that was important for business, and was why Tom had earlier advertised for casks and a cooper to travel to the Feejees). Some crew members of an American ship had deserted to spend a happy life with some friendly South Sea Islanders at Ulitea, in the Cook Islands through Fiji to Tahiti. So friendly (known by earlier trading for native artifacts) 'were the inhabitants that Mr. Reibie [sic] himself had taken a gold time keeper to friendly King Pomaree'. Amazingly, on a previous voyage Tom had been given a medallion which the chief's father, Mahee, had received some 36 years earlier from Captain Cook, when on the *Resolution.* The medallion was genuine enough:

> 'the reverse side representing two ships encircled by the words, RESOLUTION AND ADVENTURE MDCCLXXII. This medal is considerably larger than a crown piece and was originally gilt, but which from the length of time, being 36 years is now nearly worn off.' (as in July 1808).

The *Mercury* having been most happily entertained and aided by the Chief, Thomas stood towards another island, Manjee, south west of Ulitea, to meet a very unfriendly lot of south sea islanders. Fearless of the look of fire arms — or ignorant of their power — and most probably very suspicious of the seamen's intentions, these men endeavoured to lure the sailors ashore, to remove what they could from the decks as they swarmed on board; like Swift's Lilliputians they endeavoured to tow the *Mercury* ashore, and finally attacked Seaman Clark, plunging a spear into

> 'his belly. A general disposition was now manifested and, self defence became a duty. 2 musketoons [sic] were immediately discharged among the foremost; and we are not sorry to observe that the whole contents of one lodged in the body of Clark's unprovoked assailant. Their consternation at the noise they heard may easily be conjectured: they

> staid [sic] not to examine the cause of the explosion, taking to their paddles, in a few minutes reached the shore where an immense number were assembled; the *Mercury* took leave of this little inhospitable island.'

One might ask 'Well, for Heaven's Sake why should these islanders have been hospitable to an unknown schooner?' Likewise it is timely to remember that the sailors had to have great skill to manoeuvre the sails to catch whatever wind might or might not be in the immediate atmosphere; no engine here to speed the *Mercury* away from hostile shores. Steam did not catch up with Port Jackson until the late 1830s. There were many adventures such as this. Tom Reibey continued trading, using differing crews.

An interesting advertisement appeared in the *Sydney Gazette* on 10 September 1809 reading:

> 'Wanted for the schooner *Mercury,* a Chief Officer and Five seamen wanted to engage on a pleasant voyage to Otaheite with the advantage of good encouragement and liberal wages. Apply Messrs Reibey and Wills.'

The Scene on Shore.

The Reibeys' fine house built on Lot 70 on the eastern bank of the Tank Stream, which reached from the then Harbour foreshore (in line with the present Customs House) to what was shortly to be named by the great man himself after himself, as Macquarie Place. Earlier it was reported, in October, 1803, that the house was to be of faced stone, fifty feet in length, allowing for a principal and attic story. They named their home Entally House, Entally being the name today as then of a suburb of Calcutta, India. Tom had, whilst a member of the *Britannia*'s crew, visited Calcutta on trading trips; the name has now become important to Tasmanians as Thomas the second used the same name for the grand home he built at Hadspen, near Launceston. Tom and Mary's family had expanded with the births of Celia, born on 1 February 1803, Eliza born on 10 June 1805, Penelope Jane born 12 September 1807, and Elizabeth born on 15 April 1810. So Mary was more than just busy, with a seafaring husband, a husband's busy shipping line as well as ship building, not to mention the store which repeatedly was advertising cedar and boats for sale.

The knowledge of the coast had vastly extended with Bass' discovery of Bass Strait in 1791 and with Flinders' magnificent circumnavigation of the whole vast continent in 1801-2. As a side result, Bulli coal was now exported to India and the Cape. Even some woollen and linen weaving was attempted in the early years. The population was mixed and viable. As Manning Clark had noted, 'the convicts often had the strength of their hands and the sharpness of their wits which would buy property, respectability, and found families'.[234] The navy and army men among the convicts who had broken the services' codes of behaviour, included William Redfern the naval surgeon, and a friend of the Reibeys, according to Mary's 1820 diary (when travelling). Redfern had taken part in the Mutiny at the Nore.

George Howe came in 1800, transported for a political offence, a lucky break for this Colony, he becoming the editor of *Sydney Gazette.* His

John Eyre | National Library of Australia

View of Sydney from the East Side of the Cove'

Augustus Earle

National Library of Australia

'Government House and part of the Town of Sydney, NSW., 1828' delightful descriptions, as well as his most reliable reporting make some of the most valuable research material available for those early years. There are literally reams of humorous reports on daily happenings, upon the idiosyncracies of the Sydney personnel, and very dramatic news stories of the 'earth shattering' events such as the Governor's dismissal. The *Surprize* and the *Sovereign* had brought in the dour, and badly done by, Scottish martyrs — Manning Clark speaks of high minded Gerrald and Muir, of malicious Margarot, of Skirving and the Reverend Thomas Palmer. The transports from England and Scotland were largely filled with ex-thieves, but of the 2,086 from Ireland, some 600 were sent here for riot and sedition.[235] Such intelligent men might be expected to compalin occasionally.

Blood and Thunder of Revolution.

On 4 March, 1804 occurred the daring, incredible, but hopeless, uprising of 200 misled convicts in the Castle Hill area, which, when put down, caused Governor Philip Gidley King to declare:

> 'the districts of Parramatta, Castle Hill, Toongabbie, Prospect, Baulkham Hills, Hawkesbury and Nepean to be in A STATE OF REBELLION and do establish Martial Law.'[236]

The *Sydney Gazette* uses three columns in its very small paper, to describe the Insurrection, and very exciting reading it makes. The Commanding Officer at Parramatta was informed at half past eleven at night of the firing of the houses at Castle Hill and

> 'Sydney was instantly alarmed . . . the military and inhabitants were under arms . . . The Captain, Officers and Marines and ship's company of H.M. Ship Calcutta came on shore . . . all horses in the town were held in requisition . . .'

Bravely His Excellency himself 'got on horseback and proceeded unattended towards Parramatta'. With troops in pursuit, the 233 insurgents previously drawn up in a brave and foolish battle line, careered in fear through the 'woods', Philip Cunningham their leader, shouting 'Death or Liberty!' He was wounded, caught and 'suitably despatched on the stair case of the Public Store', which store they had intended to plunder. The poor, desperate, unhappy fellows had believed that 1,100 men supported them in their revolt; they had intended to plant a tree of liberty in Government House grounds at Parramatta, before marching on to take Sydney. All insurgents finally surrendered, giving up 136 musquets (sic), fourteen pistols, 'and a great number of swords, bayonets on poles and pitch forks'.

It was a truly frightening happening, giving the townspeople pause to consider the state of the Colony; causing much argument and discussion among all stratas of the 4,000 odd inhabitants. It is difficult to recreate the near panic which must have swept the little town. During these years there were many fascinating reports of incidents, including the amazing arrest of Governor Bligh in 1808.

A curious anomaly occurs in the 1806 Muster of the personnel in the Colony, for which there may be an official explanation. There is no Mrs. Reibey. Mary Reibey's short day-to-day travel Diary written in 1820-21 over nine months, notes relatives, and happenings sometimes reminiscent of her pre-transportation experience. But never once is there any hint even of a close family discussion about her experiences in 1792 upon arrival in New South Wales. There is no written record of what she did in 1793-1794; commercial tourist tales, newspaper gossip, novels and even historical notes, are largely hearsay founded, possibly, upon family legend without any substance except that she was married to Thomas Reibey in September 1794. It seems the lady known as Mrs. Reibey buried her antecedents during those Colonial years 1794 to 1806. Let there be no criticism; in that violent world of the convict community on The Rocks there was no place for the quiet balanced thinking people like her, Redfern, Wills and others. In this 1806 Muster then, there is no record of a Mrs. Mary Reibey; she appears under her maiden name. The record reads:

> 'MUSTER OF THE INHABITANTS
> List of Women in the Colony 1806
> R.Ad. [for *Royal Admiral*] Haddock Mary. C. [for convict, or concubine as a technical term] Legit chn 3m 2f (married in N.S.W.). Housekeeper.'[237]

Twenty years later, in the 1828 Census[238] Mary Reibey described herself as having come to the Colony 'Free on the *Mariner* in 1821' avoiding the truth that she had really arrived in the Colony as a convict aboard the *Royal Admiral* in 1792. This leads to a conclusion of a possible deliberate omission of the name Reibey when giving particulars to the 1806 Muster. Well, she'd been very careful long long before when maintaining her alias James Burrow. There are good and cogent reasons why she should bury her emancipated past in 1806; the store and business were prospering, she was getting more and more involved with people through the business and she had determined to give her children the best life possible with attendant upward social mobility. Mary Reibey accomplished just that. Yet so did other openly acknowledged emancipists; but they were mostly men. I tend to think Mary Reibey in those days, 1800-1806, was able to perceive the need to tailor her life as a woman to the required qualifications of the exclusives — Thomas was a retired naval officer, a free man, her children deserved that small deception, which she still maintained in 1828. They might have known of her transportation fourteen years earlier, but the neighbours certainly wouldn't find out from the Muster.

As for Thomas, the Muster reads:

> 'Thomas Reibey, Came Free, had a farm of 160 acres, which included 100 acres of pasture, the remainder under cultivation of wheat, maize and barley.'[239]

Frank Clune asserts that there is added information: 'stated the proprietor lived on the farm with his wife and children.'[240] Well, this is not completely accurate in 1806; maybe they used it for a hobby farm. Actually, Thomas was on the Hawkesbury during the 1806 floods, performing a most valiant rescue of non-swimmers — a boat of eight persons was accidentally 'rent' on a branch only a trifling distance from shore but there was a panic as the boat filled, they all called upon Reibey for assistance; but, said the *Sydney Gazette* of 6 April 1806:

> 'and all were about to grasp hold of him; but conscious that inevitable death must be the consequence to himself as well as them he threw himself into the water . . . got hold of the peinter [sic] and . . . towed her within a few yards of shallow water; but much embarrassed by the weight of his clothes and boots was obliged to relinquish his hold . . . as soon as he gained the bank he assured them he would save the whole . . . their outcries were at this moment dreadful; they were all standing in the boat which sunk gradually; Reiby [sic] tore up a sapling . . . wading . . . saved four lives, though all had sprung at the bough and two fell in . . . Reibey made towards Morris, whose cries for help had not yet ceased but . . . assistance came too late . . . his hat alone was to be seen . . . Likewise was the case with Green, who has left a widow and three helpless infants to deplore his loss.'

And this long account is not one bit redundant in its vivid picture of the helpless situation of migrant settlers — non swimmers — struggling in flood waters. But the main purpose here, of course, is to round out a little more the splendid character Tom Reibey.

Events, businesses, salutary reminders, flow through the *Sydney Gazettes* covering their last years together; they can only be mentioned as telegrams of progress. The covered waggon of William Roberts, running to the Hawkesbury every three weeks, taking sixteen hours, 27 January 1805; the bushrangers busy on the same track, 17 February 1805; the loss of that pseudo currency, the promissory bills, one in favour of Thomas Reibie (sic) for One Pound Thirteen Shillings and Ten Pence, 6 July 1807.

The most extensive coverage was given to the Jenner discovery of the Cowpox immunisation, explaining how small pox, that dreaded scourge for centuries, was to be eradicated from the world by the use of the immunisation process. Repeated editions of the *Sydney Gazette,* called upon responsible parents to avail themselves of this preventative. Tom had advertised for a soap-boiler, another of his manufacturing lines; he had been granted a wine and spirit license in 1809 among an astounding 53 licensees! The Government ship had advertised for 10,000 — repeat 10,000 — pounds of biscuits to be supplied for HMS *Buffalo*; imagine the baking business that could handle such an order, and then remember this was in a colony a mere eighteen years in existence. One glorious piece of Howe's journalism must end these short excerpts. Written, it seems surely with tongue-in-cheek, concerning a Madam, it runs thus (3 June 1804):

> "On Thursday departed this life at a very advanced age, Mary Jones, long resident on The Rocks, and one of the first European Inhabitants of this Colony. The funeral was performed the day following with a splendour suited to her avocation during her latest years. From twelve to fifteen couples of spotless damsels, robed in white, followed in procession, and after depositing the venerable remains, returned to her late apartment where spiritual consolation was duly administered."

The Bligh affair must have made every man inclined to look over his shoulder to see if his friend was indeed his foe; must have made every trader, seaman, farmer, bury himself in his own affairs rather than be involved with the NSW Corps and their determined leaders. Lieutenant Governor Joseph Foveaux proclaimed in the *Sydney Gazette,* 31 July 1808, that he 'conceives it to be beyond his authority to judge between Captain Bligh and the Officer whom he found in actual command of the Colony'. However, Lieutenant William Paterson, under a banner streamer of his name, made a grand and lengthy Proclamation on 19 March 1809. He lists the undertaking signed by both Bligh and himself, in which Bligh agreed to return to England as soon as possible, wind and weather permitting, by HMS *Porpoise.* In consideration of this agreement, all restraints had been removed from Bligh and he was allowed to return to the comforts of Government House. But (alas and alack, as is well known) 'the said William Bligh in direct violation of His Word of Honour as an Officer and a Gentleman . . . had not departed.' Furthermore, there was some hanky panky with 'certain libellous and inflamatory papers . . . intended to disturb the general tranquility . . .' And so Paterson commanded all subjects not to hold communication with Bligh or his personnel, all now on board the *Porpoise.*

Well, of course if the map is correct, then all the happenings around Government House, just across the paddock or park from the Reibey household and store, would be of anxious moment to the family. However, Tom was appointed as a Pilot in the Harbour in September of the same year. Maybe the last trip to the Feejees had been a little too much for the mariner.

Not only are boats 18 feet and 19 feet being advertised for sale in September, but Tom also has for sale 'a capital chaise with plated harness complete.'

As was required by the law, all persons leaving the Colony, even for Tasmania, were required to announce their intentions, stating by what ship, and asking for all claims to be made. Surprisingly, Tom the newly appointed Pilot announces he is leaving the Colony for travel to China and India by the *Lady Barlow* on 8 October. The *Lady Barlow* actually sailed on Tuesday 10, reaching Bengal on 29 December 1809. The purpose of his trip was to gather for the partnership of Wills and Reibey a great quantity of miscellaneous goods for the Colony, which indeed he did.

Governor Lachlan Macquarie arrived by the *Dromedary* on 28 December 1809. Here was a man of strength, who was to make tremendous and permanent changes to the newly developing City and outer settlements. Moreover he became the friend of emancipists, and immediately upon arrival he found he had a fight on his vice-regal hands. Macquarie, not surprisingly, cut down the number of licences issued for wine and spirits.

He did it by Proclamation, six weeks after landing. He meant to show his strength. Mary Reiby (sic) was among the lucky twenty to retain a licence. She thus begins to sign advertisements in her own right, so, Tom being absent on the Indian trip, she put up the Farms, or at least two of them, for lease, on 7 January 1810 'to be separate or together and to be entered on in March next, Two adjoining Farms down the River at Hawkesbury, known by the name of Reibey's Farms, lying at and situate between Cobcrafts [sic] and Roberts. Apply to Mrs. Reibey. Also to be Sold a fine new Boat 19ft keel . . . Mast, rail oars complete. Apply as above.'

So Mrs. Reibey the Businesswoman becomes a fact in the local newspaper.

Macquarie was very busy with the streets which had haphazard names, so on 6 October 1810 a grand orderly revision was gazetted. Most of it is as valid today as then. He ordered proper Posts and finger boards to be erected in conspicuous parts where streets cross each other—

> 'The principal Street in the Town and leading through the middle of it from Dawe's Point to the Place near the Brickfields where it is intended to erect the First Toll Bar, being upwards of a mile in length and hitherto known alternately by the names of High Street, Spring Row and Serjeant Major's Row is now named GEORGE STREET in honour of our revered and gracious Sovereign." . . .
>
> 'It being intended to remove all those old Buildings and Inclosures on that space of Ground which is bounded by the Government Domain on the East, by the Judge Advocate's, Secretary's, Chaplain's and the Commissary's House on the South, by the Spring of water and Stream on the West and the Houses of Mr. Lord, Mr. Thompson and Mr. Reibey on the North, and to throw the same into an open Area, the said Area or Space of Ground, has been named *'Macquarie Place,* and is henceforth to be so denominated.'

In addition Macquarie signified that a new wharf would be erected at Cockle Bay (present Darling Harbour), would be called Market Wharf and would be near the new Market Place — guess where? — why of course, between Market Street and the present Sydney Town Hall. On 6 October the *Sydney Gazette* presented the plan, the newly named streets and their locality.[241] Changes generally to the benefit of the Town came thick and fast in these early years of the new regime.

Macquarie made his grand plan for the streets of Sydney known to the citizens on the same day that Thomas Reibey was notified in the *Sydney Gazette* as returned to Sydney from Bengal. He found the business had survived very nicely; Mary had publicly been the representative nominated to receive a debt of Twenty-five Pounds from an officer; had advised of her servant, a convict, Stephen Wycombe decamping, issuing the usual warning; she had advertised a waterside house of stone near the Government Wharf, having eight years of the lease still to run and being the premises of Mr. Thomas Reibey . . ., 'Apply to Mrs. Reibie [sic] on the premises.' Was this their fine new home? It was repeated in July. Were the Reibeys planning a tour? A change? Going to Tasmania?

Thomas returned in the *Mary and Sally,* captained by Ambrose. 'She brings an investment consisting chiefly of fine teas, sugar, calicoes and China-ware the joint property of Messrs. Wills and Reibey.' Tom had been absent for more than a year. And once again there had been adventures of a sort. He was delayed at Whampo when a Chinese 'who was from the *Lady*

Barlow was found murdered in the streets'. Reibey sold his sandalwood for Sixteen Dollars and a Half a 'pekul', and went on to Bengal. He was there from 2 April to 10 June, when he sailed home in the *Mary and Sally,* sailing well west of the Straits of Sumatra which were filled 'with a swarm of privateers'. Unfortunately Tom brought home a fatal sickness, said to be caused by sunstroke suffered in the hot northern summer in Bengal's hot steamy climate. Not realising this approaching trouble, in November 1810 Mary Reibey and Sarah Wills happily sold their tremendous new stock in their separate establishments, at the new Wills warehouse in George Street and in the Reibey premises at Macquarie Place.

In March, young James Reibey, a mere fourteen years but old enough to take to the sea, sailed off in the *Santa Anna* (*Sydney Gazette,* 3 March 1811). Thomas Reibey was still advertising the Macquarie house for sale in March 'as he intends to leave the Colony', and hopefully Tom accepted a renewed Spirit Licence.

And then — and then, poor Tom died of delayed effects of sunstroke, on Friday 5 April 1811.

> 'On Friday evening died at his house in Macquarie Place, Mr. Thomas Reibey after a severe indisposition of several months . . . He was an affectionate husband, an indulgent parent, . . . and leaves a widow and large family to regret his loss.' *Sydney Gazette* 6 April 1811

Vale Thomas Reibey.

EMANCIPISTS AS A PERCENTAGE OF POPULATION OF NEW SOUTH WALES IN 1820

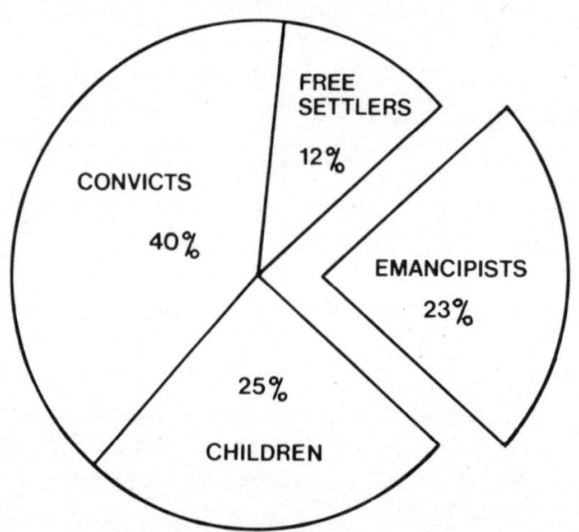

POPULATION 1820 – 24,000

Source: A.G.L.Shaw, CONVICTS AND THE COLONIES

Chapter 9
STAND UP THE REAL MARY REIBEY

The Matriarch.

Mary Reibey, the woman that Sydney knows through the legends, the lady who had a warehouse near The Rocks, whose surname graces a trendy tourist tea room and a lane near Macquarie Place, has really caught up with this tale. Most extant newspaper stories are concerned mainly with her excellent management of her Reibey inheritance as Tom's widow, her shrewd investments to which great capital gain accrued. This was very clever of her, remembering that she was a woman in a very strongly male-dominated financial world and trading centre; remembering that this was in a colony where decisions were mostly made by men. Moreover Mary was an emancipist, though it is difficult to know whether this fact was well known to her contemporaries.

Twenty years had passed since the *Royal Admiral* had sailed through the Heads. However, Lachlan Macquarie had arrived, a Governor who was to steer the Colony into a more equable balance between Exclusive and Emancipist, at least for a few years. To help her, Mary Reibey had money, property, and a well established shipping and trading company on which she was to build her empire. Not the least of her advantages was the training she had had while sturdily standing by as deputy for Thomas during those lonely years both at the Hawkesbury and in Sydney, whilst he was away at sea looking after the trading and purchasing part of the business. All of this she did, mark you, as well as bear seven children, caring for them and possibly schooling them. The youngest, Elizabeth Ann, was just fifteen months old when her father died. One can guess at the hushing of the babe, the quietening of the lusty family during those seven uncertain months of Tom's last illness. James was of course at sea. Why James? Thomas, the eldest boy, had already been indentured away, and was preparing for his entry in the business as Tom senior gently faded, suffering this sickness. Wills, the partner, died shortly after Tom.

Mary Reibey and Sarah Wills being two very different ladies, had been running separate stores, and warehouses, as retail outlets for their spouses' joint trading partnership. Not surprisingly, this partnership was dissolved very shortly after affairs were settled upon the demise of the men. Mrs. Wills earlier, writing to her mother on 1 May 1808 said 'We are still making money very fast . . .'[242] There was the immediate grief for the widowed Mary, prepared though she may have been. His gravestone, lovingly restored by great-great-grandsons, John Macdougall of Melbourne and his brother Peter of Sydney, can be seen in the Pioneer Memorial Garden in the Botany (Sydney) General Cemetery. It is very simple, reading *incorrectly*:

"Thomas Reibey, departed this life on 6th May, 1811, aged 36 years."[243]

Mary evidently had intended a very flowery epitaph, according to Fitzpatrick.

'Here lie the Perishable Remains of Mr. Thomas Reibey who came into this Colony a Free Mariner and during a residence of twenty years in this Colony always supported a fair and upright character. His conduct as a Husband and a Father needs no better eulogium than his actions have engraven in the Hearts of His Widow and children who have abundant reason to lament his loss.

He died the 5th day of April 1811 Aged 42 years.

Reader as a Mortal, think of my Mortality.
Survey thy past, and view thy present Life.
Then with thy good, compare thy evil works
And judge if thou canst die.'[244]

Now the Matriarch took over. As decided in the first chapters, Molly Haydock had had a good liberal arts education, and as a mother had undoubtedly watched over her young people and their schooling. This unused epitaph indicates her own command of the contemporary formal language; no doubt the children were accustomed to her standards, fiercely high for them. After Letters of Administration were granted she swung straight into action. One month later the *Mercury* returned to port under a hired Chief or Master, Mr. Tait, and again the *Mercury* had been in dangerous trouble with some of the treacherous natives.[245] King Pomaree had been expelled by the anti-traders tribe, but he was able to write to the Sydney missionaries, 'to the Gentlemen of the Missionary Society here . . .'. His letters are in the Otahetian language, and in an excellent hand, using the dye with which they colour their cloths and mats . . . The Chief wrote, according to the translation, 'Prosperity to you, my friend, at your dwelling place at Sydney: May you and us be saved by Jehovah, the true God of the world, that supports us.'[246] Well, I guess faith had to pave the way for trade in the early 19th century, at least in the Pacific, although Pomaree seems to have been disowned by his clan.

Mary advertised on 24 August, tactfully,

'Wanted, for the fine Schooner *Mercury,* 5 or 6 seamen to proceed on a pleasant Voyage to Otaheite . . . Apply to Mrs. Reibey . . . George Street.'[247]

Mary moved the family to No. 12 George Street, next to the Post Office conducted by Isaac Nichols near to the Kings Wharf. It was next to a hotel; we do not know whether she used her liquor licence at this hotel. A new bridge had been thrown open to the public on 20 May, 1811 connecting George Street and Macquarie Place. Maybe she saw more business opportunities in George Street. Prior to this move, Thomas the second was giving notice in the *Sydney Gazette* that he intended to leave the Colony, to sail in the *Aurora.* Born in 1796 he was now in his fifteenth year, and after all he was but following the example of his father, a confirmed naval officer by nineteen years of age. Actually in the same edition Mary made her first advertisement of goods brought in by the *Mercury* prior to the move to George Street:

Mrs Reibey informs . . . the Public . . . that she has 'Prime salted Pork and Flair for Sale at her House Macquarie Place.'[248]

(From the time of Thomas senior's death, oddly enough, the spelling of the name stabilizes.) The same advertisement appeared in the next three editions, and so, also, did the widow Wills notify the public of her sale of goods from the *Mercury*. This was probably the last joint venture of the two ladies. Sarah Wills, did not take long to remarry, and to none less than George Howe, the Editor-printer of the *Sydney Gazette*.

Thomas II did not sail on the *Aurora,* he left on the *Mercury* on 7 September 1811.[249] Just fifteen, and bound for the adventurous run to the Pacific Islands. Well, his mother at fifteen had been bound for the 'lands beyond the seas'. Did young Thomas know? In one generation things had changed dramatically; it was the son of the owner, Master Thomas Reibey, who was now on board. Very different to the sad little girl on board the *Royal Admiral* in 1792. In fact young Thomas was the heir apparent, learning to be a mariner in his own ship. Yet I guess the heart of Mary the mother warred with the heart of Mary the business lady.

The Merchant Lady.

George Street was getting busy. The traffic was often disrupted, as the Governor points out in his Proclamation on 9 June, 1811 (just as Petronius had complained of Rome in AD 50):

> 'Whereas the Public at large and Persons on Horseback and in Carriages in Particular are frequently obstructed and exposed to Risque in the Streets of Sydney, by Cars [sic — meaning bullock carts] being left in them without any person to attend to the cattle drawing them; and also, by the Drivers of the Cars and carts sitting in them, instead of being on foot with their Cattle to guide and manage them.'[250]

Well, if these men did this again within a mile of Sydney they were to be 'severely punished by Fine or Imprisonment'.

On Saturday 20 July, Mary made her big splash in the *Sydney Gazette* with a column at least six inches long advertising her sale:

> 'Mrs. Reibey informs her Friends and the Public in general, that she has removed from her House in Macquarie Place to No. 12 George Street, late the residence of Mr. Michael Hayes, where she has laid in a Variety of Articles recently imported in the Providence consisting principally of . . .'[251]

and here follows the description of nearly 200 odd goods — Mary had gone into the importing business in a big way. What is more interesting, Sarah Wills was advertising from No. 96 George Street, a very similar list, with the difference that Sarah gave the price of most of her goods, but Mary, in the best tradition of quality stores, as today, coyly makes no mention of anything so vulgar as a price! The goods included:

> 'ironmongery, including hat hooks, wood screws, guns; slops [material] and made up clothing, 'trowsers', shirts and shifts, calico by the piece . . . crockery of all varieties, basons and water ewers'

and then she tempts the carriage trade:

> 'gentlemen's fine black beaver hats, . . . ribbands, . . . muslin and cotton handkerchiefs, . . . japanned chests, black queens stuff for petticoats . . . a

> numerous assemblage of other articles . . . which she is determined to sell the same at reasonable prices assuring herself it is the best recommendation to public Patronage and Support.'

Sarah really does better at 96 George Street, for she has 'ladies' straw and other bonnets, girls' ditto . . . as well as black satin, bombazine and velvet'. My, but what those Colonials were getting into their homes in the year 1811, and the older Colonists could ruefully remember with horror those first four stark years from 1788 to 1792, just nineteen years back, when there were few utensils, few clothes, and only huts.

Macquarie.

Fine houses were now beginning to appear on the gentle hills and slopes of the Port of Sydney. Macquarie, without the blessing of the Home Office, saw his Colony as the beginning of a fine state of the British Empire. He planned accordingly. Francis Greenway arrived in 1814, convicted for a forging offence, and brought with him all his skills and vision as an architect. In Bigge's report[252] the civil engineer Major George Druitt Speaks of Mr. Greenway the Civil Architect. John Oxley[253] believed that the Governor had kept the best carpenters (from amongst the convicts) for use in erecting large and numerous buildings. Some of the speculating colonists made mistakes, as did Edward Riley; in 1816 he went to Sydney as a merchant trader, flourished and became a Director of the Bank, took over *Ultimo House,* then one of the largest homes in the Colony; but his business failed and he suicided in 1825. Mary appears never to have been in the red at all. She had an eye for the possibilities of Van Diemen's Land. Not for her, as far as records show, were the new lands around Bathurst ever attractive. Oxley spoke of the undulating hills, clear of timber in the neighbourhood of Bathurst, about 40,000 acres waiting for large holdings, unsuitable for small settlers' farms. It was a bit difficult to get there, Oxley claimed, noting the distance from the markets, with but a horse track mostly over the 136 miles; suitable only for the well supplied man with sheep as his main object. Oxley, completely ignorant of the gold lying under his exploring feet, spoke of the rocks composed of granite, quartz, limestone, marble, slate and basalt. This industrious servant of the Governor speaks equally well of the good coastal land around Port Macquarie, three days' sail from Sydney and that around Port Stephens. Later Mary invested in grants around the Shoalhaven area. Tasmania was to attract her interest and investment for her family. And why not? Governor King, anxious to forestall any French ambitions, endeavoured to secure Bass Strait against any foreign intervention in Colonial rights. Hobart on the Derwent was settled in September, 1803, the second of Australia's first two cities. In January, 1804 Collins took his unsettled colony from Sorrento, Port Phillip, across to Hobart. As Blainey notes:

> 'Bass Strait could easily become the lifeline of the colony and that, in foreign possession, the lifeline could be endangered. The only narrow strait on the entire route from Europe to Australia, it would be an ideal base for enemy raiders.'[254]

At all events, Thomas Reibey had seen the opportunity to extend his shipping activities to the Derwent and the Tamar — and his son Thomas II followed on.

Explorers and Population.

In the meantime, exciting things had happened; the Blue Mountains had been crossed in 1813; stimulated by Macquarie, Blaxland, Lawson and Wentworth, had finally conquered those formidable cliffs, which had frustrated Phillip, Tench, and later colonists. Their Diary makes fascinating reading, telling how, once they had solved the problem of the north-south ridges, they would spend fourteen days hacking at the thick tall impenetrable mountain bush to get a passage of a few thousand yards.[255] The important results stemming from the discovery of the bountiful western slopes, with the quickly following surveying of Evans, . . . and Cox's road, meant immediate relief for the cramped Colony. True, squatters and settlers were pushing back the frontier in the south, making their way to the Goulburn district, but land for flocks was urgently needed.

People were flooding into Sydney. In 1810 there were 12,000 persons in the Colony; in 1820 there were 24,000 persons in New South Wales, most coming after the Napoleonic Wars had ended. (A mere 12%, or 1,307, had 'come free', plus 1,495 who were born in the Colony — Currency lads and lasses; 159 of the convicts had received absolute pardons; 962 had received conditional pardons. Thus the Emancipated, 23%, included 3,255 time expirees; 1,422 had tickets-of-leave. Then 40%, or 9,451, were serving as convicts; 25%, or 6,000, were children.) These figures[256] alone support Macquarie in his recognition of the rapidly swelling majority of the 'new free' and the 'soon to be free', many of whom as we well know were making themselves an articulate and hard working core of the settlement. Even so, although by 1820 some 324,000 acres of land had been granted, including 243,000 acres granted by Macquarie, over 240,000 acres were held by free settlers.

Macquarie coped with the expanding population in many ways. Permanent Government structures were built, such as the Military Hospital in 1815 (now occupied by the National Trust and for many years housing the famous old Fort Street Model School, later Fort Street Girls' High School); new churches and buildings in the outer settlements such as St. Matthew's at Windsor. Many remaining lovely old homes show the inspiration of Macquarie's support and the brilliant Georgian concepts of Francis Greenway, Government Architect.

A Depression.

There was a depression between 1812 and 1815. According to B. H. Fletcher

> 'in 1811 and 1812 the retail market collapsed . . . the commercial depression . . . made worse by contraction of demand resulting from drought and the recall of the 73rd Regiment . . . replaced by half the number of men.'[257]

He notes the largest emancipist business in the Colony — Lord, Williams and Hutchinson, had collapsed; D'Arcy Wentworth, surgeon and trader (to be appointed a Justice of the Peace and Superintendent of Police by Macquarie) was in difficulties; even Robert Campbell was defaulting; and 'John Macarthur lamented that trusting had caused the ruin of every man . . .'. Despite this monetary situation, Macquarie carried on with his idea of New South Wales as an extension of Britain rather than with the British Government's idea of the Colony as first and foremost a penal settlement. The foundation in 1817 of the first bank, the Bank of New South Wales, was due to Macquarie's support of businessmen who wanted monetary reform.

There had been no set currency for New South Wales — there was a motley of coins brought out by individuals. In 1792 the *Kitty* arrived[258] with two chests of public money, silver dollars worth about One Thousand Pounds, specie necessary to pay the artificers, convict superintendents, ex-marines, and new settlers. Coins in use included the English cartwheel penny of copper, gold guinea, silver shilling; Netherlands gold ducat; Portuguese johanna; Spanish silver dollar; and others.[259] In November 1800 Governor King had endeavoured to avoid dishonest trade with this odd money by issuing a proclamation valuing the coins thus:

Spanish dollars — five shillings sterling;
Johanna — Four Pounds; Dutch guilder — two shillings;
Guinea — One Pound Two Shillings; English shilling — One shilling and Eight Pence; and 1 oz copper coin — Two Pence.

In 1812 the sloop *Samerang* came to Port Jackson with Ten Thousand Pounds of Spanish dollars from Madras. Macquarie used 40,000 of these coins to create a stable coinage. He organised the convict William Hershell to cut a circular hole in the centre of the Spanish dollars; the centre piece was stamped 'NSW 1813' with 'Five Shillings' stamped on the reverse. These were called 'dumps'. The Holey Dollar, or Ring Dollar, from 1822 onwards was recalled and exchanged for Sterling coins. From 9 September 1829 these Holey Dollars were no longer legal tender.

At first, prior to the Holey Dollar, trading ships were taking all the specie out of the Colony in payment for their goods, as for example did Captain Bond of the *Royal Admiral* in 1792. Therefore Colonial trading began to use Store Receipts issued by the Commissary, and personal Promissory Notes issued by stores, such as Mary Reibey's. There are many advertisements in the *Sydney Gazette* for lost Bills and Notes. Many Notes were forged, dishonoured and stolen. So the foundation of a Colonial Bank, the Bank of New South Wales in 1817 was important. Mary Reibey let her former home at Macquarie Place to the Bank, to become its birthplace as it were. Shann writes 'Whatever its standing in the eyes of the law, the Bank proved a vigorous custodian of the community's financial interests.[260]. . . This comment refers to the distrust the British Government had for the Bank, for Macquarie's handling of the Colony, and the ambivalent attitude of Bigge, who approved the Bank but did not recommend the renewal of its charter. Nevertheless the Bank Charter was renewed. Mary herself had no doubt promised money when Mr. Campbell in 1816 called a meeting reforming a Colonial Bank. She is, in fact, on record in the P.R.O. records as having acquired twenty-seven 'additional' shares.[261]

'Currency' referring to the odd assortment of makeshift coinage and promissory notes (see above), was a term used in a derogatory way by free newcomers to distinguish those people BORN in New South Wales from the Sterling variety — that is those persons born in the United Kingdom and therefore akin to the sterling silver coins originating in Britain. The term 'currency lads and lasses' refers to free persons, not to convicts brought out to serve a sentence. I find it strange that even today there are sixth generation Australians whose predecessors 'came free' to the Colony during those first ten years who resent the use of 'currency lad' if applied to their first Australian born ancestor. It really is a picturesque term.

And Mary Reibey? She of course would be using the odd and silver currency; she, of course, had borne seven currency children, fathered by a British naval officer. So? Mary began very quietly to prepare for her immediate future. Governor Macquarie had already made a grant of 200 acres to each widow, both grants at Airds. In 1816 Mary advertised nearly all her properties for sale, including the house, which undoubtedly was large and comfortable:

> 'premises . . . to be sold . . . consisting of a large and extensive shop, and four large Parlours or sitting Rooms [that must have been necessary for business as well as social reasons] on the first floor with a commanding Hall, five bedrooms with a comfortable garrett . . . Cellaring under the whole of the House, now in the immediate possession of Mr. Robert King, whose time expires in October next . . . extensive warehouse now in the possession of Mr. J. Binnie, George Street, . . .
> 'Likewise that well known house in Macquarie Place, the property of Mrs. Reibey . . . Also an allotment of ground in Cockle Bay near the waterside with a house and premises thereon.'

This advertisement seems to suggest that she was selling the house at 12 George Street, the first mentioned, as well as the 'well known Home in Macquarie Place'.

There is more to come; no less than twelve farms, at the Hawkesbury, Wilberforce, were for sale. They were all described as let, some out of flood reach, some partly cleared. They made good collateral, and maybe the Reibeys had earned those farms, or some of them, in this way. They were: 300 acres Ravil Farm, at the Hawkesbury; 30 acres Reibey Farm, same; Cross Farm of 30 acres; 3 ditto of 60 acres; two ditto 25 acres; and one ditto 30 acres; all these adjoining. Higgins Farm . . . one ditto; Singleton's of 40 acres; One ditto of 100 acres known as Reibey Farm, on the Lagoon bounded by Reynolds and Gosport. There were in addition 300 acres below Portland Head; one ditto in the District of Airds (she hadn't had that one very long!). So much for her farm holdings; but there was still more for sale.

> Also the good schooner *John Palmer* —
> 'this day arrived from Port Dalrymple, lately refitted with a sheating, a new suit of sail, 2 anchors and a cable . . . Likewise there are four Tuns of wood imported on the *John Palmer*. One half of the purchase money to be paid down, and twelve months Credit for the other half on good security. For further Particulars enquire of Mrs. M. Reibey, Macquarie Place.[262]

And there were reasons for her quiet rationalising of her assets. One was the approaching marriages of her two eldest sons, the other was to do with her own intended voyage across the world to seek out her relatives, and to meet with her business contacts, her old seafaring friends, the Captains of the trading vessels.

In 1817 there is renewed interest in building her fleet. She bought at auction, for Seven Hundred and Fifty Pounds, the brig *Governor Macquarie*.[263] Grants were applied for in Tasmania, for her two sons. Thomas II was acting as Master on the schooner *John Palmer* (not sold yet), sailing between the Tamar and Port Jackson,[264] announced in the *Sydney Gazette* thus: 'Arrival from Port Dalrymple . . . Mr. Reibey, Master.' Thomas junior made a most successful match, with (we are told by legend and by report) one of Sydney's most eligible and beautiful young ladies, Richarda Allen, daughter of Surgeon Allen.[265] Three weeks later, on 17 June 1817, Tom took his bride by sea on the family's ship, *Governor Macquarie,* to their future home in Van Dieman's Land. On 24 October 1817 400 acres were officially granted to Thomas Reibey on the river bank at Carrick.

For Mary, great pride, great satisfaction. The wheel was turning, so far as her fate was concerned. There were rough passages ahead; still some grief to contend with. But for the moment, Mary Reibey was on top of a wave of success. The splendid Sydney marriage, the assured security for her sons, and her own perspicacity in investing in the southern settlement; here, she had set up wharfs (called 'staiths' then), organised Huon pine shipments; her ships could carry coal and provisions for the Colonists; and she could make her sons into good business men and fine gentlemen. Where is our original sad little transportee? Macquarie's chief engineer, Druitt, retained the services of three vessels for Government shipping between the settlements, including the transportation of convicts.[266]

James Reibey, on 25 March 1816, married the young navy widow Rebecca Breedon.[267] He was not quite eighteen years old, and they bravely took off to settle on his grant of 400 acres near Hobart.

Mary was gradually spreading a net.

The Changing Situation.

Mrs Mary Reibey was aware that much political discussion was taking place in Sydney between such active emancipists as Wentworth, particularly in connection with recognised British civilian rights as trial by jury, and self government. She was aware that Governor Macquarie was losing his fight, largely through his own personal characteristics; so she decided that she must take her dear girls HOME to learn just what civilization was all about! Moreover she meant to return to England in all her glory as a wealthy Colonial widow, a shrewd business lady, to bravely and sensibly visit her own old town of Blackburn in Lancashire. She hoped to have the great pleasure of having her girls confirmed in the old church of St. John's.

In March 1820 Mrs Reibey and her two elder girls, Celia and Eliza, sailed for England on the *Admiral Cockburn.* The wheel had turned just about full cycle for Mary-Molly Incognita.

Chapter 10

THE RETURN OF THE NATIVE

The main content of this chapter consists of extracts from the copy made in 1898 by Mr G. B. Barton the Australian journalist and historian, of the so-called Diary written by Mary Reibey whilst on her return trip to her birthplace in Blackburn, Lancashire, England in 1820. The Diary deals with arrival in London, Manchester, Blackburn, Liverpool, Glasgow, Edinburgh, Blackburn, Manchester and London; including her shopping spree, finishing with a tantalizing wait at Gravesend until she and the girls finally sailed for New South Wales in the *Mariner*.

This abridged version is given for the sheer joy of hearing directly from the lady herself. Thus far the biography has been painfully built upon the evidence of others.

The Diary was made available to G. B. Barton by a grandson of the Reibey couple, Tom and Mary. He was James Thomson, settled on one of Mary Reibey's original grants at Burrier, Shoalhaven district. With James Thomson's permission Mr Barton used the extracts for an extended article in the *Evening News,* a Sydney newspaper in February 1898.[268] John Macdougall, great grandson of Mary Reibey, of Caulfield, Melbourne, most kindly passed on the material for use in this biography. John Macdougall is descended from Mary's 3rd daughter Jane Penelope. James Thomson is descended from Eliza, the 2nd daughter who figures in this Diary together with his future father 'Mr Thomson'. The Diary was much later found in the collection of Mr and Mrs A. G. Foster, and given to the Mitchell Library in 1924, Mr Foster being a descendant of Mary's sister, Elizabeth.

G. B. Barton wrote in the *Evening News*:

> 'Fortunately it [the Diary] has been carefully preserved by her [Mary Reibey's] grandson, Mr. James Thomson J.P. of Burrier to whom I am indebted for the privilege of publishing some extracts in these columns [*Evening News*] . . . It is well to remind the reader that spelling and grammar had not reached their present stage of artistic development [1898] . . . For instance it was common enough for educated people to write 'we was', 'you was', 'they was''

Like Mr Barton, as her biographer, I am deeply grateful to her descendants and have retained the 'purity of the text'. To enjoy, if vicariously, the journey made to England by Mary and her two eldest daughters, it is deemed necessary to read her personal notes, as we have a background of her earlier interesting history in our mind's eye. These impressions were made during the year she spent renewing acquaintance with her birthplace, Bury-Blackburn, and as she discovered London, Glasgow and Edinburgh, and various people. The return of this native shines vividly through her pages, just as clearly as does her affection for her home in New South Wales.

The Fosters.

We know that there was a little girl named Elizabeth Haydock, who were just five years old when her little sister Molly was born in 1777, in that Bury household in Lancashire.[269] She became Mrs Charles Foster. We know that in 1820 there was a son, Thomas, who had a little son and who lived with his family in 12 Albion Street, Salford, near Manchester, because Mary says so in this Diary.[270] From the same source we know Mary was annoyed because she had to pay Ten Shillings to collect a parcel of letters from her sister which had to be re-addressed to Mary in London from Manchester in 1820. Mary may have been a wealthy Colonial widow, but she was not happy about this impost, and says so, to her Diary at least.

The only other mention of her sister is the account of Mary's nightmare, dreaming that her sister was dead. (Mary shows herself to be both superstitious, and very much influenced and impressed by the texts used by all the clergy she so conscientiously followed during this English tour; the Scots also received their share of respectful Colonial attendance at Services.) However, Mary did visit, and receive a visit from, her nephew Thomas Foster. In an earlier chapter it was noted that the lady never at any time mentions any discussions with her relatives of the strange events of Molly Haydock's childhood. Also noteworthy is the lack of any reference to visits to Reibey relatives, if there were any, in England. One would have expected her to introduce her two daughters to their father's family.

The Charles Fosters migrated in February 1818, finally settling in Tasmania. He was granted 300 acres near Entally, according to *Historical Records of Australia,* and Parish Maps.[271]

As recently as November 1981 two most interesting letters have come to light, in the possession of Oliver Newton William-Powlett of Devon, England, a fifth generation, great (to the fifth) grandson. One was from Mary Reibey herself, dated 1825, and one was from her son James Haydock Reibey, who lived in Northern Tasmania (Van Dieman's Land), written in 1829. The letter is carefully labelled 'Private', being addressed to his mother's cousin, a solicitor of Glasgow. Amongst business and family news he tells of the troubles of the Fosters. He writes:

> 'You know long ere this that Eliza Foster [Eliza was Elizabeth Haydock Foster's daughter] was married to a Mr. Pitman, an American Gentleman from China, extremely well off and a most excellent man, but I do not expect she will live long as she is in a deep consumption. Mrs Foster her mother lives with them and she has a good farm and some other property of her own. You know old Foster was found dead supposed to be murdered, as he was on the way from the interior of New South Wales to give evidence against some cattle stealers . . . the eldest daughter Jane was some years ago married to a man of the name of Patten (formerly Master of a vessel) they keep a Public House in this Town [Launceston] and he has turned out a drunken beast . . . she is very steady and they are well off, it was an unhappy circumstance for our family they ever came here, we have never been so united since she (Mrs F) is a perfect D. . . l. . .'[272]

Augustus Earle

National Library of Australia

'June Park, Van Diemen's Land, the grand Appearance of the Country in its natural State, perfect Park Scenery'

Entally House, Hadspen (near Launceston), Tasmania, 1981

Left: Thomas II Haydock Reiby 1796-1842, son of Mary Reibey. [From a portrait painted in Plymouth, 1841.] *Centre*: Thomas III Haydock Reibey 1821-1912, grandson of Mary Reibey. Inherited *Entally* [above] — one-time Premier of Tasmania. *Right*: James Haydock Reiby 1823-1853, brother of Thomas III.

In another letter dated Launceston 18th April 1832, also marked 'Private', James tells the same cousin further about his, James', aunt:

> 'Old Mrs. Foster is now here. She has a Farm and works as a m. . . [indecipherable] settler . . . the only good one of that Family was Eliza Mrs. Pitman and she poor thing was cut off in her prime. Jane her eldest daughter is married to a man of the name of Patten who keeps a Public House and who uses her very ill. The oldest son I have never seen but he is also here somewhere but I do not know what he is doing. James the youngest is apprenticed to a Carpenter. The old man you are aware was murdered in New South Wales some years ago.'[273]

The following extracts are from the Diary irregularly recorded by Mary Reibey when she returned to the United Kingdom with her two eldest daughters, Celia aged 17 years, and Eliza, 15 years. Spelling and grammar are as in the original.

Extracts:
1820 June 20th Landed at Portsmouth 8 o'clock in the morning. Took refreshment at the Inn. Set of at 9 o'clock in the coach for London. Arrived there at 7 in the afternoon, at the Belle Savage Inn, Ludgate Hill. Took lodgings their. Wrote to Capt. Watson, my friend to procure me lodgings but through an omission in my letter of not sending my address, he could not find me out, therefore was obliged to stay their for 3 nights, not liking to go to a strange place. Next morning after I arrived I took hackney coach and went to the office of Bell & Wilkinson having business there.[1] After my arrival the first person I saw too my great astonishment was Mr. Jones, who I believe was as much amazed as I was to see me in London. However sat down and had a little talk about our Country and in came Mr. Underwood and of course another wonder was pronounced how I came their. I had then delivered my papers to Mr. Jones[2] who was kind enough to say he would do anything he could and I thought it would better had he understood the Treasury better than I where I was going after . . . if I had not found him their. Mr. Underwood walked back with me to my lodgings and took me and daughters out a little to see the Town. Treated us to Ice-cream and returned with us again, and left us immediately. I was then very anxious about Capt. Watson not comeing not knowing that I had forgot to give him my address. However it so happened that I had a letter from Mr. Atkinson[3] to his father which I mentioned to some person who told him and the old Gentleman came immediately and a finer one and a better man their cannot be. He was very much affected when he read the letter and I believe it was very Favourable to me and Daughters as he immediately asked us to his House and have kept on friendship ever since. He mentioned to Capt. Watson where we was and on the Sunday morning being the third[4] day after our arrival at the Inn he and his Two Daughters and Capt. Watson

---

1 Possibly business re James' wife's pension, she having been a widow — Rebecca Breedon — first married aged fourteen years.

2 Mr. Jones acted as her London agent.

3 Mr. Atkinson later married Jane Penelope, now in Tasmania under Tom's care.

4 22 June 1820.

came to take us away as he had got Lodgings for me next door to himself. During the time they was comeing to meet me I had taken Coach and drove off for his house when Mrs. Watson kindly asked us in, dinner was prepared for us. In about a half an hour in came Capt. Watson and very glad he was to see us. After we had dined he called a Coach and we went to the Inn, settled my account and took my baggage to my Lodging it being pretty generally known by our Sydney friends and those who had visited Sydney as Capt. of ships and otherwise of our arrival in London and we had a great deal of visitors. I then wrote to my cousin John Hope[5] in Manchester prior to our going down in the Country, but did not receive an answer in Course, owing to his having been removed about a mile and half out of town, but hearing their was a letter for him in the Post Office he immediately answered it by a very kind and affectionate letter and an invitation to stay at his House.

July 17 During our stay in London we visited the two Theatres[6] where we saw the Provoked Husband after . . . Covent Gardens, the Obitiquary after piece the Millar and his men. We did not visit many of the public buildings owing to our being so ill. We had a Medical Gentleman, Dr. White, attending us upwards of a fortnight who paid great attention to us. We arrived in the 20th June and left the 17th day of July for the country making our stay their 27 days and the day before our departure for the country I was bled and blistered and both me and Eliza was so ill we could not hold our heads up and I do not think Celia was much better.

July 18 to August 6th. We arrived in Manchester the day following after travelling 186 miles without stopping except to change horses.[7] When we came to the Mosley Arms Inn we found my two cousins, Mr. Hargreaves, Surgeon and Druggist, and Mr. John Hope waiting with a hackney coach to take us and Baggage to our Cousin Hope's, a very delightful place, a little way in the Country, where a Surgeon was sent for, Dr. Barton, a friend of my cousin Hargreaves, who took a great interest in recovering us as fast as possible. He paid all the attention was possible, we began to recover fast and Mr. Hargreaves very often came to take us out a walking. He sent us jellys, preserves and fruit and everything he could think of for comfort. As soon as we could walk about which was about 11 days we had several invitations, the first to Dr. Barton's, one of the first Surgeons in Manchester. Mrs B. a very ladylike woman and one of the most respectable about that Country was very glad to see us and treated us very kindly wishing us to renew our visit as often as we could. We took tea with my half cousin Mr. Aspinall. Dined and tead next day with Mr. and Mrs. Hargreaves, they made me promise on my return to Manchester that we should stop at their House. We staid at Manchester from the 8th July to the 6th August, being 19 days.

August 6th. We took the coach for Blackburn on the 6th where we arrived

5 A relative of the Adam Hope who headed the Petition for her Pardon in 1791.
6 London Theatre, 1820, Drury Lane. Mary would never had been to London as a child.
7 She was forcing herself and the girls, all ill, but she obviously wished to get to Manchester as quickly as possible.

about 3 o'clock in the afternoon, Mr. John Hope accompany us. It is impossible to describe the sensations I felt when comeing to the top of Derwen [Darwen] Street my native home and amongst my relatives and on entering my once Grandmothers House where I had been brought up, and to find it nearly the same as when I left nearly 29 years ago, all the same furniture and most of them standing in the same place as when I left but not one person I knew or knew me . . . but was fully requited by my Cousin[8] Miss Alice Hope who . . . met us at the door [of the Hope house] with all the affection and love of a sister. Their being beds prepared for us we became a part of the family as we had already done at her brother's in Manchester. My arrival became known to all the old inhabitants of Blackburn who had known me in my Childhood, the door hardly ever closed with people comeing out of curiosity or respect . . . I had often expressed a wish to see my Children confirmed in the old Church at Blackburn. We arrived in their on the Saturday evening and the Bishop on the Monday following (who only comes every three years.) My cousin John Hope procured certificates from the Curate of St John's and they was admitted and was confirmed with about 300 more males and females in St John's Church, the old Church being shut up.

Aug. 8. During the time we were at Blackburn we was divided betwixt my father's and Mother's relations. We had a general invitation to all their houses, especially Mr. William Haydock,[9] son of my Uncle William who is in his 74th year and Mr. Robert Brown, son of my Aunt Hindle [Brown] who is in her 76th year. I believe they thought they could not show me enough of attention but no place was so congenial to my mind as Miss Hope's, the most affectionate young woman I ever met with . . . we met Mr. and Mrs. Little an independent Gentleman who is one of the trustees to my Aunt Hope's estate . . . John Hope and he [William Hope] to settle our little business relation to the Houses,[10] . . . Mr. David Hope came . . . to Blackburn accord. to his promise (27th August) . . . We was very proud to see each other and I found him to be one of the most affectionate young men I ever met with, quite the man of business too . . .

Sept. 5th. Took tea at Mr. Wraith's next day and Whent to see the first stone laid of the old church at Blackburn.[11] It is somewhat singular that nearly 30 years ago before that Mr. David Hope and myself was at the 2nd Sept. laying of the first stone in St. John's Church.

Sept. 7th left for Preston . . . arrived at Preston in an hour and half . . . in a post chaise.

15th September . . . went to see Mr. Horrocks Mill and one of the proprietors showed us all through it, a most grand sight but the heat from the steam engine being too oppressive for me gave me a complete surfeit . . . to Blackburn . . . where I was taken very ill . . . at my Cousins, Mr. Robert

8 Alice and John were siblings and the children of Adam Hope.

9 Uncle William Haydock was brother to James Haydock, Mary's father.

10 Maybe Mary and her family had been in contact sometime in the past, since her Aunt Hope has left her three Houses.

11 There were two churches — the newer building commenced in 1820.

Brown . . . My Aunt Hindle[12] an old woman in her 76 year would insist on sitting up with me part of the night . . . to see the concern and attention was admd. . . .

From Liverpool went to Greenock Glascow by the Robert Bruce, Steam boat. Left Liverpool Tuesday, arriving 1 o'clock Friday.

October 21, 22, 23 . . . Rained very hard . . . wet feet . . . a violent cold . . .

Oct. 24 Whent to the Museum, passed through the Cottage, to the High Church, a very grand Cathedral built by the Roman Catholics 700 years ago. a very interesting sight it was . . . Whent to tea at Mr. Fleming, Mr. Hope's partner. Had a little dance among the young people . . .

Oct. 25. Wednesday whent to see the manufactorys of making cotton balls spinning machines.[13] We took a walk round by the Clyde . . . passed the Roman Catholic Chaple, a very grand building . . . the Gaol a very spacious building. Ill for 11 days . . . the doctor's bill being Five Pounds Three Shillings and Sixpence . . . very exhorbitant demand. I was bled with leeches at my temple . . .

November 14th went to see a singing iron that the muslin runs over and touching never damages the cloth altho red hot . . . Saw company at Mr. Hopes an illumination and bonfire took place on account of the bill being thrown out against the Queen . . .

15 November Celia sat for her picture. Capt. Wood called and took us to see the Lunatic Asylum . . . took a walk in Trongate and Argyle Street to see the splendid illumination.

Nov. 15 This day I sat for my picture, my two daughters went to the Trades Hall . . . a lecture on Education of Roman Catholic children which the protestant clergy has undertook providing they will allow the Bible to be read.

Nov. 17 Went this day to Paisley, a Manufacturing town about 6 miles from Glasgow . . . a Gentleman of great respectability, a fancy gauze Merchant of Paisley, waiting our arrival at the Inn . . . we availed ourselves of their [recommended friends] kind invitation to dinner after taking a glass of wine and a little Bride Cake (they being lately married) the Gentlemen took us to see the different manufactorys and what curiositys their was but their was very little except the sounding Ile attached to the old Abbey where we saw Queen Mary the mother of Robert, King of Scotland . . . we then returned and dined from a very sumptious dinner provided by our friendly host . . . So ended this day Friday.

Saturday 18th. Staid at home all day. Whent to Mrs . . . to tea, a party of about 20 Ladies and Gentlemen. Their the young people danced several country and Scottish reels. Left at ¼ past 11 o'clock. So ends this day . . . very pleasant society.

Nov. 20th. Staid at home . . . Had several visitors. Eliza sat the 3rd time

12 Aunt Hindle Brown was therefore 47 years old in 1791 when Molly was sentenced to penal servitude beyond the seas.

13 The Industrial Revolution in full swing.

to the painter . . . whent in the evening to Mr. Graham . . . Mr. & Mrs. Fleming, an American Merchant and Mrs. F. sister, both of which played on the piano very well . . . They had several dances Scotch reels, Shetspeys etc. The Company broke up at 11 o'clock. We staid to supper . . . and left at 12 o'clock in a Noddy[14] . . . So ends this day.

Nov. 21st. Staid at home. Visitors . . . Eliza and Celia sat to the painter. Whent to tea at Mr. Stuarts . . . Miss Cochrane played on the piano accompanied by Mr. Stuart with the double flagelot.[15] Had several dances . . . So ends this day.

Nov. 22nd. This morning breakfasted with Mr. Walter Wood. Met there Dr. & Mrs. Chalmers,[16] Mr. Irvin, Mr. Pratt, a Lieut. in the Army . . . and another young gentleman. Had a little conversation about indifferent matters . . . After took a walk to the observatory. Saw their Camera Obscura and the magnifying glass, magnified 1400 times . . . several visitors . . . Mr. Scott, Mr. Cochrane and sister came to take C. & E. out walking. We whent to see the panorama of the Battle of Waterloo[17] . . .

Thursd. 23rd. I sat this day to the painter. Celia and Eliza . . . went to tea to Mrs. Chartres had a great party and kept up the dancing till 3 o'clock in the morning.

Nov. 24th. I sat to the painter. . . . Capt. Wood called took out the young ladies.

Nov. 25th. Celia, myself . . . whent to Mr. John Flemings to tea . . . Cards was introduced, played a short time as Dancing seemed the most wished for. After the dancing was over a very splendid supper was sat down to where several toasts were given . . . healths named my family in N.S.Wales was drank. Broke up at 11.

Mon. 27th Took a coach and whent to Hamilton . . . 10 miles from Glascow . . . We was shown through the Duke of Hamilton's Palace where we saw a most grand collection of paintings by Reubens and others amongst them was Daniel in the Lions Den, one of the most striking pieces I ever saw. There was also King George the Third and Queen Charlotte, on each side of a throne which we ascended and sat down on. There was also a painting of Bonaparte which was done from the original. It was said to be a great likeness.

Nov. 29 Whent to see Mrs. Grants to a ball in the evening there being a great spirit for dancing 40 couples. I took a few hands of whist . . . did not break up till 3. . . . Expect company tonight to bid us farewell. Celia sat the last time to finish her likeness.

Nov. 30th Left Glascow at 11 o'clock for Edinburgh in the Coach. Changed horses at a small village called Cumbernauld. Went as far as Gieryama in the Coach where a boat was in readiness to put us on board the

---

14 A type of carriage.

15 Small wind instrument, similar to present day recorder.

16 Dr. Chalmers was a famous Glasgow preacher.

17 Battle of Waterloo was a mere 5 years past.

Steamboat tug. Arrived at Newhaven about 6 o'clock in the evening. Took coach from there to Edinburgh being three miles. Arrived in Edinburgh half after 7 o'clock. Expences being Two Pounds Eighteen Shillings and Six Pence.

Fri. Dec. 1st. Took a walk round the town. Saw the castle, gaol . . . College and several buildings. . . . At night whent to the theatre and saw performed the Tragedy of Douglas, after piece the Vampire . . .

Dec. 2. Mr. Hope took us out walking . . . Each took a basin of hare soup for which the charge 10d a basin . . . Called on Mrs. Robinson . . . found her very pleasant woman and her two daughters. Had a little conversation concerning the schools in Edinburgh. She recommended me to a Miss Duncan. Whent to the Pantheon, saw there great horsemanship by Mr. Clarke and others. Also the play the Antiquary after the piece The Way to Win a Husband. . . .

Monday 4th. Mrs. Robinson and her daughter called on us to take me to Miss Duncan, the Boarding School Governess who lives in Picardy Place. A most delightful and airy situation. I agreed with her for one year only on account of Eliza's bad health but to continue longer if her health proves well at Fiftytwo Pounds Ten Shillings per annum for board and lodgings, tuition in different branches about Twentyfour Pounds more for each young lady. . . .

Dec. 5th. Came home and was busy in the cutting out of flannels . . . and getting everything ready for them to go to school tomorrow.

Dec. 7th. Called at Miss Duncan's to see how my daughter was. Found them rather poorly owing to sleeping in a strange bed and being up sooner than usual. However they was taking a lesson in drawing, being their first attempt. . . . We sat down to dinner at half past four . . . The coach came to the door for us . . . we left the two young people at the school.

Fri. 8th. . . . took leave of my daughters . . . Arrived at Preston the next at half past 7 o'clock being the 9th.

Monday 11th visited the houses in Salford.[18]

Dec. 12th. Left Blackburn at 2 o'clock. Arrived there at ½ before two. Arrived Manchester half past 5 o'clock in company with Mr. Thomas Brown my cousin. Came to Mr. Hargreaves another cousin where I had promised to stay a month. . . . Dreamt my sister was dead.

Dec. 15th Friday 15th Mr. Hargreaves and I called on Mr. & Mrs. Marsden. She also took me to a manufacturing warehouse, Mr. Heathcote's, where I bought a piece of calico measuring 41 yds at 1/-. . . .

---

18 These were the houses, presumably, left by her Aunt. Significantly, the nephew with his family lived at No. 12 Albion Street, Salford. The nephew was her sister's son, Thomas Foster.

Dec. 17th. Sunday 17th Staid at home all day. Had company to tea and supper, Mr. & Mrs. Browns Uncle to Mr. Hargreaves[19] . . . Broke up at 10 o'c.

Dec. 18th . . . Recd a letter from Mr. Jones with two enclosed, . . . and one from Mr. Watson's sister in Sydney. Whent to the play and saw 'Othello' performed after piece '3 Weeks after Marriage.'

Dec. 19th. Mr. & Mrs. Hargreaves and myself whent to the man who is doing my carriage to desire him to have it done this week . . .

22nd Dec. Friday 22nd Dec. set out for Bury. Mr. Hargreaves has taken me in his Gig to a place called Openshawfolie where I found my old nurse and her husband who was both so gratifyed they hardly knew how to contain themselves with joy, the old lady said she was sure she could not have rested in her grave had she not have seen me. They said they was both in her eightyfirst year of their age and both looked as if they should live 20 years longer. We went to Bury about a mile further, where we put up at the Grey Mare, an Inn about 20 yds from where my mother lived[20] in the wild[21] [sic] but ALL THOSE HOUSES HAD PULLED DOWN to make improvements to the Church. Mr. Hargreaves and I took a walk around the town. There was at time a great show of wild Beast to be seen, we whent in and was highly gratified at the sagacity of the elephant. We dined at the Inn. . . . Mr. Hargreaves and I whent to the old church at Bury[22] to procure the certificate of my age. The clerk and I looked through the Register Book of parchment and I discerned it first. I was born in the year of our Lord 1777, May 12, and christened 29th.

Dec. 23rd. Mrs. Hargreaves and I whent to Market it being so near Christmas. A very throng market it was, so much so, that we lost each other. Called to see if the carriage was finished.

Monday 25th. Being Christmas day dined at home. Had no company. Mr. & Mrs. Hargreaves and I took a walk. Came home, had tea and read a few passages in the Scriptures.

Wed. 27th. Whent to see if my carriage was finished, being Christmas the workmen were away.

Thurs. 28th. Whent to see my Nephew, Thomas Foster, name of place is Albion[23] Street No. 12 Salford. He had got a little son home since last I saw him, about 10 weeks old and a very fine child he was.

Dec. 29th. Recd. letter . . . from my daughters. Whent to see if the carriage was packed up. Said it should be finished tomorrow. Staid at home all day after being ill of a cold.

---

19 Internal evidence of Mary's relatives. Hargreaves is a cousin, the Aunt Hindle Brown is his mother's sister. These clues were used when unravelling her connections in 1791.

20 Mary's mother was Jane Law. Jane Law's mother's house, Grandma's home, had therefore been moved 'to the top of Darwen Street' when she had had the care of the orphan Molly Haydock.

21 In the 'wild' is as circus in Piccadilly Circus.

22 Bury is half way between Salford (near Manchester) and Blackburn.

23 Internal evidence of the survival of Elizabeth Haydock, her marriage to C. Foster, of the birth of a son, of that son Thomas living in vicinity of Mary Haydock Reibey's inheritance, houses at Salford.

Sun. 31st. Continued to be very poorly. Mr. Buchanan brought me news of the ship *'Malabar'* having arrived from New South Wales.

Mon. Jan. 1st 1821. Still confined to my room. Mr. & Mrs. Hargreaves paying every attention to me. My old nurse and her husband came over from Bury to see me. Mrs. Hargreaves gave them a bed and every comfort that they required after so long a walk for two old people in their eightyone years. They hardly know how to express their joy at being able to see me before they died, a more venerable and better looking old man I never saw and a more healthy old woman at her age indeed she looked to live twenty or thirty years more.

Tues. 2nd. They set off home again, Mrs. Hargreaves packing them up some mince pies and a little wine and water and I giving them a few shillings to assist them by the way. They left me with a heavy heart . . .

Sun. 14th Jan. 1821. This day the carriage whent by Baches, the carrier, for London.

Sun. 28th Jan. Took coach for Blackburn . . . Slept at Mr. Browns dreamd Thomas[24] was come to England and that he said my little Betsy was very ill and subject to fits.

Mon. 29th. Sold my houses for Three Hundred Pounds.[25]

Weds. 31st. Came over to Blackburn . . . Found a letter from Mr. Jones . . . Signed over my right to the houses in Salford and recd. Three Hundred Pounds for them, being a loser of One Hundred Pounds.

Feb. 1st. To Manchester . . . to bid them goodbye.

Mon. 5th Feb. Packing up this day. Whent to see Mr. Hope's warehouse and looked at some cambric and callico. Gave him an order for a 100 pieces paid him in cash Eight Pounds for money laid down by him for me . . . Bank of England Notes. No. 28578, 28586.

Tues. 6th Feb. Took coach for London paid Three Pounds Three Shillings. My cousin John Hope and his wife and Thos. Foster dined with us at Mr. Hargreaves. They all came to see me off in the coach for London. We started at 2 o'clock in the day. Settled with Mr. Hargreaves for cash for me by him. Bothe him and Mrs. Hargreaves behaved uncommonly kind during my stay. There they wished me to stop another month or two. Mrs. Hargreaves made my two daughters Jane & Elizabeth a present of two books.[26] Mrs. Hargreaves made me a present of a book of prayers named 'Nelson's Festivals' and also the medicines both Eliza and I took.

Wed. 7th. All this day in the coach and all the preceding evening. We arrived at the White Horse Fetter Lane[27] a ½ before 7. Ingaged a bed. Capt. Dagg of the ship *Tucan* called and told me he had seen James & George very well. Made me easy. Took a walk in the Cheapside and down Ludgate

---

24 Thomas Reibey II, of Entally House, now married to Richarda for three years, and caring for Penelope and Betsy (Elizabeth Ann) in Tasmania.

25 The houses left to her in Salford.

26 Jane is Jane Penelope.

27 Near St. Paul's.

Hill . . . He [Mr Jones] gave me the news of the Tucan arriving . . . no letters for me which made me very uneasy all day. Whent to Capt. Watson. Took lodging there. At night went as far as Capt. Atkinsons. He was just reading a letter from his son which he had got out of Mr. Berry's box and he saw a packet directed for me but the officer in Charge would not let them be taken as they must go through the Post Office.

Feb. 9th. Mr. Jones & I whent to Mr. Berry's lodgings, No. 8 Size Lane back of the Mansion House. He was not within but we left a note on his table to send my packet as soon as he got it which was to be within the afternoon, expences of it at Post Office was 12/- and the Porter 2/-. I stopd. up till after 12 o'clock reading them.

Mon. 12th. Whent to the City called on Mr. Jones had a little conversation with him concerning going out to N.S.W. and about the affairs of the Colony. Recd. a pacquet of letters from my sister going through Manchester. Double postage on them 10/- expence.[28]

Wed. 14th. Capt. Watson whent on board the ship *Brixton* which was lying at the London Dock, to look at the accommodation. Found them very good but could get no decisive answer, the broker not there.[29] I purchased this day 1 doz of Bell buttons, 1 pr. of silver salts, 4 salt spoons, 1 doz. sugar stand, 7 table spoons, 18 teaspoons, 1 child's Coral, 1 silver eye glass, 4 ridicule clasps . . . 19 chair, 5 yds of sarsenet & 7/6 for a gown and lost it going home. Also a pair of chandelier candlesticks . . .

Fri. 16th. Called on Capt. McIntosh who lives on Ratcliffe Highway. He had purchased a ship called the *Hope* and intending to take passengers to N.S.W. He called a coach and we whent on board, she lying in the canal refitting but she appears to be longer before she will sail than I wish to stop. I can make no agreement. The other half owner Degraves being on board. He also is going out with his small family to settle at Van Dieman's Land and wished for all the information I could give them which I did to best of my judgement. Capt. McIntosh is quite the gentleman. We all walked back calling in our way at a pastry cooks shop and taking refreshment. We parted and each party whent their own way after they giving me an invitation to dine.

Sat. 17th. Whent into the City with a Mr. Davison, a porter to purchase a desk but there was not one to suit me. He took me through the Mansion House, Guildhall and the Bank.

Feb. 19th. Removed to my new lodgings in Postern Row, No 9 Mr. Sharp, Watchmaker at 16/- per week to find coals myself. After whent on board the *Mariner*[30] sloop lying in the Limehouse Canal. The two owners called on me in the evening to enquire into the affairs of V. Dieman's Land and Port Jackson . . .

---

28 Internal evidence about sister Mrs. Eliza Foster (formerly Elizabeth Haydock).

29 Mary Reibey from here on for nearly three months has great trouble organising a passage back to N.S.W. for her and Eliza who it appears is to return with her mother.

30 The three women eventually sailed home to N.S.W. in the *Mariner*. Hence Mary's later 'fudging' the truth in the 1828 Census, 'came free by *Mariner*.'

Fri. 23rd Feb. Whent to Moor Lane the Baches[31] the carrier to send a small box to Manchester to Mr. Hargreaves . . . Mr. Jones called on me to advise me about what ship I must take. The owner of the *Mariner* called at night and we agreed . . .

Sat. 24th. This day walked to the west end of the town as far as Grosvenor Street, the residence of Sir Robert Peel but was down in Staffordshire. Bought a canteen this day for George and 45 vols. of the British Essqyist [sic] and Gibbons History of Rome, 12 vols, from its foundation.

Tues. 27th. Bought this day 12 setts of Table Matts, 12 doz doyleys . . . Gave an order for a quantity of cutlery . . .

Wed. 28th. Staid at home all day it freezing and snowing all day. The ditch round the Tower was frozen over and the boys were skating, my window being opposite I had full view of them. This day had in 250 cakes of Windsor soap.

Thurs. 1st. At home all day. In the evening whent to see the Queen go to the Mansion House to be present for the benefit of some poor Society, but did not see her. She whent in a private entrance contrary to all expectations.

Fri. 2nd. Mar. Took a walk in the City. Whent to Wiston & Herrit Office 37 Old Broad Street, to enquire about the *Mariner* . . . Gave Mr. Davison an order for some crockery ware . . . very dity [sic] weather . . .

Tues. 6th. Very bad weather. Gave order for some stationery. Purchased some irish linens. A very bad cough on me.

Wed. 7th. Took a walk into Aldgate, Broad Street and made some little purchases . . .

Mar. 9th. Recd. two letters from Edinburgh, one from my daughters . . . Wrote one in answer . . . Purchased Clarke's Family Bible.[32]

13th Mar. Tues. Got home my miniature frames.

Wed. 14th Mar. Whent to Wakemans, the carrier to see about 3 cases with Irish & Calicoes. Ordered a double barrelled fowling piece for George. Bought the Incyclopaedia Britanica, 20 vols. 30 Guineas.

Thurs. 15. Whent on board the *Mariner* . . . Whent to the theatre, the Royality, a very miserable performance.

16th Mar. Fri. . . . a Lieut. Thomson,[33] relation of Dr. Chalmers called, brought me a note from my daughter Celia.

Sat. 17th. . . . recd. a letter from D. Hope saying my daughters would be in town if the wind was fair today or tomorrow.

---

31 Baches, the carriers responsible for her precious new carriage.

32 The Family Bible is now (September 1981) in the possession of C. A. (Tom) Harrison, at Longford near Launceston, Tasmania. This Bible was printed in 1810. On the inside leaf containing the family particulars is an inscription in Mary Reibey's own handwriting saying she had purchased the Family Bible in 1820. The book is in excellent condition showing the descendants of Thomas Reibey II. Great-great-grandson Tom Harrison is descended through Thomas II's daughter Mary Ellen who married Charles Arthur.

33 Lieut. Thomson was to eventually marry Eliza. She was then 16.

Fri. 6th. Whent to the Brokers of the *Mariner* to see when I could take my things on board. Mr. Atkinson and I went to the City Canal. Came home in a waterman's boat. Bought a piece of Irish linen. Gave a woman 10 chemise to make and 5 she has got the stay maker. Brought home 4 pr. of stays.

Sat. 7th April. Whent to Mark Lane to Buckles, Bagsters & Buchanan to inquire concerning Rebecca's pensions but got no answer.[34] . . . Lieut. Thompson called . . .

Wed. 11th. Whent on board the *Mariner* but no appearance of being ready.

Fri. 13th. Whent to Buckles Bay and Buchananan, Mark Lane 33, to enquire about Rebecca's pension but got no more information than last Sat. Off to Whitehall to get the proper forms made out but called to see William Charles Wentworth. Staid with him too long till it was too late too go.

Sat. 14th. Called on Mr. Wm. Wentworth . . . Whent to Whitehall the Admiralty Office & Army Pay Office to inquire about Rebecca's pension. Gained all I could after being referred from one to another till I was tired. Got the necessary forms from them . . .

Tues. 17th. Purchased a trunk this morning, gave 21/- for it. Celia and Eliza gone to order their pelisses & pay the Doctor's bill Five Pounds Twelve Sillings.

Apr. 18th. Wed. Whent to Broad Street 53 . . . ordered from Cooper & Eliot some looking glasses, a sofa, A Mahogany Dressing & writing case. Packed up all my luggage. . . .

Apr. 21st. Sat. Got my goods on board the *Mariner.*

Apr. 22nd. Whent to the Foundling Hospital[35] a beautiful little chaple and a most gratifying sight to see such a number of little females in such good order and an equal number of boys . . .

Apr. 25th. Whent on board. Nothing doing. Mr. Williams and I whent to Clementinas to look at a piano.

Thurs. 26th. Mr. Thomson called on us and we whent to Greenwich Hospital by water . . . Saw through the painted Hall and chaple. Came home by coach. Mr. T. spent the evening with us.

Apr. 27th. Whent on board the ship. Am afraid she will not sail this three weeks yet.

Sun. 29th. Whent to a Scotch church in Miles Lane. Mr. Thompson called and took us.

Apr. 30th. Whent on board the *Mariner.* Nothing doing. . . .

May 1st. Was taken very ill of my old complaint on the lungs . . .

---

34 James Reibey had married a widow Rebecca Breedon — Mary was seeking an official widow's pension.

35 At Coram's Fields near Russell Square, London.

Thurs. 3. Eliza & I whent on board the *Mariner*. Still very ill. Was obliged to go to bed. Mr. Thomson brought two tickets of the speaking of the Bible Society, at the King's Concert Rooms, Haymarket. Only Eliza and Mr. Thomson went, Celia staying at home with me on acct of me being so ill.

Sun. 6th. Called in a physician, Dr. Frampton this day. Gave his opinion to Dr. White.

Sat. May 12th. . . . this being my birthday 44 years of age, my complaint began to take a favourable turn.

Sun. 15th. Celia & Eliza whent to dine at Mr. Ross a little way out of town, accompanied by Mr. Hope and Mr. Thomson . . .

Fri. May 18th. Celia and Mrs. Hope going to Manchester. They left the Swan with two necks in the regulator [sic] . . .

May 19th. . . . sent the last of my luggage on board, Mr. Thompson and Eliza gone on board the *Mariner*.

Sun. 20th. Staid at my lodgings. Mr. Thompson took out Eliza a walking in the afternoon . . .

Tues. 22nd. Took coach for Gravesend where we arrived about 5 o'clock in the afternoon . . . We staid all night at the Inn *Prince of Orange*. Mr. Thomson went in quest of lodgings. I thought it best to go there [Gravesend] for the good of my health.

May 23rd. Wed. Took lodgings at Mr. Beers, Pilot, Lower Terrace at 50/- per week with the servants attendance, boarding ourselves . . .

Sat. May 26th. Mr. Thomson & I Whent amarketing. Mr. & Mrs. Dunn passengers in the *Mariner* called on us, they having been down at Gravesend 7 months waiting for a ship . . .

Wed. 30th. Whent to Market . . . few things to sell only purchased a few eggs and butter . . . Mr. & Mrs. Dunn . . . took tea with us . . . Had a few games of whist.

Thurs. 31st. Mr. Dunn called to know if I had any commands to London as he was going to settle some misunderstanding with the Brokers of the *Mariner*, Wiston & Hewitt . . .

June 3rd. . . . Ship *Lusitania* came down to Gravesend ready to clear out.

June. Mon. 4th. Nothing to do. Mr. & Mrs. Dunn called and we went out walking to a very pleasant place situate on the River Thames, a bathing house, a small park adjoining it. There are seats for the accommodation of visitors and where you have the most beautiful view of shipping sailing to & from London.

June 5th. Mr. D. . . . to London . . . We hear by advertisement in the Times paper the *Mariner* is to be down on Sunday next. *Lusitania* sailed from Gravesend.

June. Wed. 6th. I think this will now compleat my twelve months in England as we landed at Portsmouth on 21st June 1820. I am very much afraid we shall not sail for that Place before the day. Recd. a letter from Mr.

Atkinson requesting me to come up to London to put my cabin in order . . . Accordingly Mr. Thomson and I set off 2 mins. to 1 o'clock and arrived at the Dundee Arms at ¼ to 5 o'clock. We immediately whent on board the *Mariner*. It came on to rain very hard and everyone had done work on board for the day we could not do anything that afternoon . . . Walked to Mr. A [Atkinson] where they were kindly received me and I slept there all night, Mr. T going to his lodgings. Recd. a letter from Celia from Manchester. All very well.

June Thurs. 7th. This day Mr. Atkinson and I whent on board the *Mariner* . . . and made a great clearance . . . and put out of the cabin . . . trunks Nos. 7, 9, 15, 16, & 20 and 1 small bale, 1 box of Mrs. Kemps marked 21, down in the hold as the owners had charged freight on them . . . I slept there [Atkinsons][36] that night as did also Mr. Thomson. Had they been related to me they could not have been more kind.

June Fri. 9th. . . . this day came down to Gravesend . . . Mr. Thomson and Eliza took a walk to see Mr. & Mrs. Dunn.

Wed. 13th. No ship down or signs of it . . .

Thurs. June 14th. Mr. Cox [one of the prospective passengers on *Mariner*] came down this evening and brought the news that the *Mariner* could not proceed on her voyage for want of means. He also brought a letter from Mr. Jones . . . advising the passengers to seek redress . . . They in consequence are going to London tomorrow morning viz, Mr. Dunn, Cox and Thomson to join Major Homen [all passengers] in complaints to the Lord Mayor. Now this is ever since the 1st of April when he first ingaged that the ship should sail, I have been living at very heavy expence and in consequence my sickness has increased it and God only knows now when we shall get off, but I will put my trust in Him who alone can judge.

June Sat. 16th. This morning recd. two letters from Celia and one for Eliza and one for myself, wishing to go back with me in consequence I wrote her an answere to come up immediately. The Gentlemen all returned with the news the ship was to be down on Tuesday.

June Wed. 20th. This evening the *Mariner* came down to Gravesend.

June 21st Thurs. Whent on board the *Mariner*. Had some little dispute about getting into my cabin.

June 22 Fri. Mr. Atkinson came down from London and brought my daughter Celia with him. I returned with him to settle about her passage. Slept at Mr. A.

[June 24, 25, 26 are to do with the disputed passages.]

Sun. 26th. We weighed anchor and sailed from Gravesend. Whent down the River about 14 miles, was obliged to come to anchor owing to the wind being foul. Most of the ladies were a little sick owing to the motion of the ship.

---

36 Their son did eventually marry Jane Penelope, so became 'connected'.

June Wed. 27th. ¼ past 11 o'clock in the morning weighed anchor and got under weigh. Very light wind and rather heavy sea. Most of the ladies very sick . . .

Fri. 29. The Pilot left us. Passed Dover this morning.

Sat. 30. Foul winds and beating to get to Portsmouth. Anchored at Ride at the Isle of Wight . . . Some went on shore, took lodgings at 3/- per day while on shore.

July 2nd. Rained all day could not go on shore . . . went on shore at Portsmouth, found Capt. in difficulties in regard to provisions on the ship. Heard that the owner was in Gaol. The passengers were obliged to consent paying for the provisions . . .

Thurs. 5th July. This day the gentlemen went on shore and bought the remainder of the provisions . . . Had to open the Hatch to get their dollars to pay for it. Sailed from Ride [Ryde] this evening with a foul wind . . ."

This marks the end of Mary Reibey's available notes, in which the Return of the Native to England is so vividly described.

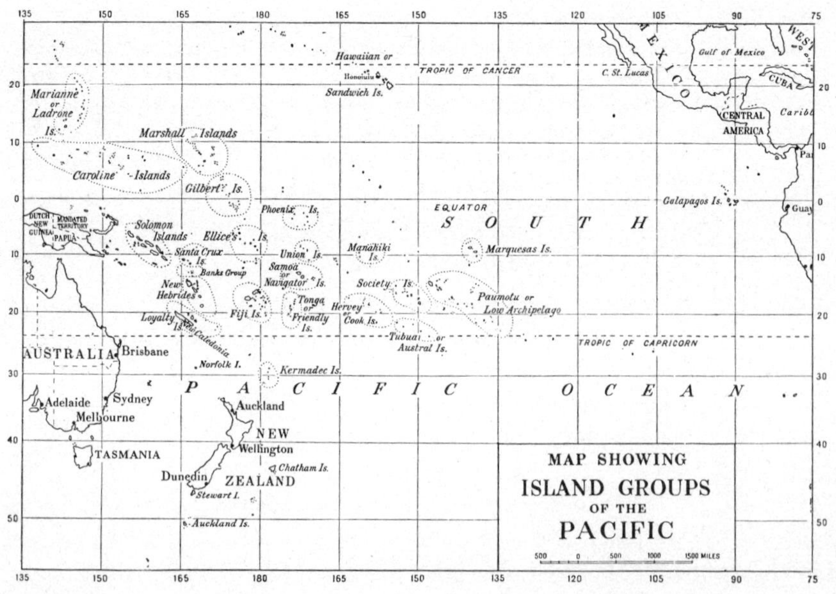

Chapter 11
HER COUNTRY — AFTER ALL

The Family

The Reibey Trio of Mary, Celia and Eliza, returned to Sydney with all their booty from England, to take up a busy family programme. For indeed, during the next thirty years, we can watch Mary enjoy family successes and endure family tragedies. When the strong matriarch finally died in 1855, it was as a survivor of a long life, outliving Celia, George, Thomas, James and Jane, and indeed some grandchildren. Only Eliza, and Elizabeth Anne who was married to Joseph Long Innes, were alive to mourn the wonderful old lady.[274] Nevertheless these last thirty years find the lady continuing with her accumulation of land in strategic areas of New South Wales and Van Diemen's Land, or Tasmania as it became known in 1853. She supported her family by seeing them settled on properties. In the case of two grandsons we are fortunate in sharing the daily record of activities that one noted in his Diary kept until the week of his Grandmother's death.[275]

Thomas Reibey the Second and Richarda, of Entally, Hadspen, Carrick near Launceston.

In Tasmania Thomas and Richarda had one little girl, Mary Allen, born 27 March 1818;[276] Richarda next presented to the Southern Settlement one of its most interesting characters, Thomas Reibey III, on 24 September 1821. (He was really No. IV since a little son, also Thomas, had survived for four days only in 1820 while Mary and the two girls were tripping around Scotland.) This lad, however, known as Thomas Reibey III, was to live till the next century, until 1912, lusty and tough from birth, living through a career as interesting and aggressively challenging as his more famous grandmother Mary Reibey. Near Hadspen, Thomas II had built that splendid home, *Entally House,* for his family. He had consolidated the shipping business, building staiths or wharfs along the Tamar and still sailing as Master on his vessels between Port Jackson and Tasmania. There is an old proverb which runs some such way as — bend the twig in the way you'd have the tree grow. This is what old Thomas Reibey had done with his sons, especially with Thomas II. Thomas II and Richarda had a third child James Reibey II. He was to inherit his Uncle James Reibey's home, *Morton* as James I and Rebecca did not have any family. More importantly, James II was to become the Reverend James in England, marrying into county carriage folk, generating a line from Mary and Thomas Reibey of Sydney. James Reibey I, married to the young widow Rebecca (Breedon) though not to enjoy family, as noted, was comfortable on some 2000 acres of very attractive Tasmanian land.

Eliza and Thomas Thomson.

Mary's second daughter who had been so assiduously courted by the Scottish Lieutenant Thomas Thomson in England and on board the *Mariner* was taken to Hobart for her marriage to this gentleman of the

Royal Marines, the wedding being celebrated on 20 November 1821 by the Reverend Robert Knopwood. The couple made their home in Tasmania at *Rosetta,* Launceston. But their son James Thomson was to become Master of *Burrier,* Nowra district, New South Wales.[277] Their two daughters were Maria and Jane. More of James later, after we have dealt with the history of his aunts and uncles. Thomas Thomson, the father was to cause great trouble by 1829.

Celia and Thomas Wills.

There was to be a wedding and one surely rather close to Mary's heart and memories; Celia was to marry Edward Wills' son, John. Thus children of the two old partners were to unite the families, even if fate was against their chances. It is an interesting commentary upon the composition of the Sydney community that these two Currency Children each had one parent who had been sent to the Colony as a convict; Mary Haydock Reibey and Edward Wills. Celia and John were married at St. Phillip's Church on 18 June, 1822.[278] Celia's death notice was to appear just fifteen months later, upon the birth of a daughter who, later, also died. Celia's miniature portrait shows a very pretty girl; it must have been a sad blow to Mary, the mother. There was more tragedy to follow.

George Reibcy.

Only one month later, Mary's second son George died in a tree felling accident at *Entally House,* Launceston. George died a bachelor.

Jane Penelope and John Atkinson.

As Mary Reibey's English Diary indicated, Mr. Atkinson senior, a Master Mariner in London, had been most helpful during the frustrating delays for Mary, Eliza and Celia when waiting for the *Mariner* to sail. John Atkinson junior had come to Hobart in 1817, after having travelled 'in his father's vessel carrying troops from Russia in overthrowing the destined Monarch of the world' — Napoleon, of course — according to a Hobart paper.[279] In 1819 John was in Sydney and there made friends with the Reibey family, and apparently, particularly with Jane Penelope. She remained at *Entally* during her mother's absence in England.

John Atkinson was warned he had a hopeless liver disease and would be dead very shortly, so he returned to Launceston, to catch the fresh restorative airs of the St. Leonards Estate where the Thompsons lived. He succeeded in catching excellent health, living to the tremendous age of 99 years. What is more, he caught Jane Penelope, and they were married on 11 September 1824 at St. Phillip's, Sydney. He had bought Mary Reibey's George Street property in 1821. The wedding was reported, 'married by Rev. Wm. Cowper, St. Philips, John Atkinson, of Atkinson & Bingle'. Nevertheless, John Atkinson took his bride to occupy one of his mother-in-law's Hawkesbury properties at Wilberforce Reach. Records show that Governor King had granted to Thomas Reibey and his heirs, in 1803 a farm at Mulgrave Place, later known as *Reibeycroft.* The Shire map of

Richmond shows Thomas Raiby [sic] as occupying 80 acres on the river bank at the area shown as Wilberforce Reach on the River. The Atkinsons' first child, a son, was born at Wilberforce on 28 March 1826; indeed three more siblings were born there, George on 26 September 1827, Jane Elizabeth Pitman on 21 December 1829, and Mary Innes born on 19 May 1832. This last child was born some thirty-six years after Mary Reibey's first son Thomas II was born in a hut very close to Wilberforce in 1796 in every rough circumstances. By the Atkinson's time, of course, doctors, hospital and midwives, and a civilized settlement dominated the Windsor district. It is interesting to watch these historical echoes of all the earlier happenings.

This second generation couple, the John Atkinsons, were a healthy, fecund pair like the first Reibeys. The couple later moved back to Tasmania. No less than seven more children came to bless the household; the first two of these were born at Blackford Hill, St. Leonards. The last five were born in Launceston. Their mother, Jane Penelope, died on 9 October 1854. But John Atkinson lived long, like his wife's flamboyant nephew Tom Reibey of *Entally,* he died on 20 December 1893. A Tasmanian newspaper of 22 December 1893 sported a long obituary telling of all his interests during the long life, of his intimate knowledge of Sydney (in the early part of the century) and of her prominent citizens. Mary Reibey's tactics became clear as her following generations are seen to spread over quite a portion of the southern island state as well as in New South Wales. Later generations are now found in Southern Queensland and the northern part of New South Wales as well as in Melbourne and Sydney, not to mention the branch planted by James II in Devon, England. The Tasmanian connections are extensive.

Elizabeth and Joseph Long Innes.

Mary and her beloved Betsy had their social life amongst the Sydney people. Mary had successfully, it seems, hidden her initial transportation. Already this biography has pointed out the ambiguous listing in the 1806 Muster, by Mary herself or by authorities collecting the Muster information, where she is listed simply as 'Mary Heydock C *Royal Admiral,* 5 legit. chn. m. Sydney.' The 1828 Census reveals a deliberate 'fiddling' with the facts; it reads 'Reibey, Mary age 50 c.f. [came free] *Mariner* 1821 Prot. R. occupation, Householder, Res. George Street. Prot.'[280] Elizabeth is registered at the same address, same religion. In the *N.S.W. Calendar and General P.O. Directory for 1832* there are two addresses, Mrs. Reibey, George Street Sydney, and Reibey Farm, Windsor.[281]

In 1827 Mary bought land with a frontage to George Street of 160 ft. for the large sum of One Thousand Pounds, which in itself is a commentary on the leaping values of George Street 150 years ago. *Entally House,* now no longer the headquarters of the Bank of New South Wales, was leased to the Church and Schools Corporation, Mary herself[282] in 1825 being elected a governor of the Free Grammar School. At that time she is also credited with owning 1,260 acres of land, as well as sheep and cattle. The *Sydney*

Gazette in June 1828 reported that Mrs. Reibey 'after having erected many elegant . . . buildings in George Street and Macquarie Place has now turned her attention towards the improvement of Castlereagh Street . . .' She gave the George Street land to Elizabeth and Joseph Long-Innes upon their marriage on 5 May[283] 1829. Captain Long-Innes was the Adjutant of the 39th Dorsetshire Foot Regiment, who had journeyed to Sydney from London on 24 March 1827, on board the *Guildford,* with prisoners. He remained in Sydney with a foot injury when the 39th returned to service in India in 1832. Governor Gipps, in 1839, appointed him temporarily to 'discharge the duties of Superintendent of the Sydney Police at a salary of Four Hundred Pounds per annum'.[284] In Hunters Hill Mary built a stone house known as Reibey Cottage. It was sold to Didier Joubert in 1847.

Elizabeth and Joseph Long-Innes had a proper-sized Victorian family of seven, four girls and three boys, thus adding to the spreading network of Reibey folk over the Colony! The first was born 9 February 1830 and the last, Reginald Gipps Long-Innes, born on 13 May 1844. Of these grandchildren, one was to be famous. *Burke's Colonial Gentry* uses two pages to account for this grandchild of Mary and Tom Reibey.[285] He is listed as Hon. Sir Joseph Long Innes, Knt. of Winslow, Darling Point Sydney and of Clover Hill, Sutton Forest, New South Wales, born Sydney 16 October 1834; m 5 July 1865 Emily Janet, eldest daughter of Hon. John Smith M.L.C.; Bathurst, N.S.W. His father, Captain Long-Innes, who had married Elizabeth Ann Reibey, had come from Ireland, he was the son of an Army Major of Clover Hill, County Leitrim. All Mary Reibey's grandchildren appear to have succeeded in achieving a very healthy, well situated niche in colonial life, and also in Devon, England.

After the Long-Innes marriage Mary apparently returned to *Entally House* in Macquarie Place for a few years. Then the old house is said to have become, in turn, the Office of the Colonial Treasurer, and temporary premises of the Royal Exchange and various trusts.[286] Allegedly *Entally House* became a 'Pub', being finally demolished in 1880. Mary herself had organised the purchase of an estate 'in the country extending for more than three kilometres'; on which in 1850 she built still another *Reibey House* in Enmore Road, Newtown.[287] Here she retired to the country, outside the City boundary.

During those last years she had the fun of watching her descendants in their various fields, law, shipping, grazing and the church. What more could the lady, the Matriarch, desire? However, there were alarums and there were deaths. There was the Catchpole Taradiddle, the remarkable changes in the Colony politically and economically, and there were the deaths. And these come so suddenly in families, devastating even to rock-like characters as enduring as Mary Reibey.

Celia and George were long since buried, as indeed was Thomas Reibey the first, when Mary's son Thomas II died at *Entally House,* Carrick, Tasmania, in 1842, leaving his elder son, Thomas III to carry on. Thomas III had been educated at Eton and Oxford (as was his brother James), had married Catherine Kyle of Scotland, and entered the Church in the Launceston area in charge of the Carrick Congregation. Brother James became Rector of Denbury in Devon, married and set up a family branch in Devon. His grand daughter, Charlotte Emily Reibey, last of the family to bear the (Mary-Thomas) Reibey surname, married Barton Newton Wallop William-Powlett of Cadhay, Ottery St-Mary's, Devon. She is still remembered and lovingly referred to by her family as 'Sugar Plum', long after her death; her charming portrait hangs alongside that of her husband.

One of their sons, Sir Peveril Reibey-William-Powlett, has served as a British Admiral and as Governor of Rhodesia. He now lives at *Cadhay* with the present owner, his nephew Oliver N. W. William-Powlett, Mary Reibey's grandson (six generation). Oliver farms his property, which surrounds the historic 16th century stone manor house, *Cadhay*; he is deeply interested in his famous ancestress, freely making available photographs of the family portraits and family papers. Lying unsuspected amongst these papers I found three (original) letters, one from Mary Reibey herself and two from her son James Haydock Reibey. Her signature is identical with that in the Family Bible, in the possession of another descendant Tom Harrison of Longford, Tasmania, and with that on the fly leaf of a library book held by the Archives of Launceston Public Library. There does not appear to be any other extant letter of our subject, and this letter of 1825 confirms opinions on her business acumen. It is superinscribed on the outside:

No 11 9 Feb; 1825

Mr David Hope,
60 Brunswick Street,
Mangles. Glasgow

and the letter paper is sealed with black sealing wax, impressed with a capital R. On the back is stamped: Ship Letter. . Plymouth.

From her Diary it is evident that she, in 1820, was very friendly with David Hope, her lawyer cousin of Glasgow, who was attending to her overseas business arrangements. It is interesting to note how short she appears to be of ready cash at a time when she was consolidating her building enterprises. For according to this letter of 1825, and her son's of 1829, she is unhappy about her indebtedness to Adam Hope, and yet the *Sydney Gazette,* June 1828, speaks of her building activities in George Street, and now, 1828, in Castlereagh Street. She writes:

Febry. 9th 1825

'My Dear Cousin, by the Ship *Mangles* and by the son of your Agent Mr Broadfoot of Leith I send you a few lines to say that with myself my family here and all well health and much the same as when I last wrote you they all desire their love and respects and are anxiously waiting letters from you. it is now sometime Since and I think it long in not receiving one from you Mr Broadfoot has been living a short time with us and says he will see you therefore he will be able to give you more Information that I can Communicate through Paper I think him a very amiable young man and very steady I have a very high opinion of him, I regret much not haveing the Money for What goods are Sold handed over to me according to Promise by this Conveyance I Should have Considered it very safe by Mr Broadfoot but so it is I have been disapointed very much which has grieved me Sorely I expect by the next vesel Sails from here in about a month I shall be able to send some part or all for What is sold I should like if Possible you to apoint an agent to receive the Money here the Agent for the the Australian Company Wld. oblige you to remit the Cash with his I have sent from the residue of the goods to my House from the Commission Wharehouse and which I will endeavour to sell myself they have offered 2 p a lb for the paints but which I Shall not take I have enclosed for your inspections the Acct Sales, if you have not laid the Money out namely the £60 Sterling which I wrote you to do for me in goods you may Keep that with the interest and put to my Credit having lately made use of some of your Goods on my own Account which you shall have a regular Acct of whenever it will be my fortune to receive the Cash for What is Actually Sold I Shall not lose a moment in remitting it I have sent by Mr Broadfoot our last years Almanack and last Sydney Gazette with o[indecipherable] No 17 newspaper the Australian, and the Pelisse for Mary, my daughter Elizabeth says She Whould wish to send you a Small memorial but will defer it till another opportunity I must Conclude this before I intended has the person has called for them and Cannot wait... now remains your ever affectionate friend and Cousins

M Reibey.'

(The spelling and punctuation is as written and is typical of many 19th Century letters.)

In James Haydock Reibey's letter to the same cousin, written some four years later, he tells of the family trouble with the brother-in-law Thomas Thomson, who has embezzled money and adds

'this I believe has prevented her (Mary Reibey) who repaid some of the missing funds to 'save him from a worse fate' (than gaol) as much as anything remitting some money she owes you she is continually talking about it & you and saying she is ashamed to write you. I was trying very much the other day to get her a Bill in England for £100 to remit you but could not succeed for her.'

And he continues

'My Mother (Mary Reibey) some time back sent me a bale of Carpetting one that came by your recommendation from some part of Scotland This carpetting I sold here on credit to a shopkeeper by the name of Ash, he shortly after failed, and having a good opinion of the Young Man and willing to assist him I advanced him large sums of money and became security for other sums including my former debt carpetting included about £1500 he repaid me some part of the Cash advances I had made him when unfortunately he was killed from a fall off a horse, leaving me minus carpetting included of £870 .. I seized all his property I could get hold of on this side and a Lawyer of the name of Butler at Hobart Town seized on all he could get hold off (sic) and as the accident happened there (Hobart) he had the start of me, this Butler was his guardian and has advanced a claim on him for some English outlays as he states before their arrivals in the Colony. 'We are at... now who will obtain Letters of Administration from the Supreme Court, but the little property left is hardly worth while contending for, and if I succeed the whole probably will be swallowed up in law expenses. . I am extremely sorry to have to send such an account of the Carpeting. I would have communicated to you before respecting it but was in hopes of something better turning up.'

One has to consider the letter in terms of the young Colony at Port Dalrymple, Launceston, in terms of the great distances between Launceston and Hobart, of the rivalry between the two districts, (which still exists in some small areas) before one can condemn James as a sharp business man. He died in 1843, a year after his elder brother Thomas II had died, and left a substantial property to his namesake, the nephew in Devon. This eventually became the property of Charlotte (Sugar Plum) Reibey William-Powlett. Not surprising, really, to find these letters in Lotte William-Powlett's grandson's collection.

Mary saw to it that there was enough money available for the grandchildren to be educated in England. At the death of her son Thomas II, her grandson Thomas III came home, not quite a graduate in theology but sufficiently so for the Bishop to appoint him as Archdeacon of the Carrick District. At the lovely *Entally House* he and his wife Catherine were leaders in the area in many ways. Mary, fortunately, lived long enough only to glory in his style and successes. She was to die in 1855, some years before the great scandal.

Thomas III was in turn Archdeacon; the instigator of a libel case, which he lost, concerning his relationship with a young married woman, an old friend of the family and mother of his godchild; a politician and the Premier of Tasmania for one year; and eventually, in retirement, the breeder of blood stock, including a runner-up to a Melbourne Cup winner. I wonder if Mary sensed in this grandson a spirit very akin to her own, tough, resilient, no matter what? The *Examiner* of 12 February 1912, uses one whole sheet in tribute, at his death, to 'this much respected old gentleman'. The serious dispute with the Bishop is tactfully glossed over, which of course required Thomas III's resignation from the Church. His main glory was as a politician, as a sturdy member and representative of the Northern settlement; he was involved in the riotous arguments in the Legislative Council, of which he was a member. In 1876 he was invited to form a Cabinet. He lasted for a year as Premier. To the curious visitor to Carrick the little church is a mystery with its walls of stone, one colour to a fair height, and then obviously completed many years later with another coloured stonework.

The explanation is simple. Tom had given a farm to pay for the erection of this church in his own district. However, with the attendant criticism of the court case, he had withdrawn all help and the building was abandoned. His Will in 1912 forgave all and left the wherewithal to complete the church. In actual fact the church was not completed till 1961 — and then by public subscription.

The Thomson Grandson.

The grandson James Thomson, who reported regularly to his grandmother Mary Reibey upon the state of his 'housekeeping' of the Shoalhaven property *Burrier,* and to whom we are indebted for allowing

Mr. G. B. Barton, in 1898, to make extractions from his grandmother's Diary of 1820 is the final descendant to tell us of happenings related to the lady in her time. John Atkinson the eldest of the Jane Penelope and John Atkinson family was for a while working with James Thomson, his first cousin. The Atkinson boy, John, sold out later to the Thomson grandson, returning to Launceston to marry, unsatisfactorily, and die in 1854. In his Uncle James' letter of 10 August 1829 from Launceston, Van Diemen's Land, we discover great family trouble with the Thomsons and can only suppose that Mary Reibey rescued the young man, giving him the opportunity of managing *Burrier* with his cousin, John Atkinson. James Reibey is writing to his Scottish lawyer cousin, explaining that:

> 'Another cause of my not writing you before was in consequence of the horrified state of my mind for the very blameable and foolish conduct of Mr Thomson [who was married to Eliza Reibey, Mary's daughter, James' sister] the event has justified my foreboding, entrusted as he was, at the Head of the Customs and Treasury of this part of the Inland with immense Sums of money with a Salary of only £300 per Annum to be careless so as hardly to keep any accounts, and to live at the rate of £800 or £900 per year All my advice and knowledge only served to irritate and make him shun my society — the Consequence is that Govt. at last took notice of it, everything he had was seized (all the property Mrs T. had from my mother included) and sold and he thrown into Prison the deficiency was about £3000 My Brother Thomas (Thomas II) and myself had at last come forward to save him from a worse fate (as was threatened) and became security for the amount to Govt. .... Mr and Mrs Thomson are living on their farm at Pattersons Plains but Ill off and he is very lazy and useless a being that he cannot turn his hand to anything. . I have no patience with him so extravagant and so careless, and to add to their misfortunes Mrs T. has just been confined of her fifth child.'

Eliza Reibey, enjoying the young Thomas Thomson's gallant attentions on board the *Mariner* in 1821, and her mother Mary could little have guessed what lay in the distant Tasmanian future. Still her son, James, was to be adequately supported by his Grandmother. This Diary notes his continuing reports to Newtown to Mary Reibey, some twenty years after his father's troubles.

The Diary was originally a gift to fourteen year old John Atkinson by his father, and the two partners used it for their recorded daily efforts, letter book and incidents.[288] In 1850 Mary was still very much alive, with her fingers firmly on the farm pulse, though living in Newtown. It is well for us to realize how extraordinarily important were the seafaring folk who kept the communication channels alive, who carried the produce and goods. There must have been quite a camaraderie between the settlers and the news bringers, as it were, from the hub of New South Wales, Port Jackson, Sydney. There are letters extant in beautiful handwriting as this one, for example, addressed to and informing Mary Reibey:

> '28th August 1847 — Having one cow calved, and that in two or three weeks we trusted to be milking five or six. . . . Sent Mr. Henry Osborne check [sic] for Twentyfour Pounds on the Commercial Bank, Sydney,

dated 20th Aug. . . . Sent for Two milk buckets . . . a new skimmer and enough stuff for three or four strainers. signed T&A.'[289]

Captain Innes had been given responsibility re the Shoalhaven affairs, hence this note:

'1st September, 1847 — Capt. Innes —
Our neighbours are sadly complaining of all our horses trespassing on their Areas, in fact one of them (neighbour) has just been doing so and has told me 'That it has now come to such a pass that if we do nothing with them, he in fact Mr. Atkinson, I must drive them to the pound' such were his words. One horse I should say was fully equal to two if not three cows, not so much for what they eat, but that they travel so far so quickly and always pick the best right over. Another damage done by them, whenever they get among other people's horses, is in consequence of there being five uncut colts among them, three 2 year olds, and two three year olds. I think it very probable that in the course of a month or six weeks some of Bessy's [neighbour] mares will be foaling. Will you be good enough just to speak to my Grandmother and see what is to be done, for it will be quite impossible for us to keep them out of any of our neighbours grounds . . .'

There is a long memo concerning goods (sent to 'my grandmother'), the necessity of 'learning from my Grandmother what stock it was her intention to reserve for herself',; a meticulous list of needs for *Burrier,* — bread, fishing lines, oil cloth for table 47½ ins. long (sic) by 31 broad; bootlaces; enclosed in a letter to Mrs. Reibey. Poor young men, they had their troubles. A neighbour was complaining 'For some time past there has been a large brindle bullock running here that we are told belongs to you although there is only Mrs. Reibey's brand on it . . . You must really very soon contrive some plan for taking them away . . .'

From 1852 James is on his own at *Burrier* and is rather strongly courting the McKenzie lass, Mary, from a property further down the Shoalhaven River called *Bundanon.* From his farm record, his daily notes to himself, the picture of his work, play and courting comes across the 130 years; a picture made before trains, cars, telephones were in the district, when there were local Aborigines to help and to hinder, when there were, as ever, floods to contend with, when the mail came by the river boats. Here are a very few extracts — often there are the words 'went down to *Bundanon*'. He later married Mary.

'Jan. 1853 Attended boat races at Wooridgee.
Jan. 27 Shooting match, won a bridle.
14 Feb. 1853 Jimmy Callaghan & mate while I was away have been digging down at the river and have found a metal exceedingly like gold. I am at present afraid to believe that it is so.
Feb. 15 My gold turned out to be copper brass.
Sunday 27th Arrived Sydney 12th March & left upon the 17th. Arrived at Woorigee upon 21st . . . day of the races. Stopped for the races, went to the race dinner . . . won a rifle at a shooting match . . . got home 25th.
Sat. 9th July 1853 . . . bought a watch from one of the sailors (damned fool I was) for Three Pounds.

Received from Hogan Twenty Pounds rent and from the Howes Fifteen Pounds.
Wed. 29th June 1853 Raining . . . a very heavy flood.
12 July . . . another flood as high as the last . . . still raining. A gentleman named Welsh apparently an architect came up to see if I would sell Burrier.
Sat. 16 . . . Recd. bill from Hyams amounting One Hundred and Seventyfour Pounds Eleven Shillings and Threepence. Isn't that stunning."
Sun. 17 . . . Went down to Bundaroon and agreed with Nicholson to build me a boat 16 ft keel for Sixteen Pounds, I find copper nails.
Wed. 10th Aug. . . . received Illustrated London News and papers . . . still raining & another flood.
Mon. 29th Went down to Wooridgee and held court. [James was a J.P.]
Sat. 3 Sept. Borrowed Two Hundred Pounds from Montgomery for which I am to pay 7%, gave him a P.N. for Two Hundred and Fourteen Pounds due 2nd Sept. 1853.
Mon. 12 . . . Planting potatoes . . . 'Lass o Gowrie' came up. Put on board 'Lass o' Gowrie' 135 bushells of wheat.
Sat. 17th Sent the three blacks with the cows [sold to a neighbour Condy] but they could not get them past Barangelly and went off to Wooridgee.
Mon. 19th All day looking for cows and then went down to *Bundanon.*
Tues. 27. Finished planting potatoes, and 4½ acres of corn.
Thurs. 6 Oct. Doctor McKenzie here and Echo [boat] at the wharf taking in Montgomery's corn.
"Thurs. 13 Raining — as yesterday.
Fri. 14 Ditto . . . all drunk.
Sat. 13 Nov. Returned to *Bundanon* agreed to sell Thomas 12 heifers for Fiftyfive Pounds.
Thurs. 8th Cutting thistles at Illaroo.
Sun. 1st Jan. 1854 Dined at *Bundanon* then came home and found that the blacks had got into the store and broached the grog . . . sent for constable.
Thurs. 5 Jan. Returned to *Bundanon* . . . paid tailor Two Pounds Five Shillings for 3 waistcoats.
Sun. 15th Jan. Went down to *Bundanon* . . . found all blacks drunk.
Sat. 14th Finished reaping and paid the blacks Eight Pounds . . . gave Jimmy 2/-.
Thurs. 16th Feb. Attended Flower Show at Kiama . . . not worth seeing.
Sun. 26 March 1854 Fishing . . . E. de Mestre here. [There are many old family names noted.]
Wed. 26 April Started for Kiama to attend Licensing Meeting . . . on my way down found Philip had killed another blackfellow, Darby Brooks.
Fri. 19th May Mr. Brown here with Jimmy Barefoot on a charge of robbery . . . took down some of the depositions . . . building again.
Wed. 24th Giving out blankets for blacks.
Thurs. 25th Went to the pigeon match . . . won a saddle. Ditto another

match Ditto.
Fri. 26th Hanging about doing nothing.

In May and June — busy building . . .

"Wed. 18th July Finished chimney.
Sun. 29 Miss McKenzie & others here.
August 25, 26, 27 Partitions in new home . . . slabbing and splitting . . .
Sept. 20th Went down to Bangelly Creek & brought up the cedar . . . got swamped.
Thurs. 28th Splitting shingles . . .
Oct. 9, 10, 11, 13, 16 Made shutter and door, making doors & windows, flooring room in kitchen [which would be separate for fear of fire from cooking] making doors & windows, went out walking.
"Tues. 7 Nov. Arrived at Wooridgee, bought following things, 1 doz ale One Pound; 4 bottles gin One Pound Seven Shillings; 6 bottles wine Seven Pounds Ten Shillings.
Thurs. 16. Just commenced burning shell [which had been sent up by boat to be used for mortar].

There is little else, and a break of five months — until:

'Thurs. 30th May 1855 Recommenced journal . . . Pulling corn . . . Heard of my Grandmother's death [Mary Reibey] left for Sydney . . . borrowed Twenty Pounds from Hitchcock.'

That is almost the last entry.

The Shoalhaven Shire Maps show Mary Reibey as being the holder of *Burrier* of 800 acres, frontage on the Shoalhaven River about 11 miles from Nowra in the Parish of Illaroo. Adjoining are grants in the names of Mary and James Thomson. Mary Reibey is also shown as the holder of *Illaroo,* of 928 acres on the Northern bank of the River. James' father, Thomas Thomson, died in 1844 in Launceston, still another death preceding Mary's. This diary, such as it was, is relevant to the later years of Mary Reibey, showing how her grandson faithfully fulfilled requirements in caring for the property. He and his Mary McKenzie lived to raise another generation, with family members still living in the district.

The Cathpole Taradiddle.

This was an unnecessary worry for the old lady, and she nearly lost her superb poise . . . poise which had carried her safely through those trying days in August, September and October 1791. The Reverend Richard Cobbold wrote a fictionalised account of a single woman, Margaret Catchpole, a convict who had stolen a horse and who had finally reached Sydney in 1802. Cobbold wrote a story which the London Press acclaimed as the story of 'our convict people' and the book became a 'sellout' success in 1849. Mr Cobbold assured his readers 'they might depend upon the truth of its main features'. Rumour had it that another person, not Margaret Catchpole, was buried in St Peters cemetery Richmond N.S.W. (in 1819) and that the girl was identical with the wealthy respectable widow, Mrs Reibey.

Mr G. B. Barton, in 1924, endeavoured to put the story into its proper perspective.[290] The girl, Margaret Catchpole, if the story is possibly even half true in fact, survived some incredible dangers and experiences, long before she left England, all because of her passionate devotion to a wild smuggler. She was gaoled, escaped and recaught in the well known boy's clothing made out of her prison sheets. She came from Suffolk, and apart from the stealing of the horse and the homemade boy's clothing there is no similarity, really, with the Molly Haydock story. For one thing Molly-Mary was tried in August 1791; Margaret Catchpole's sentence for Botany Bay was in 1800. Mrs Cobbold had been the lady who had employed her, befriended her, and was finally put into the position where she had to surrender Margaret Catchpole to the authorities. Margaret was a most illiterate girl, having learned what little literary skill she had from the Cobbold children. G. B. Barton quotes one letter from her, which forever more reveals that she was not the cultivated Mary Reibey. Margaret Catchpole wrote to her uncle and aunt Palmer:

> 'may th 02, 1803.
> my Dear uncle and aunt i hav sent you 2 newespapers the onely i Cold git at this time so i hop you will faver me with sum of ipswich papers when you right to me and send me that when i made by ascap out of prison . . .'

There is much more in similar style, and it finishes 'Loven Cusan, Margaret Catchpole.'

When Mary Reibey heard these rumours she felt that the bottom had fallen out of her carefully built respectable world. The Bishop of Tasmania, about to visit England, was asked to help allay the rumours, and this, I think, is where arose the oft repeated story of the innocent girl condemned for a childish frolic. A letter was sent to Dr Nixon, stating Mary Haydock, a Lancashire woman of a respectable family, was at boarding school and ran off in the night for a frolic with a pony in the neighbouring field, with no intention of stealing it. The Bishop added, apparently, that he thought there were some very strong extenuating circumstances as he noted the sentence was only for seven years instead of death, and the Bishop suspected that she had run away on account of a youthful love affair. Which only goes to show how mixed up the Bishop was about the whole affair. Apparently the rumour was scotched, Mary was at peace, and Margaret Cathpole lay quietly in her 1819 Richmond grave. Her death is recorded in the records of St. Peter's Church, Richmond, N.S.W. And all this taradiddle because the Reverend gentleman wrote a good story, and the Press took it up.

Before she died, Mary saw St. Leonards, the North Sydney, New South Wales, area declared as part of Sydney, and many people had crossed over the Harbour to build on the North Shore. She saw the ferry from Dawes Point carry vehicles across to the point where now Blues Point Tower arises. That punt and its successors lasted till the Sydney Harbour Bridge arose a century later. She watched with approval the grazing success at Camden Park, the spreading of the Squatters, the road to Yass which was met by a track from the new settlement at Melbourne. The fortnightly mail coaches met at Yass to exchange people and goods and mail. She watched the new ferry routes in Sydney Harbour to Parramatta and to Lane Cove and indeed to Neutral Bay.

During those years sectarianism became a fighting point, but not necessarily among the humble people who worked and lived happily enough. Van Diemen's Land achieved Trial by Jury by 1840. The *Sydney Gazette,* now run by Richard Jones, a Tory, had for her and others lost its neutral touch. Mary had become indifferent, apparently, to the squabbles between the Exclusives and the Emancipists, just as the *Sydney Morning Herald* began to look at the problem as at 18 April 1831 with a more statesmanlike, balanced view.[2 1] Like others, Mary had had to weather the Depression of the early 1840s but she of course was well prepared. In the country, as we have seen in her grandson's Diary, there were District communities with their Shows and Race Meetings, and their neighbourly helpfulness. She had shuddered, no doubt, at the Myall Creek massacre, wondering if the settlers were living in a climate of fear and were therefore not acting responsibly when apparently sponsoring such a frightful revenge (if that was what it was). She would remember their own fearful days on the banks of the Hawkesbury.

Mary had enjoyed the cultural growth of the town, the substantial development of theatre, no longer the limited attempts of 1798, and had lived to see a beginning of responsible government.

More than anything else, I think she would have enjoyed driving in the new streets of the City, admiring those lovely stone buildings which we can still enjoy. There were the stores at the Quay side; the Argyle Cut; the wonderful introduction of gas lighting in 1841; the hotels the *Lord Nelson* and the *Hero of Waterloo* at The Rocks; the marvellous military Hospital; the houses in Fort Street, and Cadman's Cottage still nestling down by the Quay. The Government stables, the creation of Francis Greenway, stood on the Eastern slope, heralding sometime in the future a new Governor's residence. There were to be seen Hyde Park Barracks, the graceful St. James' Church and there were *Cleveland House,* and *Elizabeth Bay House.* She saw the Darlinghurst Gaol begin, a masterpiece of the time. Paddington was sporting the lovely *Juniper Hall,* still situated on the corner of Oxford and Ormond Street.

One could continue to revel in all the tremendous building activities which had taken place since our fearful Molly-Mary reached Sydney in October 1792. Her life had been full; she had lived through the founding and growth of our country, which became her country, her home. She felt as her friend W. C. Wentworth felt — it had been a good life. She died at Newtown on 30 May, 1855 at the age of seventy-eight and was interred with her husband, her son Thomas and daughter Celia Wills in the Family Vault, re-erected at the Sydney Burial Ground, Elizabeth Street from the Old George Street Burying Ground.[292] It only remains to say:

We salute you, Mary Reibey.

11

[illegible]

My dear Cousin,

by the Ship Mangles and by the Son of your Agent Mr Broadfoot of Leith I send you a few lines to say that with myself my family here are all well health and much the same as when I last wrote you they all desire their love and respects and are anxiously waiting letters from you. it is now some time since and I think it long in not receiving one from you Mr Broadfoot has been living a short time with us and says he will see you therefore he will be able to give you more information than I can Communicate through Papers I think him a very amicable young man and very steady I have a very high opinion of him, I regret much not having the Money for what goods are sold handed over to me according to Promise by this Conveyance I should have Considered it very safe by Mr Broadfoot but so it is I have been disappointed very much which has grieved me sorely I expect by the next vessel sails from here in about a month I shall be able to [illegible] some part or all for what is sold I should like if possible you to appoint an Agent to receive the Money [illegible] the Agent for the Australian Company Mr [illegible] on to remit the same with his [illegible]

for the residue of the goods to my House from the Commissary
Storehouse and which I will endeavour to sell myself they
were offered 2 att for the point but which I shall not
take I have inclosed for your inspection the Acct
Sales, if you have not laid the Money out namely the £60
Sterling which I wrote you to do for me in goods you may
Keep that with the interest and put to my Credit
having lately made use of some of your Goods on my
own Account which you shall have a regular
Acct of whenever it will be my fortune to receive
the Cash for what is actually sold I shall not
lose a moment in remitting it I have sent
by Mr Broadfoot our last years Almanacks and
last Sydney Gazette with one No 17 newspaper the
Anothetam, and the Bell ring for Mary, my daughter
Elizabeth says she should wish to send you a
small memorial but will defer it till another
opportunity I must conclude this before
I intended has the person has called for
them and Cannot wait Pray and remain
your ever affectionate friend and Cousin

M. Reibey

SHIP-LETTER
PLYMOUTH
No 11
7 Feb: 1825

REFERENCE NOTES

1 The Bishop's Transcripts, Parish Registers, 910, Vol. 111 Ref. 551.
2 Abram, William Alex., *History of Blackburn,* 1877, pp. 267, 395, 483, 638, 640, 670.
3 Varied spelling as Haydock, Heydock.
4 Mary Reibey . . . Travel Diary notes 1820-1821, Mitchell Library.
5 Shaw, J. G., *Bits of Old Blackburn,* 1889, pp. 48-51.
6 Abram, op. cit., p. 592.
7 Ibid., p. 593.
8 Op. cit. The Bishop's Transcripts. "James Haydock m Jane Law by licence at St. John's C of E Parish Church — Blackburn, Lancs. Celebrant Rev. John Hewetson."
9 Mary Reibey op. cit., 22 December 1820.
10 Abram, op. cit., p. 267.
11 Mary Reibey, op. cit., 18 July 1820.
12 Abram, op. cit., pp. 638-640.
13 The Petition of Friends to King Geo. III., 5 November 1791.
14 The County Archives, Preston, Lancashire.
15 Bury, Blackburn Church register . . . James Haydock m. Jane Law 22 May 1771.
16 Macdougall papers, Elizabeth Haydock 1772-1849, see Chapter 10.
17 Bishop's Transcript, op. cit., Burials 1779.
18 Cousins Haydock, bearing same given names, appear in records. Identification by dates and residence.
19 Mary Reibey, op. cit., 6 August 1820.
20 Ibid., 22 December 1820.
21 Ibid. 6 and 12 December 1820.
22 The Petition, op. cit.
23 Ibid.
24 Mary Reibey, op. cit., 5 September 1820.
25 St. John the Evangelist C of E Parish Church, Blackburn, celebrated 150th Anniversary, 1939.
26 Trevelyan, G. M., *Illustrated English Social History,* Vol. III, Vol. IV, 1960.
27 Mary Reibey, op. cit., 7 November 1820.
28 The Petition, op. cit.
29 Holliday, *A Brief Sketch of Schools,* VCH Vol. 11, pub. London 1908, Ref. 25.3, p. 590.
30 Mary Reibey, op. cit., 22 December 1820.
31 Ibid., 1 January 1821.
32 Trevelyan, op. cit., pl. 35 Vol. III.
33 Ibid., p. 103, Vol. III, James Woodford Diary.
34 The Petition, op. cit., "her lately deceased Grandmother had . . . enjoined her to the practice of every moral religious duty."
35 Mary Reibey, op. cit., 6 August 1820.
36 Ibid.
37 The Petition, op. cit.
38 Bishop's Transcript, op. cit., James Borrow Christening April 1777 Burial September 1789.
39 Virginia Woolf, *Orlando,* Hogarth Press, London, Panther 1977, Chapter II, p. 41.
40 Ibid., Chapter III, p. 78.
41 The Petition, op. cit., 5 November 1791.
42 Ibid.
43 Ibid.
44 Portrait, Mary Reibey, Mitchell Library, Sydney.
45 Trevelyan, op. cit. Vol. 3, pp. 148-156.
46 Plumb, J. H., *England in the Eighteenth Century,* p. 144. Vol. 7. *The Pelican History of* England.
47 Trevelyan, op. cit., on tea smuggling. Vol. 3, p. 169.
48 Ibid., public hangings. Vol. 3, p. 103.
49 Halliday, *Bibliography on Blackburn.* A. O. Lancs. Livěsey on roads. "The narrowness [of the highway], the steepness of many hills, nature of the soil, the carriages frequenting the same — the roads became ruinous." 25.3-35.1.

50 Bury Records, op. cit. — James Borrow. Bishop's Transcript.
51 Evidence — John Commander — Summer Assizes, Stafford 1791.
52 Report from Mr. Justice Heath, 18 November 1791.
53 Op. cit., The Petition.
54 Op. cit., Evidence — John Hughes. Report — Mr. Justice Heath — John Sorton was uncle and owner, John Sorton Hughes the nephew giving evidence.
55 Op. cit., The Petition.
56 Op. cit., Evidence — Hughes.
57 Op. cit., Silvester, Mr. Justice Heath's Report.
58 Ibid.
59 Op. cit., Trevelyan, Vol. 3, p. 146.
60 Ibid., note 76 on Plate 76.
61 Ibid., Vol. 3, p. 51.
62 Op. cit., Mr. Justice Heath's Report.
63 Op. cit., Assizes Evidence of Francis Emborton.
64 Ibid., Evidence, John Hughes, 18 August 1791.
65 Ibid., Evidence, John Commander, 18 August 1791.
66 Op. cit., Trevelyan, Vol. 3, p. 151.
67 Ibid.
68 Op. cit., Assizes 1791, Evidence, John Commander, 18 August 1791.
69 Ibid., Evidence, William Moore.
70 Ibid.
71 Ibid.
72 Op. cit., Summer Assizes 1791, Evidence, John Commander.
73 Op. cit., Evidence, John Hughes.
74 Op. cit., Trevelyan, G. M., *English Social History,* Vol. 3, p. 97; Shaw, A. G. L., *Convicts and the Colonies,* p. 39; *H.R.N.S.W.,* Vol. 2, p. 426 Conditions of County Gaols; Manning Clark, *A History of Australia,* pp. 61, 65, 69.
75 Howard, John, State of the Prisons 1777-1784; The Gaol Act 1823.
76 Bentham, Jeremy — quoted by A. G. L. Shaw, op. cit., p. 57; Principles of Penal Law 1789, p. 57.
77 Op. cit. Shaw, The branding of criminals, including army deserters, was not discontinued in England until as late as 1879; p. 129.
78 Op. cit., Shaw, p. 29, p. 42: Hanging days, eight in number at Tyburn each year, were holiday fare, quote Radinowicz, W. P., 1948-56, *History of Criminal Law,* calculations to 1819 show that less than 200 were hanged yearly throughout the U.K.
79 Preamble to *The Transportation Act,* July 1718.
80 Op. cit., Shaw; some first offenders by "benefit of the Clergy" escape capital punishment, and in its place, were transported, p. 25.
81 Op. cit., The Petition, November 1791.
82 Op. cit., Court List, Assizes 2, X/108670 P.R.O., London.
83 Op. cit., Evidence before John Wright — John Commander, 18 August 1791.
84 Loc. cit., Evidence, William Moore.
85 The indictment: the sentence. Assizes 5/111 4181 P.R.O., London.
86 Op. cit., Petition, November 1791.
87 Op. cit., Assizes 2, X/208670, P.R.O., London.
88 List 1, Staffordshire Summer Assizes, 1791 — Records.
89 Op. cit., The Report of Mr. Justice Heath, 18 November 1791, see appendix.
90 Op. cit., List 1, Staffordshire Summer Assizes.
91 Loc. cit.
92 Loc. cit.
93 Op. cit., The indictment.
94 Op. cit., Mr. Justice Heath's Report.
95 Gillian Richards, Wahroonga, N.S.W.
96 Jane North's Reprieve; S/L08670; by John Heath, 29 November 1792.
97 Op. cit., Records, P.R.O., Stafford Summer Assizes.
98 Manning Clark, *A History of Australia,* Vol. 1, Chapter 6, pp. 102-103; and *HRNSW.* Vol. II, p. 7 on 6 February 1791 — Surgeon Kent on board *Boddingtons:* complaint — re male convicts ". . . symptoms of fever very apparent among them tho' they were properly wash'd and cleans'd."
99 Op. cit., *HRNSW,* Vol. 1 Pt. 2, p. 59, Phillip to Nepean.

100 Op. cit., The Petition, 5 November 1791.
101 Ibid.
102 Op. cit., Report of Mr. Justice Heath, 18 November 1791.
103 Ibid.
104 Mr. Justice Heath's Report, November 1791.
105 Diary, Mary Reibey, 17 July 1820.
106 Op. cit., Mr. Justice Heath's Report.
107 Chapter 1 — The Background Material.
108 Op. cit., Diary, Mary Reibey.
109 Ibid.
110 Ibid.
111 Op. cit., The Petition.
112 Op. cit., The Bishop's Transcripts.
113 Op. cit., The Petition.
114 Ibid.
115 Manning Clark, *A History of Australia* Vol. I, p. 71 1962 MUP; and quote from *HRNSW,* 1, pt. 2, p. 14.
116 Dundas to Lord Grenville, 17 December 1789, *Historical Manuscripts Commission,* p. 555.
117 Op. cit., Manning Clark, Vol. I, pp. 94-98.
118 Ibid. p. 178.
119 Noah, Wm., *Voyage to Sydney in the Hillsborough,* 1798-9. 1978 LAH.
120 George Barrington, *HRNSW,* Vol. 2, p. 771, letter to his wife.
121 Ibid., Letters from the Dublin Chronicle, 31 July 1790, p. 754; from the Gazetteer 29 December 1790, p. 758.
122 Watkin Tench, *Sydney's First Four Years,* p. 39 Reprint 1979 LAH.
123 A. G. L. Shaw, *Convicts and the Colonies,* 1978 MUP, p. 56.
124 Stafford Assizes — 26 — X/L08670, P.R.O., London.
125 Journals of the House of Commons, Vol. xl, p. 1161.
126 *The Sun,* 18 January 1981, on the occasion of the Annual Sydney Harbour Ferry Boat Race. *Karingal* 106 tonnes, *Lady Cutler* 350 tonnes, *Lady Woodward* 339 tonnes, *Kanangra* 300 tonnes: 1 tonne = .98 ton.
127 Op. cit., *HRNSW,* Vol. II, p. 58, 1893.
128 Op. cit., *HRNSW,* Vol. I Part 2, p. 367, Captain Hill, letter.
129 Ibid., p. 386, Rev. Johnson, letter.
130 Op. cit., *HRNSW,* Vol. II, p. 770, George Barrington, letter.
131 Noah, William, *Voyage to Sydney 1798,* L.A.H. 1978, p. 11: Orlop deck — O.E.D. Lowest deck of ship with 3 or more decks.
132 Ibid.
133 Op. cit., Noah, p. 21.
134 Op. cit., p. 49.
135 *HRNSW,* Vol. III, p. 701, Governor Hunter to Under Secretary King.
136 Collins, David, *Account of the English Colony,* Reed 1975, Vol. 1, p. 150.
137 HRNSW, Vol. 2, ed. 1893, p. 450.
138 Ibid., p 51, Report of Evans, Read and Marshall, 30 June 1791.
139 Ibid., p. 792, Reprinted from *Dublin Chronicle,* 12 January 1792.
140 Ibid., p. 783, *Western County Magazine* 1792, George Barrington, letter.
141 Ibid., p. 792, Reprinted from Dublin Chronicle, 17 December 1791.
142 *HRNSW,* Vol. 1 Pt. 2, p. 623, Henry Dundas to Gov. Phillip, 15 May 1792.
143 Log Book, *Royal Admiral,* Foreign and Commonwealth Office, India Office, Orbit House, London. Frank Clune, *Bound for Botany Bay,* Chapter 12.
144 Microfilm, Reel 2427, A.O.N.S.W.
145 *HRNSW,* Vol. 1 Pt. 2, Grenville to Phillip, p. 458.
146 *Sydney Morning Herald,* May 1980; *Time Magazine,* 1980.
147 At 14 March 1973, Portuguese fort, Isle Bahrain; Malacca, west coast Malay: N. Irvine, unpublished travel report.
148 East India Co. Agreement with Britain, *HRNSW,* Vol. 2, p. 9.
149 Op. cit., p. 48, East India Co. Agreement with Britain, discussed by Lieut. Bowen to Under Secretary King.
150 Op. cit., Phillip, p. 220, Navy Office Accounts, June 1793, Final settlement.
151 Op. cit., Collins, p. 199.

152 Op. cit., Phillip to Dundas, *HRNSW,* Vol. 1 Pt. 2, p. 299 and Cobley, p. 319: "At this moment the Colony is approaching to that state in which I have so long and anxiously wished to see."
153 Op. cit., *HRNSW,* Vol. 2, p. 86; Collins, p. 203.
154 Op. cit., Phillip, *HRNSW,* Vol. 1 Pt. 2, p. 111.
155 Op. cit., Nepean, p. 80.
156 *HRNSW,* Vol. 2, p. 779.
157 Op. cit., Noah, Wm., *Voyage on Hillsborough,* p. 11.
158 Op. cit., *HRNSW,* Vol. 2, pp. 250, 305, 332.
159 Cobley, John, *Sydney Cove — 1791-1792,* Sydney 1965, p. 316.
160 Ibid., p. 351.
161 Ibid., p. 350.
162 Op. cit., Collins, p. 200.
163 Ibid., p. 572n.
164 Op. cit., *HRNSW,* p. 75, p. 332, letter, Richard Alley, 22 March 1790.
165 Op. cit., p. 767, letter, female convict, reprinted *Dublin Chronicle* 4 August 1791.
166 Op. cit., Cobley, p. 79.
167 Ibid., p. 93.
168 Op. cit., *HRNSW,* Vol. 2, p. 470.
169 Thompson, George, *An Account of the Miseries at Botany Bay,* Ridgway, 1794.
170 Op. cit., *HRNSW,* Vol. 2, p. 479, James Lacey, letter from the *Royal Admiral,* 19 August 1792.
171 Op. cit., Thompson, p. 7.
172 Op. cit., Manning Clark, p. 71.
173 Fletcher, B. H. Intro. to Collins, op. cit., page xix.
174 Op. cit., *HRNSW,* Vol. 2, p. 479.
175 Op. cit., Cobley, p. 318.
176 Op. cit., Collins, p. 199; *HRNSW,* Vol. 2, p. 467.
177 Op. cit., *HRNSW,* Vol. 1 Pt. 2, p. 665, Phillip to Henry Dundas, 11 October 1792.
178 Op. cit., Collins, p. 205.
179 Op. cit., Cobley, p. 316, reported from Atkins, Richard, Journal 1792-1810.
180 The Mutch papers — ref. 11 Reiby (sic) Thomas, buried 7 April, 1811 aged 42 years ex ship *Britannia* 1792.
181 Op. cit., Collins, p. 198.
182 Op. cit., *HRNSW,* Vol. 1 Pt. 2, p. 652, Major Grose to Governor Phillip 4 October 1792.
183 Ibid. Phillip to Dundas, p. 651, 4 October 1792.
184 Op. cit., Collins, p. 198.
185 Op. cit., p. 187.
186 Op. cit., p. 201.
187 Op. cit., p. 377.
188 Blainey, Geoffrey, *The Tyranny of Distance,* p. 66.
189 Op. cit., Collins, p. 199.
190 Op. cit., Collins, p. 200.
191 Ibid.
192 Op. cit., p. 205.
193 Op. cit., Thompson, George, quoted in *HRNSW* Vol. 2, p. 796.
194 Ibid.
195 Plummer, T. W., quoted by Ruhen, D. and Shearer, J. D., *Bound for Botany Bay,* 1976, p. 32.
196 Ibid.
197 Op. cit., *HRNSW* Vol. 2, p. 392.
198 Op. cit., Tench, Watkin, *Expedition to Botany Bay,* Chap. IX, p. 39.
199 Banks Papers, ML "R. H. to J. Banks, 13 December 1786."
200 Op. cit., *HRNSW,* Vol. 2, p. 746, letter from a female convict.
201 Op. cit., Collins, p. 94.
202 Op. cit., *HRNSW,* Vol. 2, p. 767, letter reprinted from *Morning Chronicle* August 1791.
203 Conrad, Joseph, *The Shadow Line,* the story of the experiences of a young seaman's first command in the Malay Straits.
204 Op. cit., Collins, p. 198.
205 Ibid.
206 Op. cit., *HRNSW* Vol. 2, p. 218, Captain Raven to Lieut. Governor Grose, 1 June 1794.

207 The Mutch Papers, St. Phillip's Church Records, ML.
208 Denholm, D., *The Colonial Australians,* p. 19.
209 Op. cit., Tench, Watkin, p. 228.
210 Op. cit., *HRNSW* Vol. 2, p. 794, George Thompson — Extracts, October 1792.
211 Op. cit., Lieutenant Governor Grose to Secretary Dundas, p. 238.
212 Op. cit., Mrs. Macarthur, letters, p. 508.
213 Ibid.
214 Op. cit., *HRNSW* Vol. 2, a soldier's letter, p. 815, 13 December 1794.
215 Ibid., Grose to Dundas, 31 August 1794, p. 258.
216 *J.R.A.H.S.* Vol. ii, 1925, p. 104, Source 1/A.
217 Op. cit., *HRNSW* Vol. 2, p. 210.
218 Bowd, D. G., *Macquarie Country,* Ch. 1.
219 Op. cit., Tench, Watkin, p. 253.
220 Perry, T. M., *Australia's First Frontier.*
221 Op. cit., Collins, *An Account of the English Colony,* p. 326.
222 Ibid., p. 348.
223 Smith, Bernard, *Boyer Lecture No 2 1980,* A.B.C.
224 Op. cit., Collins, p. 349.
225 Ibid. 338.
226 Op. cit., p. 347.
227 Ibid. 382.
228 Ibid. 383.
229 Op. cit., *HRNSW* Vol. 2, p. 310.
230 The Mutch Papers, Ref. 14, 19.
231 Op. cit., *HRNSW* Vol. 3, p. 291.
232 Ruhen, Olaf, and Shearer, J., *Bound for Botany Bay,* p. 9.
233 *ADB* Vol. 2, p. 374.
234 Op. cit., Manning Clark, pp. 97-99.
235 Ibid.
236 *Sydney Gazette* Vol. 2, No. 54, 11 March 1804.
237 *A.O. N.S.W.* The 1806 Muster.
238 Sainty, M.R., and Johnson, K. A., (eds), *Census of New South Wales,* November 1828, (Sydney 1980).
239 Op. cit., *A.O. N.S.W.* 1806 Muster.
240 Op. cit., Clune, Frank, p. 101.
241 *Sydney Gazette* 6 October 1810, Macquarie's Plan.
242 Op. cit., Frank Clune, p. 103.
243 Reibey Monument, Pioneers Garden, Botany Cemetery.
244 Fitzpatrick, J.C.L., *Those Were the Days,* p. 131.
245 *Sydney Gazette,* 4 May 1811.
246 Op. cit., 25 May 1811.
247 Op. cit., 24 August 1811.
248 Op. cit., 8 June 1811.
249 Op. cit., 7 September 1811.
250 Op. cit., 6 July 1811; and Petronius, *Satyricon.*
251 Op. cit., 20 July 1811.
252 Ritchie, John, *The Evidence of the Bigge Report,* 1971.
253 Ibid.
254 Op. cit., Blainey, p. 75.
255 Diary of Blaxland, ML, A record of the expedition 1813.
256 Op. cit., Shaw, p. 21.
257 Op. cit., Fletcher, B. H., *Landed Enterprise and Penal Society,* p. 144.
258 Op. cit., Collins, p. 206.
259 Webster, Colin, *Coins, Gemcraft,* Melbourne 1979, p. 61.
260 Shann et al, *Business Archives and History,* p. 58.
261 Public Record Office Registers 64/83 Records 1813-1817, 27 additional shares.
262 *Sydney Gazette,* Vol. 14, 1816.
263 *A.D.B.* Vol. 2, p. 374.
264 *Sydney Gazette,* 17 May 1817.
265 St. Phillips records; the Mutch Papers, ML.
266 Op. cit., Ritchie, J., *Evidence of the Bigge Report,* Druitt's evidence.

267 St. Phillips records, Mutch Papers, ML.
268 Barton, G. B., Article from *Evening News,* a Sydney Newspaper, 20 February 1898 — newspaper out of circulation from 1930.
269 Op. cit., Bishop's Transcripts, County Archives, Lancashire.
270 Op. cit., Reibey, Mary, Travel Diary 1820-1821.
271 Op. cit., *HRA* Vol. 2, p. 492.
272 Reibey, James Haydock, letter to his cousin D. Hope, Glascow, 10 August 1829.
273 Reibey, James Haydock, letter to D. Hope, Glascow, 18 April 1832.
274 Op. cit., The Mutch Papers, reference 27.
275 Thomson, James, Daily record for *Burrier* Station, Shoalhaven, NSW 1840-55.
276 Op. cit., Family Bible, in possession of Tom Harrison, Longford, Tasmania.
277 Op. cit., James Thomson.
278 Op. cit., Mutch Papers.
279 *The Mercury,* Hobart, 21 December 1893, Report of death of John Atkinson.
280 Op. cit., *Census of NSW 1828,* Ed. Sainty, M. R. and Johnson, K. A. (1980) p. 314.
281 *NSW Calendar and General Post Office Directory, 1832.* (Facsimile edition 1966).
282 Op. cit., Clune, Frank, p. 172.
283 Ibid.
284 Ibid.
285 *Burke's Colonial Gentry,* p. 580. Long-Innes.
286 *Daily Mirror,* 13 December 1972. Sydney newspaper.
287 *Sydney Morning Herald,* 6 January 1979. Joseph Glascott, Suburban Walkabout.
288 Op. cit., Thomson, James,
289 The Macdougall Papers.
290 Barton, G. B., *The True Story of Margaret Catchpole.* Eagle Press Waterloo, 1924: Cobbold, Richard Rev. *The History of Margaret Catchpole, A Suffolk Girl.* R. E. King & Co. 110 Tabernacle Street, London EC. 1849.
291 *Sydney Morning Herald* Editorial 18 April 1831 specifying *non* desirable political aims for the new paper — "A system of exclusion gives a character of selfishness . . ." Facsimile reproduction — 1981.
292 Johnson, K. A. and Sainty, M. R. *Gravestone Inscriptions N.S.W. Sydney Burial Ground* (1973) pp. xvii, 11-12.

ABBREVIATIONS:

ABC — Australian Broadcasting Commission.
ADB — Australian Dictionary of Biography.
AO NSW — Archives Office of New South Wales.
HO — Home Office.
HRA — Historical Records of Australia.
HRNSW — Historical Records of New South Wales.
JRAHS — Journal of the Royal Australian Historical Society.
ML — Mitchell Library.

BIBLIOGRAPHY

ABRAM, William Alex., *History of Blackburn,* 1877.
ARCHIVES of Lancashire, Archives Office, Preston, Lancs. U.K.
ATKINS, Richard, *Journal 1792-1819,* NLA.
AUSTRALIAN DICTIONARY OF BIOGRAPHY (8 volumes), MUP, 1966-81.
AUSTRALIAN ENCYCLOPAEDIA (8 volumes), Grolier Society of Australia, 19 .
AUSTRALIAN SCRAP BOOK 1777-1866, F 980, NLA.

BANKS, Sir Joseph, Banks Papers Vol. 22, ML.
BARNARD, Marjorie, *Macquarie's World,* MUP, 1946.
BARRINGTON, George, *Voyage to New South Wales,* J. Swain, New York, 1801.
BARTON, G. B. & BRITTON, Alex., *History of New South Wales from the Records,* 1894 (2 volumes).
BARTON, G. B., *The True Story of Margaret Catchpole,* Eagle Press, 1924.
BARTON, G. B., Newspaper story, *Evening News,* Sydney, 1898.
BENTHAM, Jeremy, *Principles of Penal Law,* 1789.
BIBLE, HOLY, Printed 1810, Glasgow, Tom Harrison, Longford, Tasmania.
BIGGE, John T., *Oral and Written Evidence of the Report,* ed., John Ritchie Heinemann, 1971.
BISHOP'S TRANSCRIPTS, Lancashire Archives, Preston, Lancs. U.K. from 18th Century Vol. 111 Ref. 551, Parish Registers of Blackburn & District.
BLACKBURN PARISH CHURCH RECORDS.
BLACKBURN PETITION, 5/11/1791, Family (Macdougall) Papers.
BLAINEY, Geoffrey, *The Tyranny of Distance,* Sun Books, 1966.
BLAXLAND, LAWSON, WENTWORTH, Daily Account of expedition over the Mountains, AONSW.
BORROW, James, pseudonym for Molly Heydock, Evidence of, in Staffordshire Assizes, August 1791, PRO, London, Assi 5, 111, Part 1.
BONWICK, James, The Bonwick Transcripts, *First Twenty Years of Australia,* Sampson Law, Searle & Revington, London, 1882.
BOWD, D., *Macquarie Country,* LAH, 1978.
BRITTON, Alex., and BARTON, G. B., *History of N.S.W. From The Records,* Potter, 1889.
BURY PARISH CHURCH RECORDS, contiguous to Blackburn, Preston, Lancs. U.K.
BURKE'S PEERAGE AND COLONIAL GENTRY, London.

CENSUS OF NEW SOUTH WALES, November, 1828, Sainty, M. R. and Johnson K. A. (eds), LAH, 1980.
CHAPMAN PAPERS, Letters 1819, Macquarie to James Chapman.
CLARK, C. M. H., *Select Documents in Australian History.*
CLARK, C. M. H., *A Discovery of Australia,* 1976 Boyer Lectures.
CLARK, C. M. H., *Sources of Australian History,* OUP, 1957.
CLARK, C. M. H., *A History of Australia,* Vols. 1-5, MUP, 1962-1981.
CLUNE, Frank, *Bound for Botany Bay,* Chapters 12-18, 1964.
COBBOLD, Richard, Rev., *The History of Margaret Catchpole — A Suffolk Girl,* R. E. King, London, 1846. A "biography" much circulated in England, and quoted in daily press.
COBLEY, John, *Sydney Cove 1791-1792,* A & R, 1965.
COBLEY, John, The Convicts 1788-1792, Wentworth Press, 1965.

COLLINS, David, *An Account of the English Colony in New South Wales,* first pub. 1798, published RAHS, A. H. & A. W. Reed, 1975, ed. Brian Fletcher.
COLONIAL MUSTERS AND CENSUS RECORDS, AONSW.
COLONIAL SECRETARY'S REPORTS, AONSW.
COMMANDER, John, Evidence in facsimile Stafford Assizes, 5 August, 1791.
CONGREGATIONAL COUNCIL FOR WORLD MISSIONS, PRO, London, Box 16.
CONRAD, Joseph, *The Shadow Line,* J. M. Dent, London, 1969.
COUNTY ARCHIVES, Lancashire Office, Preston, Lancs. U.K.
CUNNINGHAM, Peter, Two Years in New South Wales, first pub. 1827, re-pub. RAHS, A & R, 1966.
CUSACK, Dymphna, *The Peaceful Army,* ed. M. B. Eldershaw, 1938, chapter "Mary Reibey and her Times".

DAILY MIRROR, 13/1/1972, Sydney newspaper.
DENHOLM, David, *The Colonial Australians,* Penguin, 1979.
DIARY/JOURNAL, Mary Reibey 1820-1821. Original ML. Copied from extracts by G. B. Barton, *Evening News,* 1898.
DIARY OF JAMES THOMSON of 'Burrier', Shoalhaven, 1851-1855 (grandson of Mary Reibey).
DONKIN, Nance, *An Emancipist Convict Girl,* NLA.
DUNDAS, Henry, Secretary to Lord Grenville, *HRNSW.*

EAST INDIA COMPANY RECORDS, Foreign and Commonwealth Office, India Office, Orbit House, London as at December, 1980.
ELDERSHAW, M. B. (ed), *The Peaceful Army,* p. 37, Chapter by Cusack, Sydney, 1938.
EMANCIPISTS' PETITION, 20/10/1821.
EMBORTON, Francis, Evidence from Stafford Assizes, Assi 5, PRO, London.
ENTALLY HOUSE, Brochure, Tasmanian Government.
EXAMINER, Tasmanian Daily newspaper, Launceston, 1870.

FITZPATRICK, J. C. L., *Those Were the Days,* N.S.W. Bookstall, 1923, quoted by Frank Clune. Fitzpatrick found handwritten notes by Mary Reibey on back of *Sydney Gazette,* Vol. 1810-1811, ML.
FLETCHER, Brian, *Landed Enterprise and Penal Society,* SUP, 1976.
FLETCHER, Brian, (ed), *David Collins,* Account, RAHS Edition, 1975.
FLINDERS AND PRICE, *Governor Hunter's Papers.*
FORDE, J. M., Genesis of Commerce in Australia, NLA.
FORDE, J. M., The Catchpole-Reibey Tangle, NLA.
FREAME, William, Relics of Old Sydney, *Windsor & Richmond Gazette* 25/10/1929.

GLASCOTT, Joseph, *Sydney Morning Herald,* December, 1978, "Suburban Walkabout".
GRENVILLE, LORD, to Governor Phillip, Vol. 1 *HRNSW,* Memoranda.
GRIFFITHS, Arthur, *Memorials of Millbank,* London, 1884, quoted in Trevelyan.
GROSE, Francis, Governor, Recorded letters, *HRNSW, HRA.*

HALLIDAY, T., *Bibliography of Articles on Blackburn,* Lancashire Archives.
HARRISON, Tom, great-great-grandson of Mary Reibey, of Longford, Tasmania, holder of the Original Bible bought by M.R. and inscribed by M.R. with date 1821, printed Glasgow, 1810.

HEATH, Mr. Justice, His Report, Macdougall papers, obtained from Sir Peverill B. W. Reibey William-Powlett, great-great-grandson, of Devon, U.K. Heath was Trial Judge at the Summer Assizes, August, 1791.

HISTORICAL RECORDS OF AUSTRALIA, quotations acknowledged in text.

HISTORICAL RECORDS OF NEW SOUTH WALES, Vols. 2 and 3, Barton/Britton, 1894.

HOLLIDAY, J., *A Brief Sketch of Schools 18th Century,* Vol. 11, London, 1908, Ref. 25.3., P.R.O.

HOWARD, John, *State of the Prisons 1777-1784; The Gaol Act 1823.*

HUNTER, John, Governor, *Papers,* ed. Flinders and Price.

HUGHES, John, Evidence given at Stafford Assizes, Assi 5, August, 1791, P.R.O.

INDENTURE OF CONVICTS, Royal Admiral, 1792, ML.

INDICTMENT, Assizes Stafford, August, 1791, PRO, London, 5/11/4181.

IRVINE, E. Marie, *Certain Worthy Women,* ed. Eldershaw.

JOHNSON, K. A. and SAINTY, M. R., *Gravestone Inscriptions — N.S.W. Sydney Burial Ground,* Sydney, 1973.

JOHNSTONE, C., *Once More Margaret Catchpole and Mrs. Reibey,* 1906, NLA.

JOURNAL FROM THE HOUSE OF COMMONS, Vol. XI.

KENT ARCHIVES OFFICE, County Hall, Maidstone, U.K.

KING, Philip Gidley, Governor, Papers and Journal, *HRNSW.* Further papers Vol. 8.

LEROY, Paul Edwin, *The Emancipists from Prison to Freedom,* The Active Freeman. Microfilm Inc YSA, Ann Arbor.

LIST OF DEFENDANTS, List 1, Staffordshire Assizes X/208670, PRO, London.

MACARTHUR, Elizabeth, Letters, *HRNSW.*

MACARTHUR, John, Letters, *HRNSW.*

McCARTEY, John, *Review in Business Archives and History,* Vol. 4, August, 1964.

MACDOUGALL PAPERS, Christopher, John and Peter, great-great-grandsons of Mary Reibey, Collection of records and diaries.

MANDER JONES, P., (ed), *Manuscripts in the British Isles relating to Australia, New Zealand, and the Pacific,* P 459 Transportation from Lancashire Prisons.

MAPS. Copies of *Hawkesbury Leases, Shoalhaven Leases,* and *Sydney in 1800,* from the Richmond Shire, Illaroo Shire, and facsimile of Sydney.

MARINE RECORDS, 1600-1822, PRO. Shops Logs 1702-1856 L/Mar/B/1.

MOORE, William, Evidence, Assizes, Stafford, August, 1791, x/108670 PRO., London.

MUTCH PAPERS, Records from Registers of St. Phillip's Church, Sydney, ML.

MUSTER OF 1806, N.S.W., AONSW.

NATIONAL INDEX National Registers, PRO, London.

NEPEAN DISTRICT HISTORICAL SOCIETY, *Reibeycroft,* pamphlet.

NEWGATE CALENDAR 1782-1853.

NEW SOUTH WALES P.O. Directory 1832, facsimile, Public Library of N.S.W., 1966.

NEW SOUTH WALES STATE ARCHIVES Reel 2427.

NICHOLS, G. R., *History of the Hawkesbury,* Book No. 1.

NOAH, William, *Voyage to Sydney in the Hillsborough 1798,* LAH, 1978.

O'BRIEN, Eris, *The Foundation of Australia 1786-1800,* A study of English Criminal Practice and Colonization in the 18th Century, London, A & R, 1950.

PALMER, Freda Annie, *Freeman's Reach and the Cattai,* Brochure 14, Nepean Historical Society.

PETITION OF FRIENDS TO King George III, November, 1791, PRO, London.

PETRONIUS, *Satyricon,* Penguin.

PHILLIP, Arthur, Governor, *HRA, HRNSW,* and Collins, Letters to London.

PLUMB, J. H., Book 7, *England in the 18th Century.*

PUBLIC RECORD OFFICE, H.O. 13 Criminal Papers — Entry Books 1782-1871, H.O. 26 Criminal Registers, Series 1, 1791-1891, Registers T.46, 46/22, 64/83.

PULLEN, Kathleen, *From Convict to First Lady of Trade,* Ure Smith, 1975.

RADINOWICZ, W. P., *History of Criminal Law,* CUP, 1946.

RAVEN, Capt. Wm., to Lieut. Grose, Letter, *HRNSW* Vol. 11, ed. F. M. Bladen, 1893, Potter, Govt. Printer.

RAVEN, Capt. Wm., Letters to sundry persons and from Government authorities, *HRNSW,* Vol. 11.

REIBEY, Mary, Diary/Journal 1820-21, Ref CY Safe 1/24 CYC24, AONSW.

REIBEY, Mary, Letter 1825 to D. Hope, Glasgow.

REIBEY, James Haydock, Letter 1829, to Glasgow.

RICHARDS, Gillian, Question-Answer Paper, fourteen year old girl, Wahroonga, NSW, paralleling Mary-Molly Heydock.

RITCHIE, John, (ed), *The Evidence of the Bigge Report,* Heinemann, 1971.

ROBSON, L. C., *The Convict Settlers of Australia 1786-1800,* MUP, 1965.

ROYAL ADMIRAL, Ship's Log, Foreign and Commonwealth Office, India Office, London.

RUHEN, Olaf, and SHEARER, J., *Bound for Botany Bay,* Lansdowne Press, 1976.

ROYAL AUSTRALIAN HISTORICAL SOCIETY JOURNAL, Vol. 11, 1925.

SAINTY, M. R. and JOHNSON, K. A. (eds), *Census of New South Wales, November 1828,* Sydney 1980.

SALMON, M., *Pioneer Australians,* Newspaper cuttings V. 25, ML.

SCHOONERS AND SHIPS RETURNS, *HRA,* Vols. I, IV and V.

SCOTT, Ernest, *A Short History of Australia,* OUP, 1937.

SHANN et al, *Business Archives and History,* Vol. IV, John McCartney, 1964.

SHAW, J. G., *Bits of Old Blackburn 1889,* Lancashire Archives.

SHAW, A.G.L., *Convicts and the Colonies,* MUP, 1978.

SHEARER, J. D. and RUHEN, Olaf, *Bound for Botany Bay,* Lansdowne Press, 1976.

SILVESTER, Evidence in Stafford Assizes, August, 1791, Assi 5, PRO, London.

SMITH, Bernard, *Boyer Lectures 1980,* ABC.

SOLDIER'S LETTER, *HRNSW,* Vol. 11.

STAFFORD ASSIZE Records for August 24, 1791, PRO, London, 5, iii Part 1, X/108687.

ST. PHILLIP'S CHURCH, Sydney, Records as in Mutch Papers, ML.

ST. JOHN THE EVANGELIST C. OF E. PARISH CHURCH Records, Blackburn, Lancs. U.K.

SYDNEY GAZETTE, Vols. 2, 3, 4 and 5, 6 and 7, 8, 9, 2-8 from facsimile issued by State Library of NSW, Vol. 9 from Roebuck Press, Canberra.

SYDNEY MORNING HERALD, Sydney, 1980, Facsimile April 18, 1831, to January 2, 1832.

SUN HERALD, Sydney, 18 January, 1981, Article, Glascott.

TASMANIAN HISTORICAL RESEARCH ASSOCIATION Brochure, *Entally House,* Launceston.

TASMANIAN newspaper, *Examiner,* Launceston 1860-1870.

TENCH, Watkin, Capt., *Sydney's First Four Years 1788-1791,* LAH, 1979.

THOMSON, James, Diary or Farm Account of Burrier, South Coast. Grandson of Mary Reibey.

THOMPSON, T. R., A Catalogue of British Family History, Lancashire Archives.

THOMPSON, George, Gunner, Journal — *An Account of the Miseries and Starvation at Botany Bay,* J. Ridgeway, St. James Square, 1794; also included in *HRNSW,* Vol. VII.

TRANSPORTATION ACT 1718, quoted by A. G. L. Shaw, *Convicts and the Colonies.*

TREASURY BOARD RETURNS, PRO Reels 3553 T1/689/701/704.

TREVELYAN, G. M., *Illustrated English Social History,* Vols. 3 and 4, Pelican, 1964.

VICTUALLING LIST REGISTER T46, PRO, London, 1763-1795.

WARD, Russel, *The Australian Legend,* OUP, 1958.

WATSON, Frederick (ed), *The Beginnings of the Government in Australia,* Gullick, Sydney, 1917.

WEBSTER, Colin, *Coins,* Gemcraft Pub., 1979.

WESTERN COUNTY MAGAZINE 1792 quoted (Letters) in *HRNSW,* Vol. 2.

WHITE, Charles, *Early Australian History, Convict Life in N.S.W. and Van Diemen's Land,* Bathurst C7S White 1889 Part 11.

WOODFORD, James, Diary quoted by J. M. Trevelyan, Vol. 111.

WOOLF, Virginia, *Orlando,* Hogarth Press, London, Panther, 1977.

WRIGHT, John, Justice, of St. Mary's Parish, Stafford 1791, Evidence, in Stafford Assizes, August, 1791.

Staffordshire · Sum' Ass. 1791. [24/8/1791]

At the assizes and general delivery of the gaol of our Lord the King holden at Stafford in and for the County of Stafford on Wednesday the twenty fourth of August in the thirty first year of the Reign of our sovereign Lord George the third King of Great Britain &c before Sir James Eyre Knight Lord Chief Baron of our said Lord the King of his Court of Exchequer at Westminster John Heath Esquire one of the Justices of our said Lord the King of his Court of Common Pleas at Westminster and others their fellows Justices of our said Lord the King assigned to deliver his gaol of the said County of Stafford of the Prisoners therein being —.

Moreton Walhouse Esquire Sheriff.

Sarah Bull ---- for fel. & privily steal. from the person of John Harris (without his knowledge) one Silver Watch Val. 40s. & two steel seals Val. 9d. goods of s. John Harris 9th May 31st Geo: 3. par: of Colton.

Guilty
Thomas Jones —— for fel. assaulting Wm. Millington in the Kings highway putting him in fear & taking from his person and against his will one Pistol mounted with Iron Val. 5s. — par: of Stone - 2nd April 31st Geo: 3.

Guilty
Jane Watt ———— for fel. breaking & entering the dwelling house of Henry Clemson (no person being therein) and steal. therein One Velveret Waistcoat Val. 10s. One Silk handkerchief Val. 5s. 1 pair of Cotton Stockings Val. 3s. two Linen Shirts Val. 14s. One pair of Silver Sleeve Buttons Val. 2s. Goods & Chattels of s. Henry Clemson. One Callico Gown Val. 10s. One Cotton [illegible] handkerchief Val. 4s. One Lawn handkerchief Val. 1s. two Muslin aprons Val. 4s. and one Linen Apron Val. 1s. — par: of Bobbington - 29th March 31st Geo: 3rd

Guilty of simple felony.
Ann Thompson ..... for privately and fel. steal. in the Shop of John Hanbury Twenty One Yards of printed Muslinet Val. 52s. — Property of s. John Hanbury par: of Wolverhampton 6th April 31st Geo: 3.

Guilty
James Burrow --- for fel. steal. One Bay Mare Val. £10 property of John Sutton par: of Saint Mary - 13th August 31st Geo: 3rd

Guilty
Job Bratt ———— for fel. steal. 24 Iron Locks Val. 10d. property of Joseph Marygold - par. of Walberton 30th March 31. Geo: 3rd

Not Guilty
Thomas Baxter —— for unlawfully assaulting Jos: Watson an Ass.t Keeper of Barton Ward in Needwood Forest & fel. beating & wounding him in the Exec. of his Office contr. to Stat: 11th July 31st Geo: 3.

John Brough — for fel. steal. 60 cwt. weight of Lead Val. 5s. property of The Most Noble Granville Marquis of the County of Stafford -- par: of Trentham 24 October 30th Geo: 3

1, 2, 3. Lists of Prisoners, Stafford Assizes, August 1791

(Ref: PRO ASSI 2 26 X/L08670)

Staffordshire Summer assizes 31st Geo: 3rd — Informations Depositions Examinations & Confessions

1 Ann Garrat. Thomas Bickley and John Salt - Infns — Thomas Ainsworth
2. Edward Billingsley, Joseph Smith and Mary Knight Infns — John Badger.
3. Jane Becket. Thomas Page & Nancy Ward Infns — Wm Nightingale and Joseph Perry.
4. Infn of Sarah Whitehouse. Wm Hendrick John Salt and Benjamin Willetts — Susannah Perks and Susannah Bradley.
5. Henry Taylor Infn — Richard Bradley.
6. John Hanbury, Jos: Cordell, Fred Atkins, Infns — Ann Thompson
7. Depns of Benj: Clarke - Geo: Murray, Tho. Webb Mary Gold — Job Bratt.
8. Confn of Priscilla Cockin. Infn of Samuel Bickley — Priscilla Cockin
12 - 11 - 10 - 9. Thos Standley. Wm Marston. Eliz: Pesllow. Sarah Yardley Depns — Eleanor Stanley and Samuel Jones
- 13. Samuel Pearson, Eliz: Pearson, R. Smallman Francis Wildey, Sarah Wildey, & Saml Hanson Infns — Wm Walters
- 16 - 15 - 14. John Stephenson and Wm Dutheridge Infn. Infn of Wm Challenor - Thos Lees, Enoch Leggs - Thomas Hawe - Richard Firkin — George Betts and Zachariah Sharp
- 18. - 17. Confession of Seth Bassett. Infn of Thos Yeats. Wm Robinson — Seth Bassett
21 - 19. Infn of Joseph Moss and Eleanor Hyde. ~~Confn~~ of Thomas Watton als Guy — Thomas Watton als Guy
20. Samuel Morris. Exon. Richard Bird — Murder of a Male Child.
- 22. Jos: Riley & Wm Hipling. Exns — James Cewley and Thomas Cotton
23. John Commander. Exn. Wm Moore, & John Sorton — James Burrows
24. Thomas Horwood — John Brough.
25. Lucy Rose Infn — Thomas Rock.
26. ~~Wm~~ Infn of William ~~Bircher~~ Coates — William Bircher
27. ~~B~~ Infn of William Coates — Dange Roe
28. Infn of Thos Eccleston. Eliz: McDougall. Mary Holt. Edward Hart. Eliz: McDougall — Jane North
- 30 - 29. Jos: Turner Infns Eliz: Turner. Eliz: Guest. Edward Guest Jos: Perks, Wm Roberts - John Hall & Thos Thornton — Mark Wilde
- 31 - Confn of James Briggs — James Briggs
- 32. Robt Parks Infn. Wm Thornton & Jas Parke — Wm Greenough
- 33 Wm Millington. Jas Pilsbur Infn — Thomas Jones
- 34. Exn of John Holmes & Jas Hawkins — Thomas Hodge
- 35. John Vernon. Infn. & Thos Turner and Thos Mckin — Peter Burnside
- 36. Jos: Free. Robt Johnson & John Smith Infns — Thomas Shuttelwood
- 37. Infn of John Harris and Robt Bailey — Sarah Bull
38. Mary Waylor. Infns Sarah Page. Norris Best — Samuel Harper.
- 40 - 39. Willm Hinch. Robt. Matthew Corbett. — Jas Briggs
- 42 - 41. Francis Ralph. Infns & Benjamin Hide — William Glover and William Smith

(Ref: PRO ASSI 2 26 X/L08670)

Staffordshire Summer Assizes 31st Geo: 3rd. - - - Recog. to prosecute and give evidence?

-2-1. Henry Clemson P. E. — Susannah Gould - E. - - - Jane Watt.
-5-4-3- Jos: Smith and Samuel Salt - E - Thomas Knight & Mary & Edward Billingsley — John Badger
-7-6- Thomas Page - E - Jane Beckett P. E. — William Nightingale and Joseph Perry
-9-8- Sarah Whitehouse - P. E. - - John Salt. Benjamin Willets and Samuel Salt. — Susannah Perkins, Susannah Bradley.
-13-12-11-10 Samuel Pearson - E - - Eliz: Pearson - Francis Wilday and Sarah his wife - E - John Pearson - E. — William Walters
-16-15-14- John Walthouse, Joseph Cardall. E - Jane Atkins E - John Hanbury P. E — Ann Thompson.
-19-18-17 Susannah Allen - William Day and Wm. Terry E Samuel Bickley P. E. — Priscilla Cockin
-21. 20. Thos. Bickley and John Salt - E - Ann Garratt P. E. Thomas Ainsworth
-23-22. Eliz: Peploe - and Sarah Yardley P. Wm. Marson P. E. — Samuel Jones and Eleanor Standley.
-24- Henry Taylor P. E. — Richard Bradley
-27-26-25. Enoch Lees.. Wm. Ditheridge - Wm. Challenor - Thos. Hand - Saml. Addison - Thos. Hawe - Henry Brushfield - Richd. Firkin & John Stevenson E - Samuel Ward P. E. — George Betts and Zachariah Sharp.
-[illegible]-28 Thos. Geast & Wm. Robinson - E. Robert Wilson P. E. Seth Bassett
-30-29 Wm. Bennett - P. E - Jos. Moss & Eleanor Hyde E. Thomas Walton
-33.32 John Commander & William Moore - P. E. Thos. Sorton E. James Burrow
-35-34. Jos: Riley - E - Wm. Kipling Nicholas Boden and David Wynn E — James Clewley and Thomas Cotton
-36 Thos. Horwood P. E — John Brough
-37. Wm. Coates P. E — Danger Roe and Wm. Bircher
-38. Rose - P. E. — Thomas Owen
-40-39. John Worsey - P. E. Thomas Ecclestone E. - Jane North.
-42-41 John Vernon P. E - Thos. Turner & Thos. Mekison E. Peter Burnside.
-44-43 Wm. Millington P. E - Jas. Whitlow & Jno. Leader E - Thomas Jones
-46-45. Jas. Hawkins E. - John Holmes - P. E — Thomas Hodge.
-48-47- Robt. Johnson & Jno. Smith E. Jos: Free P. E - - - Thomas Shuttlewood
-50-49. Robt. Parke P. E. - Wm. Shenstone & Jas. Parke E. Wm. Greenough
-52-51. John Sansam - P. E - Mary Taylor - John Page - Norris Best. — Saml. Harper.
-54.53 Jos: Turner - P. E - Jos. Perks - Thos. Thornton - and John Hall E — Mark Wilde
-56-55 - John Harris P. E Robt. Bailey - Thos. Wollyscroft - Sarah Bull.
-58-57- Wm. Finch P. E - Matthew Corbett - E — James Briggs
-60.59 - Francis Ralph P. E. - Benjamin Hide. E - William Glover and William Smith

(Ref: PRO ASSI 2 26 X/L08670)

The Examination and Information of John Commander of the said Borough Baker taken on oath before me John Wright Esquire Mayor one of his Majesty's Justices of the peace in and for the said Borough the 18th day of August 1791.

This Informant saith that a young man who calls himself James Burrow did early on Saturday morning last offer a bay mare to sale to this Informant within the said Borough, and this Informant ~~suspecting~~ from the appearance of the said James Burrow suspecting that the said Mare was stolen communicated his suspicion to William Moore of the said Borough Yeoman who happened to pass by at the time when the said James Burrow offered to sell the said Mare and that this Informant and the said William Moore immediately seized the said James Burrow with the said Mare in his possession And this Informant further saith that the said James Burrow now present is the same person who was so seized with the said Mare in his possession, and that the Mare which he hath this day shewn to John Sorton Hughes of the City of Chester ~~[illegible]~~ West Glover is the same Mare which the said James Burrow offered to sell to this Informant

John Commander

[illegible] Mayor

Tuesday 18/8/1791

4. Evidence given by John Commander

(Ref: PRO ASSI 5 III part I X/L08687)

The examination of John Sorton Hughes of the City of Chester
taken on oath before me the before named Justice the
and year before written.

This examinant saith that a bay mare the property of John Sorton
of the City of Chester aforesaid Merchant was stolen out of a Field
adjoining the City of Chester in the night of the eleventh of
August instant, and that the Mare this day shewn to him by
John Commander and William Moore of the Borough of Stafford
aforesaid is the property of the said John Sorton this examinant
having well known the said Mare for the space of ten years
last past

John Sorton Hughes

Taken and sworn the day and year
first within written before me.

John Wright Mayor

5. Evidence given by John Sorton Hughes

(Ref: PRO ASSI 5 III part I X/L08687)

Borough [illegible] } to wit The Examination of William Moore of the said Borough [illegible] taken on oath before me the said Justice the day and year above written

This Examinant saith that about five o'clock on Saturday morning last, as he was passing in the Street, John Commander of the said Borough Baker, came to this examinant and told him that the aforesaid James Burrow (who was then in the Street with ~~the said~~ a Mare in his possession) had offered the said Mare to sale to him the said John Commander, and this examinant and the said John Commander suspecting that said Mare was stolen, immediately seized the said James B[illegible] with the Mare in his possession, and that the said James now present is the same person who was so seized with [illegible] his possession and that the Mare which this examinant [illegible]

this morning shewn to John Sorton Hughes of the City of Chester [illegible] is the same mare that was so seized as aforesaid William Moore

Taken and sworn before me }
[illegible] Mayor }

[Thursday 18/8/1791]

6. Evidence given by William Moore

(Ref: PRO ASSI 5 III part I X/L08687)

To the Kings most excellent Majesty

These are most humbly to certify to yr. Majesty that the following persons were attainted before us respectively your Majesty's Justices of Assize & Genl Gaol Delivery on the East Oxford Circuit but divers favorable circumstances appearing in their respective cases they were respectively reprieved & are humbly recommend them as fit objects to receive your Majesty's pardon on the sevl. conditions following if your Majesty shall so think fit (that is to say)

James Rea & Stephen Lewis at Worcester for the co: of Worcester (that is to say) the Sd. Jas. Rea of killing a sheep with intent to steal the carcass and the sd. Stephen Lewis of horsestealing On condition as to the Sd. Jas. Rea & Stephen Lewis of their being respectively transp. beyond the seas for 7. years

John Weston at Monmouth in & for the county of Monmouth of housebreaking On condition of his being transported beyond the seas for the term of his life.

Ja Eyre

Saml Dent at Glocester for the co: of Glocester of horsestealing On condition of his being kept to hard labour in the House of Correction for the sd. county for three years.

Thos Godwin at Hereford in & for the co: of Hereford of stealing the value of 40s. in a dwellg. house On condition of his being transported beyond the seas for seven years.

Jane Watt Jane North James Burrow Thos Jones and Willm. Greenough at Stafford in & for the co: of Stafford (that is to say) the sd. Jane Watt of house breaking the Sd. Jane North of murder the sd. James Burrow of stealing a mare the sd. Thos. Jones of an highway robbery and the Sd. William Greenough of sheepstealing On condition as to the sd. Jane Watt James Burrow Thomas Jones & William Greenough of their being respectively transported beyond the Seas for the sevl. terms following (that is to say) the Sd. Jane Watt for the whole term of her natural life as to the Sd. Jas. Burrow Thos Jones & William Greenough for the term of 7 years & as to the Sd. Jane North without any condition whatever it havg. appeard to me by the examination of the Surgeon who could not attend at the trial to give his evidence that the Sd. Jane North was insane at the time of committing the Act

John Heath.

7. The application for commuting sentence to transportation

(Ref: PRO ASSI 2 26 X/L08670)

Whereas Jane Watt James Burrow Thomas Jones and William Greenough were severally attainted at this assizes of the sev^d. capital fel^s. follow^g. (that is to say) the s^d. Jane Watt of housebreaking the s^d. Ja^s. Burrow of stealing a mare the s^d. Thos. Jones of an highway robbery & the s^d. William Greenough of sheepstealing but his Majesty hath been graciously pleased to extend his royal mercy to them respectively on condition of their being severally transported to the eastern coast of New South Wales or some one or other of the islands adjacent for and during the sev^d. terms following (that is to say) the s^d. Jane Watt for and during the term of her natural life and the s^d. James Burrow Thomas Jones and William Greenough respectively for and during the term of seven years It is therefore ordered that the s^d. Jane Watt James Burrow Thomas Jones and Willm Greenough be transp^d. accordingly as soon as conveniently may be purs^t. to the sev^d. Acts of Parliam^t in this case made and provided and that John Williamson Esq & Joseph Dickenson Clerk two of his Majesty's Justices of the Peace for the s^d. county of Stafford do contract with any person or persons for the performance of the s^d. transportation and order such and the like sufficient security to be taken for the same as the s^d. Acts of Parliam^t. direct^s and also cause the s^d. sev^d above named persons purs^t. to such contract or contracts to be delivered over by the gaoler of the s^d. county of Stafford (in whose custody they now are) to the person or persons contract^g. for them or to his or their ass^s. & certify such contract or contracts and security so to be taken at the next ass^s. & gen^l. gaol delivery to be holden for the s^d. county of Stafford in order to have the s^d. certificate and contract or contracts and security filed among the records of this Court.

By the Court
Price

[Thursday 19/9/1791.]

8. Recording of the commutation

(Ref: PRO ASSI 2 26 X/L08670)

"TO THE KING'S MOST EXCELLENT MAJESTY

The humble petition of Adam Hope Woollen draper and others whose names are hereunto subscribed residents in the Town of Blackburn,

Most respectfully Sheweth

That Mary Haydock (a girl only *fourteen years of age*) was convicted at the last Stafford assizes of Horse-stealing for which she is now under sentence of transportation for 7 years to parts beyond the seas.

That the said Mary Haydock being a poor helpless Orphan was prevailed on by another young girl to leave her situation in the month of June last, and in order that they might not be discovered they purchased Boys Clothes and changed their names; the said Mary Haydock then assuming the name of James Burrow — that they immediately came for Chester and the next day they parted — that the said Mary Haydock (then Burrow in boy's clothes) on her way to Stafford was accidentally overtaken by a man with 2 horses who desired her to ride one and he would please her and that the man fearing a discovery left her in Stafford with the horse and she showing inexperience in offering it for sale was apprehended upon suspicion of having stolen it, and committed to the prison there under the name of James Burrow.

That your Petitioners are advised that the above circumstances appeared on the said Mary Haydock's trial [did not appear — see trial] and if true (of which the Honourable Mr. Justice Heath who tried her will be best able to inform your Majesty) seems to be favourable in the said Mary Haydock's case as from thence it does not appear that she had any hand in the original Act of stealing the horse but that she has been drawn in by the wicked contrivance of some evil minded person or persons to share solely the whole blame of the business; and when the circumstances of her very tender years is considered it appears still more unlikely to your Petitioners that she alone could have formed a scheme so daring as that of stealing a Horse, but that the business must at least have been suggested to her by some evil disposed person or persons.

That your Petitioners have known the said Mary Haydock from her Infancy she being a Native of Blackburn but could never suppose her capable of committing any such offence as that of a stealing a horse especially as she had had a good education and every endeavour has been used by her lately deceased Grandmother in whose custody she was for some time to enjoin her to the practice of every moral religious duty.

Your Petitioners therefore most humbly pray that your Majesty considering the pitiable situation of her the said Mary Haydock, will be graciously pleased to extend to her your royal pardon and forgiveness, so that she may not be doomed to a miserable exile, but be freed from her present miserable confinement, and again be restored to her relations and friends.

ADAM HOPE, Woollen Draper
JOHN PARKER
JN. FISHER, Surgeon
DAVID GARDINER, Tea Dealer
JOHN THOMSON, Cotton Manufacturer
DONALD M. LEAN, Cotton Manufacturer
PETER WYLIE, Linen Draper
CHRIST^N IRVING, Linen Draper
HUGH JAMIESON, Cotton Manufacturer
? & WM. SMALLEY, Merchants

GEO. & THOS. WALMSLEY, Attornies at Law.
S. Mc QUHAE, Dissenting Min^r
REVD. SAMUEL DEAN, Headmaster of the Free Grammar Schl.
CHARLES WAUGH, Woollen & Linen Draper
JAMES TIPLADY, Tallow Chandler and Soap Boiler,
ROBERT SMALLEY, Gentleman
REVD. RICHARD SMALLEY"

Letter from Thomas Harkie, the Minister at Blackburn forwarded it to the Right Honourable Henry Dundas (Secretary of State).

"Nov. 5th, 1791

Sir,

I transmit to you the enclosed petition accompanied with the request of the friends of the unhappy young Girl who is the object of it, that you would forward it to the Secretary of State for the purpose of having it presented by him to his Majesty. Not knowing the young girl personally I could not with propriety put my name to the Petition. Her relations in this town are very respectable people, and I hope her extreme youth will entitle her to the royal Mercy.

THOS HARKIE"

"Report from Mr. Justice Heath upon the Case of Mary Haydock

Received 18th Nov. 1791

— a Capital Respite not recommended for further extension of Mercy.

My Lord,

In humble obedience to his Majesty's Commands signified to me by your lordship, I report the case of a Person who was tried before me at the last Stafford Assizes for stealing a Bay Mare of John Sorton, which person then answered by the name of James Burrow but according to the Petition presented to his Majesty is a Girl of the name of Mary Haydock.

Robert Silvester who keeps the Swan Inn at Stafford deposed that he saw the Prisoner on the 12th [Friday] of the then Instant August towards the evening on Horseback who offered to sell him the horse saying that it belonged to his Uncle Darbin who lived about five miles from Chester. The witnesses told him to go about his business. It was a Bay Horse with a longish tail.

Francis Emborton Hostler to the last witness swore that he saw the Prisoner between the hours of 5 and six in the morning of the 18th [13th?] inst. riding the mare — he refused the price the Witness offered for her saying that he would rather stand the Horse Market with her. The prisoner asked Thirteen Pounds for her and said that she was aged about 4 past — the witness looked into her mouth and thought she was as old as he was. The witness suspected her to have been stolen and that the Prisoner tho' very young as to age was an old offender. He examined him more strictly. The prisoner said that the Mare was the Property of his Uncle who lived at Darbin. Being further asked how it happened that one so young as he was should be entrusted with selling a horse, he readily answered that once before he had sold a horse for his uncle for more money than he could get for her and for that reason he was employed again. The prisoner asked Four Pounds for the saddle and bridle. The prisoner afterwards walked the mare into Stafford when he was apprehended by Wm. Moore. It was a Blood Mare — she had a spavin on one leg and the remains of a spavin on the other hind leg.

W Moore apprehended the prisoner, who said she brought the mare from her uncle, a grocer at Darbin, one John Burrow. The witness inquired of the Chester Carrier but he knew no such person there. The prisoner then said that his uncle kept the Black Crow and let out a Post Chaise. The Carrier denied that there was any such Sign. The prisoner being further pressed said that he brought the mare from Thos. Lyster who keeps the White Lyon at the Back of the Exchange in Chester. The prisoner [witness] then delivered the mare to J. Hughes.

John Hughes deposed that the mare he received from the last witness was the property of the prosecutor, he knew her by her marks and particularly the spavins. She was stolen off a Common near Chester and was missed on the 12th inst. The prosecutor is his Uncle.

The Jury found the prisoner guilty on this Evidence and I was then and still continue to be perfectly satisfied with the Verdict. On compassion to the tender age of the prisoner, I humbly recommended her as a proper object of the royal Mercy so that her Punishment might be mitigated to Transportation. I have perused the Petition presented to his Majesty praying a free pardon on the suggestion of her perfect innocence. I am humbly of the opinion that there is no grounds for this suggestion and I am afraid that on the contrary from the artful manner with which she conducted herself that there is so much reason to suspect with Francis Emborton that she is an old offender or at least that it is not her first offence. If there were any respectable persons "who would take charge of her and enter into the cognizance that she shall not commit any Felonies for 4 or 5 years to come, I think that she might be justly entitled to the Royal Mercy. Otherwise come, I am humbly of the opinion that under the present circumstances it is more advantageous for the prisoner herself and expedient for the Public example that she should be transported. All which is most humbly submitted to the royal Wisdom and Consideration.

I am My Lord
Your most Obedient
Humble Servant

JOHN HEATH.

To the Right Honourable Lord Grenville."

APPENDIX B

GENEALOGY

These tables record the direct descendants of Mary and Thomas Reibey covering the years 1796-1960, through the four children who had issue: Thomas Reibey II, Eliza (Reibey) Thomson, Jane Penelope (Reibey) Atkinson, Elizabeth Ann (Reibey) Long Innes. The list has been compiled through the courtesy of family records. It covers six generations where known, excluding children who died in early infancy, and children of the seventh generation.

In every profession, in politics and rural pursuits, descendants of this early pioneer family have served, often with great distinction. They are now, 1982, spread throughout Tasmania, and New South Wales and to a lesser extent, in Melbourne, Perth and Queensland, and in Devon, U.K.

The names are listed in family groups, showing the second, third and fourth generations separately, followed by the fifth and sixth generations.

Mary Reibey's first son, Thomas Reibey II 1796–1842 married Richarda Allen and had issue – see over.

Mary Reibey's second son James Haydock Reibey 1798-1843 married a widow, very young, Rebecca Breedon. There was no issue.

Mary Reibey's third son was George Haydock Reibey 1801-1826. He was accidentally killed at his brother's home, Entally House, Hadspen, Tasmania, in a tree accident. He died unmarried.

Mary Reibey's fourth child was Celia Reibey 1803-1823. She married Thomas Wills in 1822 and died in childbirth in 1823; issue from this marriage, only child, Alice, died in 1824.

Eliza 1805-1870 married Thomas Thomson and had issue – see over.

Jane Penelope 1807-1854 married John Atkinson and had issue – see over.

Elizabeth Ann 1810-1876 married Joseph Long Innes and had issue – see over.

THE REIBEY LINEAGE

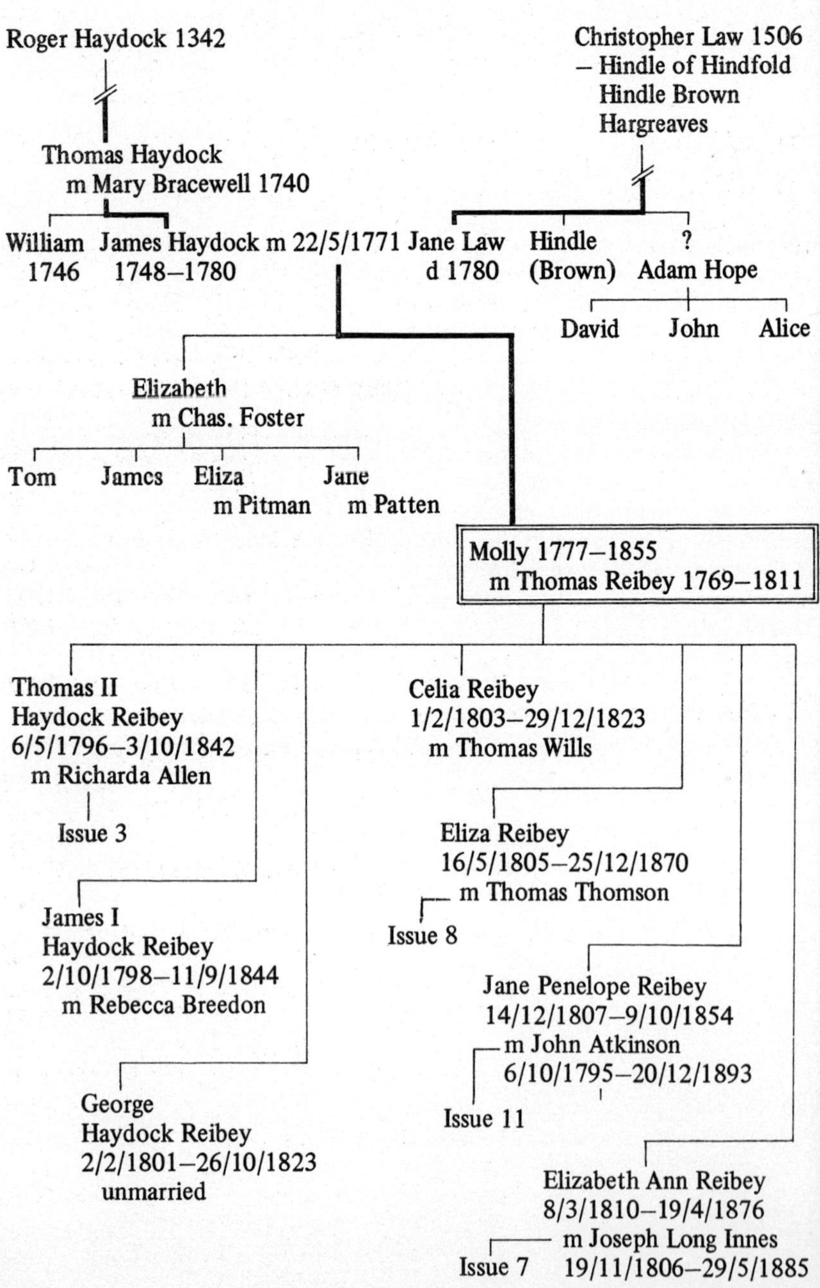

DESCENDANTS THROUGH THOMAS HAYDOCK REIBEY (THOMAS REIBEY II)

FIRST CHILD WITH ISSUE

Second Generation	Third Generation	Fourth Generation	Fifth and Sixth Generations
1: Thomas Hay-dock Reibey II 1796–1842	A: Mary Allen Arthur née Reibey 1818–1895	(i) Charles Reibey Arthur 1837	(a) Charles James Arthur 1871–1894
			(b) Montague George Arthur 1874– Barbara (Thorold) Roberts née Arthur Barry Arthur
			(c) Lionel Thomas Arthur 1875–1916
			(d) John Albert Arthur I 1877 John (Jock) Arthur 1924–1961
			(e) Mary Kate Arthur 1879–1894
			(f) Frederick Alfred Arthur 1880–1932 Frederick Frere Arthur 1927– Lucilla Nora Arthur 1956– Allan Arthur 1958– Charles Arthur III 1961– Lindsay Arthur 1966–
			(g) Lucilla Harrison née Arthur 1882–1964 Charles Arthur (Tom) Harrison 1914– Philippa Leake née Harrison 1948– Susan Webb née Harrison 1950– Louise Gatenby née Harrison 1952– Robert Harrison 1952– Lucilla Meredith née Harrison 1915–1945
		(ii) Mary Mason née Arthur 1839	(a) Harriett St Hill née Mason 1877– Harry Reibey St Hill Felix Arthur St Hill Loudon St Hill

Second Generation	Third Generation	Fourth Generation	Fifth and Sixth Generations
1. Thomas Haydock Reibey II 1796–1842 (cont'd)	A: Mary Allen Arthur née Reibey 1818–1895 (cont'd)		John St Hill 1942– Marian Hodgman née St Hill 1949– Annabell Larkey née St Hill 1951 (b) Gertrude Mason
		(iii) Richarda Emily Arthur 1841–1871	
		(iv) Thomas Reibey Arthur 1843–1919	
		(v) Kate Nelson née Arthur 1845–1869	(a) Sybil Arthur (b) Millicent Arthur
		(vi) John Lake Arthur 1847–1877	
		(vii) George Arthur 1849–1931	(a) George Arthur II (b) Charles Frere Arthur 1885–1887 (c) Mary Youl née Arthur (d) Dora Arthur 1887–1888
		(viii) Charlotte Vosper Jakins née Arthur 1851–	(a) George Jakins 1879–1963 Helen Parker née Jakins Nancy Lamberton née Jakins William Jakins Patricia (i) McCulloch (ii) Willis née Jakins Freda Crisp née Jakins

Second Generation	Third Generation	Fourth Generation	Fifth and Sixth Generations
1. Thomas Haydock Reibey II 1796–1842 (cont'd)	A: Mary Allen Arthur née Reibey 1818–1895 (cont'd)		Susan Griffiths née Crisp Barbara Crisp Thomas Crisp (b) Hilda Mary Bell née Jakins 1881–1951 Alfred Bell Mary Harrison née Bell Nesta Shaw née Bell (c) Catherine Carmichael née Jakins 1883–1960 (d) Charles Jakins 1884–1919 Catherine Jakins Marjorie Tippett née Jakins Thomas Jakins –1923 (e) James Albert Jakins 1884–1948 Jack Jakins 1922– Stuart Jakins 1950– Pamela Cording née Jakins 1952 William Jakins 1953
		(ix) Albert Frederick Arthur 1854–1890	
	B: Thomas Haydock Reibey III 1821–1912	No issue	
	C: James Haydock Reibey II 1823–1873	James Clack Reibey III 1850–1871	(a) Emily Charlotte William-Powlett née Reibey 1871–1954 Newton James William-Powlett 1896–1963 Ann Thistlewaite née William-Powlett 1930 Oliver Newton William-Powlett 1933

Sara Bruce née William-Powlett 1936

Peveril William-Powlett 1898–

Olivia Wood née William-Powlett 1925

Helen Bruce née William-Powlett 1927

Judith Colman née William-Powlett 1936

Oliver William-Powlett 1900–1921

Peter Vernon William-Powlett 1903

Mary Janson née William-Powlett 1936

Barton William-Powlett 1938

DESCENDANTS THROUGH THE FIFTH CHILD, ELIZA REIBEY 1805–1870 WHO MARRIED THOMAS THOMSON.

Second Generation	Third Generation	Fourth Generation	Fifth and Sixth Generations
V. Eliza Thomson née Reibey 1805–1870	A. Mary Helen Thomson 1822–1866		
	B. James Thomson I 1824–1899	(i) Thomas McKenzie Thomson II 1860–1911	(a) James Beardmore Thomson II 1903–1972 Thomas Leslie Thomson III 1947– Neville Thomson 1949–
			(b) Ethleen May Butler née Thomson 1904– Graham John Butler 1930– Patricia Pickering née Butler 1933– Geoffrey Butler 1937–1968
			(c) Frederick Reibey Thomson 1906–1907
			(d) Marjorie Lamacraft née Thomson 1907–1963 Richard Lamacraft 1948–
			(e) Owen Thomson 1908–1911
			(f) Frank Haydock Thomson 1910–1943
			(g) Julie Kennedy née Thomson 1912–1939 William Kennedy 1941 Frank Kennedy 1944
		(ii) Murdo Thomson 1861–1911	(a) Murdo II Four children
			(b) Muriel Redmond née Thomson 1894–
			(c) Hilda Walker née Thomson 1903– Three children
			(d) Enid Rooney née Thomson 1910 Joe Rooney
			(e) 5 others

Second Generation	Third Generation	Fourth Generation	Fifth and Sixth Generations
V. Eliza Thomson née Reibey 1805–1870 (cont'd)	B: James Thomson I 1824–1899 (cont'd)	(iii) May Thomson 1863–1879	
		(iv) Julia Shannon née Thomson 1865?	(a) Maurice Shannon 1894 Two sons, one daughter (b) James Shannon One daughter (c) Ruth Mary Hennessy née Shannon One son (d) Olive Alexander née Shannon Issue (e) Margaret Hungerford née Shannon
		(v) Hugh Thomson	(a) Caroline Thomson (b) Reibey Thomson Issue 3 (c) Netta ? née Thomson Two sons (d) Geoff Thomson One son, one daughter (e) Mary ? née Thomson Two daughters, two sons
		(vi) Eliza III Willis née Thomson	(a) Molly Willis (b) Kenneth Willis (c) Helen Thomson née Willis (d) James Willis (e) Thomas Willis (f) Robert Willis
		(vii) Netta Crashaw née Thomson 1877	(a) Eileen Spring née Crashaw (b) Robert George Crashaw (c) Mary Rance née Crashaw (d) Betty Moss née Crashaw Two sons

Second Generation	Third Generation	Fourth Generation	Fifth and Sixth Generations
V. Eliza Thomson née Reibey 1805–1870 (cont'd)	B: James Thomson I 1824–1899 (cont'd)	(viii) James Thomson II 1880–1951	(a) Edna Kilgour née Thomson One son and two daughters (b) James Thomson III One son and one daughter (c) Julie Piesley née Thomson Issue (d) Bunny ? née Thomson Issue (e) Shirley Newsome née Thomson Issue (f) Kenneth Thomson (g) Donald Thomson (h) Mac Thomson (i) Mavis Crump née Thomson
		(ix) Kenneth Thomson 1880–194? (twin of James)	
		(x) Jane Gunther née Thomson	(a) Patricia ? née Gunther (b) Pamela Woodger née Gunther Lynn Grant née Woodger (c) Sybil ? née Gunther Issue – six sons
	C: Margaret Uniacke née Thomson 1826–1869	(i) Richard Uniacke (ii) Norman Uniacke (iii) Redmond Uniacke (iv) Arthur Uniacke (v) Cecilia Thorn née Uniacke	
	D: Eliza II Ann Thomson 1827–1899		

Second Generation	Third Generation	Fourth Generation	Fifth and Sixth Generations
V. Eliza Thomson née Reibey 1805–1870 (cont'd)	E: Jane Penelope Eliott née Thomson 1829–1919	(i) Kate Steedman née Eliott 1856–	(a) to (d) Two sons and two daughters
		(ii) Isobel Mary Elliott 1857–1858	
		(iii) Gilbert Eliott II 1859–1940 married his cousin Emily Palmer	(a) Gilbert Eliott III 1888–1912 (b) Keith Eliott 1895–1943 (c) Joan Hirschfield née Eliott 1897–? Brian Hirschfield 1926– Ann Loveridge née Hirschfield Keith Hirschfield Hilary Vowles née Hirschfield 1935– (d) Emily Innes Newman née Eliott 1901– Paul Newman Noel Newman (e) Eliza Loveridge – 2 Madden née Eliott 1901–
		(iv) Helen Mackenzie née Eliott 1862–	(a) Hector Mackenzie Helen Mackenzie II Gordon Mackenzie (b) Elsie I Shaw née Mackenzie I 1882–1937 Elsie Beggs née Shaw II 1908– Margaret Jane Shaw 1910– Patricia Shaw 1913– Dorothy Shaw 1916– Kathleen Drew née Shaw 1920

Second Generation	Third Generation	Fourth Generation	Fifth and Sixth Generations
V. Eliza Thomson née Reibey 1805–1870 (cont'd)	E: Jane Penelope Eliott née Thomson 1829–1919 (cont'd)		(c) Ronald Mackenzie I ?–1963 Jean Mackenzie Ronald Mackenzie II (d) Gordon Mackenzie
		(v) Blanche Eliott	
		(vi) Harry Eliott 1866	(a) Grace Penelope Eliott
		(vii) Maud Loveday née Eliott 1868–	(a) to (g) Five sons and two daughters
		(viii) Constance Tooth née Eliott 1871–	Seven children
	F: Maria Radford née Thomson 1831–	(i) Charles Radford – three children (ii) Edith Thomson née Radford (iii) Inez Radford	
	G: Jessie I Guthrie née Thomson 1837–1904	(i) Charles Guthrie 1858	(a) Jessie Brown née Guthrie
		(ii) Mary Miller née Guthrie 1860	
		(iii) Constance Guthrie 1862–1863	
		(iv) Jessie II Baker née Guthrie 1864–1942	(a) Molly Parmeter née Baker

Second Generation	Third Generation	Fourth Generation	Fifth and Sixth Generations
V. Eliza Thomson née Reibey 1805–1870 (cont'd)	G: Jessie I Guthrie née Thomson 1837–1904 (cont'd)	(v) Florence Guthrie 1865–1878	
		(vi) Hugh Guthrie 1867–1921	
		(vii) Norman Guthrie 1869–1909	(a) One child
		(viii) Quentin Guthrie 1873–1874	
		(ix) Alice Hope Guthrie 1874–1952	
		(x) Wemyss Guthrie 1877–1953	(a) Alison Guthrie 1908–1972 (b) Hugh Guthrie III 1910– David Guthrie 1947– Katherine Guthrie 1950– Richard Guthrie 1952– Elizabeth Guthrie 1952– Margaret Guthrie 1957–
		(xi) Agnes Guthrie 1880–1942	
	H: Thomas Thomson II 1840–1883	(i) Annie Elizia Thomson (ii) Ada Mary Thomson (iii) Augusta Thomson (iv) James Thomson	

DESCENDANTS THROUGH THE SIXTH CHILD, JANE PENELOPE REIBEY WHO MARRIED JOHN ATKINSON

Second Generation	Third Generation	Fourth Generation	Fifth and Sixth Generations
VI: Jane Penelope Atkinson née Reibey 1807–1854	A: John Reibey Atkinson II 1826–1854		
	B: George Atkinson 1827–1829		
	C: Jane Elizabeth Laidley née Atkinson 1829–1903	(i) William Laidley 1855–1856	
		(ii) Emily Merivale née Laidley 1856–1881	(a) One son (b) Annabel Merrivale 1884–
		(iii) Melanie Laidley 1858–1869	
		(iv) Shepheard Edgcliffe Laidley I 1861–1945	(a) Consett Steven Laidley died 1935 (b) Barbara Street née Laidley 1905–. Jennifer Thorpe née Street 1928– John Street 1930–
		(v) Reginald William Laidley 1863 m	
		(vi) Norman Wyld Laidley 1868–	

Second Generation	Third Generation	Fourth Generation	Fifth and Sixth Generations
VI: Jane Penelope Atkinson née Reibey 1807–1854 (cont'd)	C: Jane Elizabeth Laidley née Atkinson 1829–1903 (cont'd)	(vii) Consett I Laidley 1868–	
		(viii) Mabel Gay née Laidley 1870–1914	(a) Penelope Gay (b) Patience Gay Laidley Gay Shepherd Laidley II Gay
		(ix) Mildred Mary Laidley 1873–1878	
	D: Mary Innes Palmer née Atkinson 1832–	(i) Celia Palmer	
		(ii) Edith Palmer	
		(iii) Mabel Thomson née Palmer	
		(iv) Ada Thomson née Palmer	(a) Boyd Thomson
		(v) Emily Eliott née Palmer	married her cousin, see Thomson line.
	E: Eliza (1) Madden (2) Hobkirk née Atkinson 1834–1916	(i) Mary Madden 1852–1879 (ii) Neville Charles Hobkirk 1879–1885	
	F: Charlotte Hobkirk née Atkinson 1836–	(i) Charles Hobkirk	(a) Kathleen Hawker née Hobkirk Frances Jackson née Hawker

Second Generation	Third Generation	Fourth Generation	Fifth and Sixth Generations
VI: Jane Penelope Atkinson née Reibey 1807–1854 (cont'd)	F: Charlotte Hobkirk née Atkinson 1836– (cont'd)	(ii) Louis Hobkirk 1861–1917	
		(iii) Mildred Hobkirk 1869–1926	
		(iv) Nellie Martin née Hobkirk	(a) Marcus Martin (b) Phyllis Outhwaite née Martin (c) Joan Martin
	G: Celia Atkinson 1839–1845		
	H: James Reibey Atkinson I 1841–1919 m twice (1) Henrietta Garrett	(i) Celia Mary Atkinson 1866–1885	
		(ii) John Garrett Atkinson 1868–1901	(a) Ruth McManus née Atkinson 1902– William McManus 1932 Elspeth McManus 1926 Pamela McManus 1934 Phillipa McManus 1939 Marcus McManus 1941 (b) Joyce Carvosso née Atkinson 1904– Elizabeth Carvosso 1936– Margaret Palm née Carvosso 1938
		(iii) James II Atkinson 1870–1936	(a) Sidney Atkinson 1899– (b) Margaret Appleby née Atkinson (c) Horace Reibey Atkinson

Second Generation	Third Generation	Fourth Generation	Fifth and Sixth Generations
VI: Jane Penelope Atkinson née Reibey 1807–1854 (cont'd)	H: James Reibey Atkinson I 1841–1919 m twice	(iv) Thomas Atkinson 1872–1936	
	(1) Henrietta Garrett (cont'd)	(v) Norma Atkinson 1874–187?	
	(2) Sarah Garrett	(vi) Helen Ione McDougall née Atkinson 1879–1980	(a) Dougald McDougall II 1902– Dougald McDougall III 1934– Three children Patricia Hood née McDougall 1932– Two children Ian McDougall 1935– Three children Malcolm McDougall 1938– Five children Ailsa Forster née McDougall 1939– Three children (b) Archibald McDougall 1903– (c) Peter McDougall 1905– Penelope House née McDougall 1932– Digby McDougall 1934– (d) John McDougall 1906– (e) Quentin McDougall 1908– Ewen McDougall 1937– Three children Duncan McDougall 1938– Three children Katherine Waterworth née McDougall 1941– Three children (f) Christopher McDougall 1910– Andrew McDougall 1949– Alison McDougall 1959–

Second Generation	Third Generation	Fourth Generation	Fifth and Sixth Generations
VI: Jane Penelope Atkinson née Reibey 1807–1854 (cont'd)	H: James Reibey Atkinson I 1841–1919 m twice (1) Henrietta Garrett (cont'd)	(vii) Rita Joan Atkinson 1883–1970	
		(viii) Norman Atkinson 1885–1956	
		(ix) Kathleen Jones née Atkinson 1887–	(a) Barbara Mackintosh née Jones 1925– Two children (b) Gwyneth Bret née Jones 1926– Two children (c) Olwen Caswell née Jones 1927– Four sons (d) Llewellyn Jones 1929–
		(x) Derrick Atkinson 1890–1970	
	I: Thomas Reibey Atkinson I 1844–1902	(i) Thomas George Atkinson 1889–1978	(a) Thomas Alan Atkinson 1920– Kaye Frances Atkinson 1952– James Atkinson III Three children Sally Johnston née Atkinson 1956– (b) Diana Groom née Atkinson 1956– Susan Wilkinson née Groom 1947– Charles Groom 1948– Janet Bradley née Groom 1950– James Groom (c) Hilary Cleland née Atkinson 1927– Five children
		(ii) Alan John Atkinson 1892–1971	(a) David Atkinson 1936– Two children (b) Margaret Napier née Atkinson 1937– Four children

Second Generation	Third Generation	Fourth Generation	Fifth and Sixth Generations
VI: Jane Penelope Atkinson née Reibey 1807–1854 (cont'd)	I: Thomas Reibey Atkinson I 1844–1902 (cont'd)		(c) Juliet McKinnon Brown née Atkinson 1940– One child
		(iii) Russel Owen Atkinson 1895–	(a) Rosemary Bowman née Atkinson 1923– Peter Bowman 1949– David Bowman 1952– (b) Geoffrey Russel Atkinson 1924–1924 (c) John Atkinson III 1927– Prudence Radamski née Atkinson 1953– Nicholas Atkinson 1958–
		(iv) Alison Mary Atkinson 1902–1933	
	J: Emily Clara Mason née Atkinson 1846–1925	(i) Mary Mason 1867–1942	
		(ii) Gertrude Mason 1870–1948	
		(iii) Celia Mason 1875–1885	
		(iv) Annie Grace Mason 1878–1892	
		(v) John Mason 1880–1888	

Second Generation	Third Generation	Fourth Generation	Fifth and Sixth Generations
VI: Jane Penelope Atkinson née Reibey 1807–1854 (cont'd)	J: Emily Clara Mason née Atkinson 1846–1925 (cont'd)	(vi) Thomas Mason 1884–1885	
		(vii) Kath Mason 1885–1886	
		(viii) Nina Helen Mason 1882–1883	
		(ix) Edward Mason	
		(x) Frank Mason	
		(xi) Edith Mason	
		(xii) Arthur Mason	
		(xiii) Doris Mason died 1969	
	K: Kate Atkinson 1848–1849		

DESCENDANTS THROUGH THE SEVENTH CHILD, ELIZABETH ANN REIBEY WHO MARRIED JOSEPH LONG INNES

Second Generation	Third Generation	Fourth Generation	Fifth and Sixth Generations
VII: Elizabeth I Long Innes née Reibey 1810–1870	A: Elizabeth II Jane Heath née Long Innes 1830–	(i) George Heath (ii) Charles Heath (iii) Herbert Heath (iv) Celia Morse née Heath (v) Ethel Armstrong née Heath (vi) Isabel Heath (vii) Beatrice Heath (viii) Evlyn Heath (ix) Vivian Heath	
	B: Celia Pym née Long Innes 1831–	(i) Edward Innes Pym 1858–	
		(ii) Erskine Travers Pym	
		(iii) Elizabeth Sankey née Pym	(a) Crofton Sankey (b) Celia Sankey (c) Margaret Sankey (d) Joyce Sankey
		(iv) Clara Pym	
		(v) Ethel Pym	
		(vi) Cecile Pym	
	C: Joseph Long Innes 1834–	(i) George Massey Innes 1866–	
		(ii) Edward Long Innes 1868–	

Second Generation	Third Generation	Fourth Generation	Fifth and Sixth Generations
VII: Elizabeth I Long Innes née Reibey 1810–1870 (cont'd)	C: Joseph Long Innes 1834– (cont'd)	(iii) Reginald Long Innes 1869–1947	(a) George Innes (b) Joan Price née Innes (c) Barbara Watson née Innes
		(iv) Clive Long Innes 1871–	
		(v) Mary Long Innes 1873–	
		(vi) Eleanor Long Innes 1874–1877	
		(vii) Percival Long Innes 1879–	
		(viii) John Long Innes 1884–	
	D: Herbert Munro Long Innes 1839–	(i) to (ix) children	
	E: Mary Arm- strong née Long Innes 1842–	(i) John Armstrong	
		(ii) Christian Armstrong 1871	
		(iii) Mary 1873–	

Second Generation	Third Generation	Fourth Generation	Fifth and Sixth Generations
VII: Elizabeth I Long Innes née Reibey 1810–1870 (cont'd)	E: Mary Armstrong née Long Innes 1842– (cont'd)	(iv) Frances	
		(v) Kathleen	
		(vi) Eileen	
	F: Reginald Gipps Long Innes I 1844–	(i) North Clara Long Innes 1876	
		(ii) Reginald Long Innes II 1877–	
		(iii) Selwyn Long Innes 1878–	
		(iv) Barbara Grace Long Innes 1879–	
	G: Clara I Selwyn née Long Innes 1845–	(i) Stephen John Innes Selwyn	
		(ii) Margaret Innes Selwyn	
		(iii) Rebie Innes Selwyn	(a) Dorothy Theresa Selwyn (b) Mary Geraldine Selwyn
		(iv) Clara II Innes Selwyn	

INDEX